Derek Fowlds

My autobiography

A Part Worth Playing

with Michael Sellers

fantom
publishing

First published in 2015 by Fantom Films
fantomfilms.co.uk
Reprinted in paperback 2017

A catalogue record for this book is available from the British Library.

Hardback edition ISBN: 978-1-78196-148-3
Paperback edition ISBN: 978-1-78196-291-6

Typeset by Phil Reynolds Media Services, Leamington Spa
Printed and bound by CPI Group (UK) Ltd, Croydon, CR0 4YY

Front cover photo © Lisa Bowerman

For Jo
and my wonderful family
whom I love to infinity and beyond

Contents

Foreword

Actor, friend, eternal Peter Pan – like many others, I've known and loved him boy and boy.

– Diana Hoddinott

I had known and admired Derek's work for centuries, but it was not until 1981 that we met, and started laughing together. In 1991 he was cast in *Heartbeat* as a very young Police Sergeant that grew into Oscar Blaketon. What a pleasure for me to observe this 'national treasure' develop.

– William Simons

I first saw Derek being terrific in *The Miracle Worker* and *Chips with Everything* during the sixties, little thinking that forty years on he would become a dear, dear friend.

– Peter Benson

Thank goodness Mr D has finally written all his stories and anecdotes down for you all to enjoy. I've had the pleasure of hearing them all (eight or nine times each!) from the horse's mouth, and never grown tired of them.

My very great friend is the most loyal, wise and generous of men, and I count myself extremely lucky to have spent so much time and shared so many happy experiences with him. From Bowood to Chart Hills, from the White Hart to the Fox and Pheasant, from Stamford Bridge to Wembley, he is as consistent and entertaining a man as you could wish to meet.

Oh! – and by the way – he's a very, very talented actor as well, but I'll leave him to tell you that.

– Clive Mantle

Chapter 1

A pair of long trousers if I passed

SO MANY OF MY FRIENDS AND COLLEAGUES have written funny, moving and thoroughly entertaining biographies, and I've enjoyed reading them all. I've been asked many times to put down my own story, but I've only ever got as far as the title; well, five of them really. It was always going to be called *Just One of Those Things*, a phrase my dear mum would say when I was a young actor going up for a job and not getting it. Other titles were *What Was That All About* and *Puppets, Politics and Montgomery Clift*. People have said, we understand puppets and politics but what does Montgomery Clift have to do with it?

When I was a boy I always wanted to be Montgomery Clift. He was my favourite screen actor in the fifties and early sixties. *A Place in the Sun*, a film he made with Elizabeth Taylor, is still one of my best loved films. *The Young Lions*; *From Here to Eternity* – he was a great actor.

But what I think my book will be called, if I ever get to write it, is: *Derek Fowlds – A Part Worth Playing*.

So where do I begin? Do I start with the classic opening line 'I was born' (or 'It was a dark and stormy night') on 2nd September 1937 when I came into this world? No, I think I'm going to start when I failed my eleven-plus examination, and return later to my first decade. It was the exam that really changed my life.

I went to school in Berkhamsted in Hertfordshire. There was the Berkhamsted Grammar School and the Ashlyns Secondary Modern School. My mother helped out at the Grammar School. She worked in the bookselling trade, in a bookshop – T. W. Bailey in the High Street – who organised all the books for the school and also arranged the tickets for the school plays. Mum got to know most of the masters and she was asked to go along to the productions and tear the tickets. And I went with her. That's when, I suppose, I started to get interested in acting. It was the boys who played all the parts. I remember *St Joan* and *Richard of Bordeaux* and I just got fascinated by these plays. Little did I know that one day I would be up there doing it myself.

In 1948 when I took my eleven-plus Mum promised me a pair of long trousers if I passed. I was desperate for long trousers. But sadly I didn't pass. I failed. So, instead of going to Berkhamsted Grammar school, I went to the top of the hill to Ashlyns Secondary Modern School. In those days if you didn't pass your eleven-plus you were denied a proper education. You learned how to read, write and add up but I never took an examination – no O or A levels. But I did have a lot of fun and, remembering the boy actors at Berkhamsted Grammar school, I started to act at Ashlyns, just for kicks. I enjoyed mucking about on the stage.

The first play I did was a Chinese play called *Lady Precious Stream*. I remember getting my sword stuck up somebody's skirt. I couldn't retrieve it and I heard the sound of audience laughter for the first time in my life and I was just knocked out. I did another play and this time it was Shakespeare. I'd never read Shakespeare in my life, I had no idea what it was all about. It was *A Midsummers Night's Dream* and my wonderful English teacher Enid Watling (she became a mentor and great friend to me) cast me as Bottom. I had a wonderful time doing it; it was my first Shakespearean play and Enid taught me what it meant and opened my eyes to the wonderful language of the Bard.

The last show I did at school was an operetta, would you believe. It was called *Dogs of Devon*, and I played the mayor of Plymouth. I still have wonderful memories of the production.

My childhood life in Berkhamsted was a joy. The acting was then just a hobby, like playing football or cricket or tennis. I was a cub, then a scout, and eventually a senior scout; and I remember all the boys, our gang, the boys who lived near me in Ellesmere Road and George Street. There was a recreational ground in George Street, a vast open playing area with swings and a roundabout. In the summer we played cricket and in the winter, football. It was surrounded by woods where we acted out Robin Hood and The Three Musketeers, making swords and lances out of broken branches.

Alan Reedman, known as 'Skinny', and Johnny Wheeler ('Killer') were in the gang, as were Pete Spanswick, Bobby Stiles, Johnny Sanders and Frank Hulat. Brian Bandy (strangely known as 'Widdle') was our hero, being good at everything: best footballer, best cricketer, fastest runner. Brian was also much taller and wider than the rest of us. We were always outside doing something – hitting, throwing, kicking a ball, fishing. We were hardly ever indoors. There was no television then.

As we lived near the railway we used to take copper halfpennies, climb down the bank and place the coins on the track. In our minds, after being flattened by the giant trains, our halfpennies became pennies, so doubling their worth. We never realised that playing this prank put us all in great danger.

I still, on rare occasions, see Pete and Bobby back in Berkhamsted, both married with grown-up children. Sadly Brian Bandy collapsed in Berkhamsted High Street with a massive heart attack. He was still in his fifties when he passed away.

Johnny Wheeler emigrated to Australia and was killed in a motor-bike accident in 1988. Childhood friends stay with you forever.

I also started ballroom dancing, winning a silver medal when I was 17 which followed my hard-earned bronze with my wonderful partner Vivien King. I wonder where she is now?

Growing up, the thought of acting for a living had never crossed my mind. I wanted to be a footballer or some other kind of sportsman.

Saturday morning pictures was a big thing for us boys who didn't have televisions at home. In Berkhamsted there were two cinemas: the Rex and the Court. The Court put on a Saturday morning show; entry sixpence, ninepence or a shilling. We paid sixpence (the price for the front seats) and waited for the lights to dim when we could creep back to the shilling seats. Cowboy movies were our favourite – Johnny Mack Brown, the Lone Ranger with his mate Tonto, and Gene Autry, the singing cowboy. We also loved the early Tarzan, Herman Brix, swinging on jungle vines, and *Flash Gordon* with Buster Crabbe in the lead, supported by Jean Rogers as Dale Arden and Charles Middleton as Ming the Merciless. All in black and white, of course.

In those days the grown-up films changed every three days, and if the opportunity arose and time permitted I used to bicycle to one of the cinemas, place my bike under the small open window of the toilets and clamber in. If I liked the film and an actor or scene inspired me I stopped outside a butcher's shop on the way home. The shop window was slightly darkened and provided excellent reflection for my re-enactment of the remembered scene.

(Many years later the film *We Joined the Navy* was shown at the Rex. I joined my family and all my friends for the screening. What a hoot!)

For a while the only television in our road belonged to my dear friends Lionel and Olive Bachelor. It was in their front room that I watched the coronation of Queen Elizabeth in 1953; and every Sunday night from the age of 15 we watched *Have a Go* with Wilfred Pickles, *What's My Line* and the *Sunday Night Theatre*. I saw Peter Cushing in one of those plays, and years later I worked with him in the film *Frankenstein Created Woman*.

We got our television when I was 18 and the first programme I saw was *Robin Hood* with Paul Eddington as Will Scarlet. Coincidentally, Paul later became a dear friend and colleague when we worked together in *Yes Minister*.

*

My childhood was a loving one. My mother had a very strange name, being called Ketha. I never found out why she was called Ketha. I was too young to ask Gran, my mum's mum. My mother had no idea where her name came from.

She was a very special lady, my mum. Her father was Frederick Treacher, a butcher; and Mary, her mother, was a cleaner. When Mother left school she was quite bright and worked in a bookshop. In the shop she had a lot of dealings with salesmen, selling books and stationery goods, and she was asked if she would like a job in London.

Of course she discussed it with her mum. At that time she was engaged to a man called Walter Hawkes. I don't know when that was called off.

She went to London, to Battersea Rise in Clapham, and she worked in Lovell's Libraries. She loved being up there. She had digs with Edie and Harry Bennett, wonderful people who became my Auntie Edie and Uncle Harry. Edie looked after my mum when she was there, and one day she said to Mum that she wanted her to meet a friend, Mrs Fowlds, who lived at 88 Northside, Clapham Common, which is not far from Battersea Rise. Mrs Fowlds had three sons: Albert, who was a tailor at Bentalls in Kensington High Street; Jack, who was in insurance; and Jim, the rogue and vagabond, known to everyone as 'Smiler' Fowlds. He was a steward aboard ship and used to go backwards and forwards to Australia. Mrs Fowlds was very worried about Jim and wanted him to stop going to sea, and to find him a nice young lady.

Later Mrs Fowlds introduced my mother to Jim and they fell in love. They must have married in 1932 and had a flat in 105 Stormont Road, just round the corner from my nan. Jim stopped going to sea which was the object of the exercise. They had a little newsagent's at the end of Stormont Road and Jim also became a tallyman for a tailor, collecting money owed on hire purchase schemes. My sister was born in 1934; I followed three years later in 1937 and, shortly after, war broke out.

I don't remember much about my early childhood – I think I must have been two when they started the bombing. When I was three my mum used to put my sister Babs and me down in the coal cellar whenever we were naughty. It was also the place we went to when the bombs started falling. I also remember going around to my nan during the blackout. I used to peek out at the enormous barrage balloons up in the sky and the searchlights on Clapham Common. I thought that was very exciting.

My nan used to say, 'Close the curtains, close the curtains.'

And then, for the family, events became threatening. My dad was called up. He wanted to go into the Navy because he loved the sea, but they said he wasn't fit enough so put him into the Army, in the infantry, which I've never really understood.

My parents decided to evacuate my sister and me down to Berkhamsted, Mum's home town, where my gran was. This was simply to get us both out of London.

Off we went. I was three and Babs six. Babs got involved in primary school. I couldn't go to school until I was five; I couldn't go anywhere – there were no play schools. But I had a wonderful, wonderful gran who looked after me. As I've said, a very loving childhood.

My dad got cancer when he was in the Army. I do remember him coming back to Berkhamsted; I remember him cleaning his webbing, pressing his uniform on the kitchen table and being taken with my sister to Clapham Common. My last memory was when my mother picked me up and took me to see him in the hospital and I waved to him in the corner bed and he waved back. And later, sadly, he passed away. He was only 41. My mum was devastated and she didn't see us for six months after Dad died. She stayed in London, so Gran looked after the two of us. I was only five when my dad died.

Gran was deaf and had a hearing trumpet. I supposed that's when I started to project, to shout, so I could have long conversations with her. When Mum came back from London to live with us she returned to her job in the bookshop.

At one point we had five people living with us in the house: lodgers in the spare room, and a Mrs and Miss Thorn who ate and slept in the front room. I slept in the front bedroom with my mother and sister, my gran in the middle room and cousin Pam and her nan in the other room.

We lived in Ellesmere Road, a long road of terraced houses, opposite the railway. From the front bedroom I could watch the trains. I loved steam trains, taking their numbers for a long time. Like most boys, I suppose, I wanted to be a train driver when I grew up.

We had a scullery with a copper and a mangle, and a kitchen where we lived out our day; and there was a front room which was only used at Easter and Christmas and the occasional Sunday when we had visitors. We had an outside toilet. In the winter I used to take a candle, and on the wall was this tin bath that was brought in on Friday nights for me to have a bath in front of the fire. In the summer, bath nights took place in the scullery. If by chance my sister Babs was at home a towel was held in front of me so that Babs couldn't see. Mum sat one side of the bath holding a corner of the towel and my granny the other. They had this saying, started by one of them and finished by the other, which had them both falling about with laughter. It went: 'You wash up as far as possible, you wash down as far as possible, then you wash the possible.' Hoots of uncontrollable laughter followed.

There was a gas mantle above the kitchen table, lit only in the winter when the curtains were drawn. It was a warm, cosy and loving home.

We went to our Congregational Church on Sunday mornings. Our tyrannical vicar was called Lansdown West. I've never forgotten him. The Sunday School was great fun. We were not allowed to go anywhere on a Sunday apart from church – couldn't watch sport, and unheard of to go to the cinema. In those days the upbringing was quite strict. Mum had a cane behind the mirror above the fireplace which was brought out on occasions, until one day I stopped as she was chasing me around the kitchen table and I said, this is silly, and broke the cane. The joke from this story came much later when my darling Jo asked me if I was 24 at the time. I think I was 12. There were many women in my life as a child and I loved them all.

I started primary school when I was five. I think that was the year I got 'married' for the first time. I know I nicked my gran's net curtains for the bride's veil. Her name was Margaret. I do remember Margaret. She was my first girlfriend – the first of, I'm ashamed to say, a long list.

Mum was successful at T. W. Bailey's bookshop in Berkhamsted. She earned the money, and in a way became our father. Gran, meanwhile, became our mother, for it was she who brought us up. She spoiled us rotten. I was surrounded by women: my mum, my gran, my sister, and there were three maiden aunts who visited Gran every Thursday – Auntie Hannah, Auntie Kit and Auntie Sarah, who all seemed to have warts and hair coming out of their chins. There was also another lovely lady who came called Miss Philpot, a great friend of Gran's; and there they sat, five of them, having tea.

When I came back from school I used to fall through the door with lipstick in the corner of my mouth and pretend I was dead just to give them a shock. Auntie Hannah was always up for a wrestle and when I went to bed at seven o'clock I had to go around and kiss them all. So began my love of women, I think. I've always enjoyed the company of women which has got me into some hot water in my lifetime.

I suppose my first brush with showbiz was when I was about 10 years old. My mother, my two grandmothers, my sister, my cousin Eileen and I would go to Margate for our summer holidays.

I was always a bit of a loner and quite shy so when my mother told me to take my pullover and shirt off to let the sun in, I resisted.

I can hear myself saying, 'I don't want to take my clothes off in front of all these people.'

So I used to sneak away to the other end of the beach where I could watch the Uncle Tommy Follies with beautiful dancing girls and crazy sketches. People were performing, playing make believe and enjoying it. It was loud, colourful and dynamic. I sat all alone in a deckchair and was transfixed. I escaped my family whenever I could.

My special treat during the holiday was a knickerbocker glory – at one shilling and sixpence.

At the age of 12, Valerie became my girlfriend. Her brother asked me to go to the woods where Valerie wanted to play the game 'I'll show you mine if you'll show me yours'.

Around about that time I used to travel to Clapham Common to see my nan. Mum put me on the train to Euston Station, then I caught a number 88 bus that stopped outside my nan's house. I often played with my cousin Bernard who lived nearby, and one Saturday he offered to take me to the football.

'What team do you support?' I asked.

'Chelsea,' he said with a hint of triumph in his voice. That day a new fan was born. My favourite player was Roy Bentley, a centre forward. I think they played the two, three, five formation that I played in at school. I played for my school and also for Hertfordshire, my county. My position was on the wing, number 7.

Mum so wanted me to go to the Grammar School, and years later she was told that, because of her connections with the school through the bookshop, she could have pulled a few strings to get me a place. But Mum never thought about that. She wouldn't have done it anyway; she was goodness personified. So it was a huge disappointment that I failed my eleven-plus.

For me, though, it was quite exciting as I went instead to the school on the hill. Ashlyns Secondary Modern School came about after the amalgamation of the Thomas Coram School with the 'town kids'. The foundling children were there – it was their home. I loved it and, as I've already mentioned, it was where I began acting, encouraged by Mrs Watling, the English teacher, who taught me a great deal.

My first pair of long trousers arrived on my 12th birthday. They were grey flannel, with turn-ups, and never stopped itching.

At 15 we had to leave school. It was so sudden. I started work straight away at the local printing works. I spent six months in the office, and then transferred to the factory to be an apprentice printer.

I worked at the Clunberry Press in Berkhamsted which was the printing office of Cooper, McDougall and Robertson, who made aerosols. Although I was 15 I looked about six, and there I was making tea and sweeping up in the composing room and helping Bill Brewer in the Reading Department, and going to Watford Technical College to learn about printing.

It was about this time I got my first bank account in which I banked 10 shillings a week. My pay was 30 shillings but I handed over a pound to my mum.

I loved the people I worked with and the excitement of being out in the world, although in 1953 it was a very different world to what it is today. But I hated the job and felt, is this all there is? Is this it? And I thought, no, no – something's going to happen. Then I joined the Cooper Players, which was the company's drama group. And that's what I began to live for. I performed in *Pink String and Sealing Wax*, *The Paragon*, *Why Not Tonight*. Being in all these plays, meeting new people, opened up a new world to me.

While I was rehearsing with the Cooper Players I had my first experience of real grief. When I got home and Gran wasn't there, I asked where she was. They told me she had gone away for a few days, nothing to worry about and to carry on rehearsing. When it came to opening night I asked again where Gran was. They said she's coming back very soon. At the end of the week after four performances I was told she had passed away.

It was really hard. She'd brought me up from the age of three, fulfilling my mother's role. I remember I used to sit on her knee when I was younger and she read *Rupert* to me, the story of Rupert Bear. I had a *Rupert Bear Annual* every Christmas. She also read the

Enid Blyton stories of the Famous Five, and the Biggles books by Captain W. E. Johns – they all came from my gran.

When I got to about 13 I knew exactly where she kept her purse. I'm ashamed to say that I used to go into her room in the afternoons when she was asleep and nick threepence and go round to the shop on the corner and buy some sweets. That's a terrible thing to admit; but losing her was devastating to me. It was the first time that I felt this pain of loss. She was a great, great woman.

Chapter 2

Square-bashing in West Kirby – *Reluctant Heroes* in Malta

IN 1956 NATIONAL SERVICE HERALDED ANOTHER BIG CHANGE in my life; I signed up for two years. I had no idea if I would be placed in the Army, the Navy or the Royal Air Force. To my surprise it was the RAF; I think because, in Berkhamsted at the age of 16, I had joined the Air Training Corps. I hadn't enjoyed it much and stayed only for six months; it was too regimented for me, too disciplined for a free-thinking youth.

So when I was 18 I joined the RAF. I had completed three of my seven years' apprenticeship as a printer, and in a way I was quite relieved to be called up to do my two years even if it meant leaving home for the first time. Something in me wanted adventure, and taking myself out of a cosseted and predictable home and work life seemed to me to offer an opportunity to do something different, to be someone different.

I knew I would miss my mother and sister but I felt determined, and this was backed up by my mother's special strength (and perhaps foresight). I wrote to her the day after I arrived and continued to write every week.

We all gathered, all 18-year-olds, at RAF Cardington in Bedfordshire where we were kitted out with rucksacks with standard and dress uniforms, boots and a rifle, and told where we were going to be for the next two months.

I have to admit the pride I felt in first putting on the blue uniform. I suspect the services can be hell for some and a saviour for others. For me, it just felt right. I think I had realised that, although I

12

would miss my work colleagues, I would not miss the work. An important and worthy job, being a printer; but not for me, not for the rest of my life.

While I was there I met a really nice guy who became a lifelong friend. His name was Colin Hull and he was an apprentice electrician. I was born on the 2nd of September, Colin on the 4th of September. We had a lot in common, Colin and I. We were both really pleased when we were posted to West Kirby, near Liverpool, to do our square-bashing together.

It was quite something, square-bashing – eight weeks of torment! Up at six in the morning for seven o'clock parade; then nigh on a twelve-hour working day.

The corporals shoved us around, shouted and screamed at us, taught us the drill, how to fire a gun.

We would be ordered into their huts, stood straight, upright, without moving a muscle. The corporal would strut around us, stopping in front and pushing his face only inches away from ours.

I can see him now, the peak of his cap on the end of his nose with his narrow beady eyes burning into mine.

'You're an 'orrible airman,' one corporal said to me. 'What are you?'

I had to repeat, 'I'm an 'orrible airman, Corporal.'

'And again,' he shouted.

'I'm an 'orrible airman, Corporal,' I squeaked.

I remember in the first or second week a little Scottish lad in our hut was found hanged in the toilet and we were all very upset about that. Colin thought we might get demobbed. Compassionate demob, or something like that. I pointed out that we'd only been there for two weeks. Of course we didn't and we carried on for another six weeks.

At the weekends when we had a few hours off we had to polish the billet floor, until it was so shiny you could see your face in it. Boots got a similar treatment. On sunny days we were told to dig a garden with our bayonets: no spade or fork, no trowel. Now that was silly. And we were pretty good with the rifle. The drill required the skills of a juggler, throwing the rifle about: stand at ease, stand easy, stand ready, present arms, ground arms, take up arms and so on. Shooting was much more satisfactory. Good luck or a good eye gave me a high success rate on still and moving targets.

It's funny that years later, in 1963, I was in America on Broadway doing the play *Chips with Everything* which is about National Service lads and their two years' duty, written by Arnold Wesker. We had to do a drill and passing out parade. It all came back to me, my real National Service days.

The RAF wanted us to fill in a form saying what we would like to do for the rest of our two years. It was difficult to be objective about that, having been kicked around and shouted at for eight weeks by these corporals. There was a Corporal Slater – I didn't like him at all; and Corporal Lewis, who was much nicer. Most of all I remember Corporal Maund who had a room at the end of our billet. With his cap over his eyes he never stopped staring at us, shouting at us and giving us a hard time. When I played Oscar Blaketon in *Heartbeat* years later I modelled Oscar on Corporal Maund.

Anyway, we filled in this form and (for a bit of a laugh) I put at the top I would like to be a drill instructor even if I wasn't the smartest airman in the camp. I think they just laughed at that. So they gave me my second choice which was a wireless operator. Colin came too. We had to go to Compton Bassett, in Wiltshire, which is very near to where I live now. We stayed for eight weeks. We had to learn Morse code and to pass out at twenty-five words a minute which was fast when you compare it to the Army who passed out at twelve words a minute.

At weekends we boys used to go into Calne, a small town nearby. There was a dance hall where, I confess, our intention was to 'pick up' girls. And to be fair to us, the girls were there, eager to be 'picked up'. I was always grateful that I had gone to dance classes when I was younger, the foxtrot and waltz steps coming back naturally.

The other thing I remember about Calne is Harris's sausage factory. It stank.

When we were coming to the end of our Compton Bassett Morse code training we were asked if we would volunteer to go abroad. Colin didn't volunteer, for reasons I didn't at first understand. One night he was visibly upset and I asked him what was wrong. He said that he'd just had a letter saying his girlfriend was pregnant.

He said, 'I'm only 18!'

I asked him if he loved her. He said he did, so I said you've got to write three letters: one to her, one to your mother and one to her mother and you just say that you love her and want to marry her.

In fact, months later he did get married and I was best man. So Colin decided to stay in England.

But I was lucky to be posted to Malta. To Malta for the rest of my National Service! I'd always wanted to visit another country and to fly for the first time. What an experience that was for me: ten per cent nerves, ninety per cent excitement. It wasn't a troop carrier as we know them today, it was a prop-driven conventional passenger plane, with RAF personnel filling all the seats.

As it turned out Malta was a pretty good posting for me. The weather was fantastic (so our uniforms were lightweight and khaki coloured). Tennis was my sport, and I was picked to play for the RAF; if you played a sport you got a lot of time off.

One of my pals in our billet said to me one day, 'You're an actor, aren't you?'

I said, 'No, I'm an apprentice printer, but I enjoy acting – I've acted at school and as an amateur.'

He said, 'Well, there's a Shakespeare recital at the Malta Amateur Dramatic Club, the MADC, and they're doing a production, so why don't you go down and join?'

I said I would and went down to the Palace in Valletta which was the home of the High Commissioner. (By an extraordinary coincidence my future father-in-law, the father of Wendy, became High Commissioner to Malta years after my stay.)

The Palace was an incredible building. I walked up these vast stairs and along a long corridor with armour-plated soldiers and tapestries.

At the end of the corridor were two little old ladies and they said, 'Hello, good evening.'

(I didn't realise then that these two ladies were the locally famous Warren sisters who ran the Drama Club. Later in life, when I did a film with Alec Guinness, Alec told me he once served in Malta, had joined the Drama Club, and remembered the Warren sisters with great fondness.)

I said to the sisters, 'Hello. I'm Derek Fowlds, I've been told you're having a recital this evening and I'm interested in joining the club.'

'Are you an officer?' they asked.

I said, 'No, I'm an LAC.'

'What's that?'

'It's a leading aircraftman.'

'So you're not an officer?'

'No, I'm not.'

'Well you can go in and watch. This drama club is an officers-only club.'

Blimey! I went in and I sat down. It was a Shakespeare recital. A lot of blokes and gals got up who were terribly terribly pukka and did bits from *Romeo and Juliet* and *Cymbeline*; and then suddenly this young guy got up, a bit older than me I thought, tall with long hair. He did a passage from *Macbeth* and I thought, golly, he can act, he's really good.

Anyway, when they broke for coffee I stood there like a lemon because no one came over to talk to me. So I just left.

When I got back to the billet I told my mate, 'That was a waste of time; I went down there and listened to this Shakespeare. None of them could act except this one boy and I never got to speak to him and they told me it was a club for officers only.'

I suppose about two months later the same mate said, 'You know that MADC recital you went to? Well, they're doing a production of *An Inspector Calls*, a J. B. Priestley play. You'd be great in it. Why don't you have another go?'

'I'm not going down there again.'

'Go on,' he insisted.

So in the end I got a copy of the play, read it and thought, there are some good parts in this, perhaps one for me. So I went to the same building, walked down the same corridor and the old sisters at the end were still there.

I said, 'Hello, I'm Derek Fowlds, I'm an LAC. I'm not an officer.'

'Oh'.

'I came here to a Shakespeare recital a while ago and I would really love to audition for *An Inspector Calls*.'

'This is a club for officers only.'

'Well,' I said, 'please can I talk to the director?'

'He's sitting over there at that table.'

I went over and said, 'Excuse me,' and this lovely guy looked up.

'Yes?'

I said, 'I'm Derek Fowlds, stationed at Ta Kali. I would love to audition. But I have to tell you I'm not an officer.'

When he looked up there was a twinkle in his eye. I thought he was ancient but he was only 29 years old. He later became my mentor, a lifelong friend. His name was Lieutenant Commander Bruce Wansbury, and he was First Officer on HMS *Forth* which was the flagship in Malta then.

He looked at me and told me to sit down. When the auditions started he did it by character. First the girls went up, then the mother and father and daughter, and then he said that he was going to audition the part of Eric, the headstrong young son.

Three or four guys went up with posh accents. I thought they were awful. At the end he said, 'Derek Fowlds?'

I said, 'That's me.'

'Come on, let's hear you read.'

I went into the centre of this room and started to read the part. As I did I saw the door open at the back of the room and in walked this tall blonde guy that I had seen at the Shakespearean recital. I thought, if he's auditioning he'll definitely be offered a part.

I read the part of Eric to total silence.

At the end Bruce said, 'Thank you very much, it's all very good and what we'll do now is have a coffee break. I want to discuss with my assistant director and we will announce our decision after you've had coffee and biscuits.'

When I went to get coffee no one came up to me at all. And then suddenly there was a voice behind me saying, 'I know exactly what you're going through.'

I turned around and there was this lovely actor, the boy I had seen doing *Macbeth*.

I said, 'Who are you?'

'My name is Donald Douglas; I'm a sergeant in the Army.'

I said, 'You're a sergeant! How did you get into this club?'

He said, 'I'm the only other rank in the club. They took me because I auditioned for *Hamlet* and they gave me the part.'

I said, 'I'm Derek Fowlds and I'm an LAC.'

He said, 'Keep your fingers crossed. I think you'll get that part. You were best at it, the best reading, I thought.'

We chatted and he told me he broadcast on the service radio every Sunday morning. 'You may have heard me.'

I said, 'Yes, *Letters from Home*. That's your programme.'

'Yes. It's on nine o'clock every Sunday morning.'

'That's brilliant.'

I did get the part and so began a wonderful relationship with Bruce, the director. He directed me in three further plays: *Reluctant Heroes*, *Flare Path* and a play we did at the camp called *Morning Departure*.

As Bruce and I became great friends he taught me to drink. I remember him saying to me one evening, 'Derek – come to a cocktail party aboard the ship.'

'Do you mean on your ship?'

He said, 'Yes, we're having a cocktail party.'

I said, 'What's a cocktail party?'

'What do you mean?'

I said, 'What do you do?'

'First of all it's half past six for seven, and when everyone's there we have drinks and we chat, have canapés.'

I said, 'What's a canapé?'

He laughed and said that afterwards we might go and have dinner somewhere.

Being a well-brought-up boy from Berkhamsted, I arrived at quarter past six. Of course nobody was there, but I was piped aboard as Bruce had previously told me all his guests would be.

I asked for Lieutenant Commander Wansbury and a sailor told me to follow him. Seconds later Bruce said, 'You're early.'

'You said half past six for seven.'

'Most people arrive quarter to seven, seven o'clock. Have a drink.'

By the time the first guests arrived I was totally out of it. I was bladdered, plastered. I could hardly stand. I never went out to dinner. A major known as 'Pip' Thomas, who was going to be in the production of *An Inspector Calls*, volunteered to take me to my billet in his chauffeur-driven car.

Screams, catcalls and expletives greeted our arrival back at the camp. At that time the major was in civvies so my friends had no hesitation in hurling abuse at me as I climbed/fell out of the back seat of the car.

Major Thomas didn't pull rank and saw me through to my bed, leaving me to suffer the most monumental hangover.

Major Thomas played the Inspector in *An Inspector Calls*. It was such an enjoyable production. After rehearsals I was invited back to the officers' mess for drinks, and the major and I became good friends. Years later, after he retired, I visited him at his home in Spain. He once came to a recording of *Yes Minister* with his wife and daughter.

Because of my tennis 'prowess' and drama activities I spent less than a quarter of my working day actually working. I 'plotted' few fighter planes and 'operated' few wireless transmissions. When I did, it took place in an underground headquarters we called 'Lascaris Ditch'.

During the Suez crisis everyone in my billet was due to be posted to Cyprus to back up operations near the action. All six wireless operators, including me, were listed to go. At the time I was rehearsing a play, so I spoke to one of the few female flight officers.

I can hardly believe it now but I said to her, 'Ma'am, I don't think I can go to Cyprus.'

Flight Officer Marr glared at me. 'Why?' she asked.

'Because I'm rehearsing a play.'

'Play!' she said. 'This is war! The Suez Canal has been seized and we want you and all the operators in Cyprus.'

To this day I do not know what happened or who did what, but I wasn't sent to Cyprus – I stayed behind to do the play. The other five operators went to Cyprus without me, and when they came back they gave me such a hard time and never let me forget it.

*

Donald Douglas came to me one day and said, 'I'm going to RADA.'

I said, 'What's that, an electric light company?' I had no idea.

'No, it's a drama school.'

'What's a drama school?'

He said, 'You go to a drama school and learn to act.'

'But we can act, can't we?'

'You get training. Voice, breathing, modern drama and classics.'

'How long is the course?' I asked.

'Two years.'

'Two years! I'm an apprentice printer.'

He said, 'I'm going for a scholarship and a grant.'

'What does that mean?'

'A scholarship means you get your fees paid, and with a grant you get paid each week.'

I wrote to my mother who replied that she was not going to consider this, adding that I must return home and finish my apprenticeship. You are not going to a drama school, she said!

Nevertheless, Bruce and Donald wrote to RADA, enrolled me for an audition and got all these papers. They coached me, saying you have to learn that, read that. I didn't understand what Richard II was saying half the time. I did a bit from *School for Scandal* and Chekhov's *The Seagull*.

In the evenings I used to go up to see Bruce and, in between playing tennis, he spurred me on with RADA in mind.

Donald had already gone; when he left he recommended me to take over his record show, which I did. So *Letters From Home* with Donald Douglas became *Letters from Home* with Derek Fowlds. I had to choose my own signature tune; I chose Glenn Miller's 'Moonlight Serenade'. I used to say, '"Moonlight Serenade" introduces you to another *Letters from Home*. I'm Derek Fowlds.'

It was way over the top and all the boys in my billet used to shout, 'Get off! Rubbish!'

I enjoyed being in the Maltese sunshine, playing tennis. At that time, 1956 to 1958, there was only one hotel on the island which was the Phoenicia in the capital Valletta, and all the other bays – St Paul's Bay, Paradise Bay, Hyntaphia Bay – were totally unspoilt. The other lads and I used to hire a car and go off at weekends and swim. I say swim; to my shame I hadn't learned how to swim so I used to paddle in the shallows, avoiding any depth. Not knowing my lack of swimming skills, some of them pushed me playfully into deep water; it wasn't long before they realised that my cries for help were real and to a man all dived in to rescue me.

Instead of ridiculing me they set about, on many afternoons, teaching me how to swim in a nearby pool.

What could have been more embarrassing was that I never sprouted enough hairs on my chin to shave, so I used to go to the washroom armed with a bladeless shaver and pretend. They never found out.

Malta was wonderful then. The Maltese people were always so kind, very Catholic with rosaries around their necks, fingering them as they took the garlic-reeking old bus into town.

I haven't been back. People tell me it's so built up, with hotels on all the bays, and extremely commercialised.

When Bruce said goodbye to me it was the beginning of 1958. I remember he gave me a big hug, wished me good luck and asked, 'Let me know how you get on.'

It was a valuable two years for me, for without it I wouldn't have met Donald Douglas and Bruce Wansbury and never would have become an actor. I would have returned to Berkhamsted, finished my apprenticeship, probably married the girl next door and had six kids.

Chapter 3

RADA – *Gunga Din* got me in – *School for Scandal* saw me out

I ARRIVED AT RADA FOR MY AUDITION on a Monday in February 1958. I had left home early that morning and took my seat in the third-class carriage of the train. It was still a steam train in those days with a first, second and (for working-class folk like me) third class. I carried a small, slightly tatty briefcase in which, safely stowed, were my much rehearsed lines. As the train sped to Euston Station my whole being was seized with fear, trepidation and anxiety about what was to happen. It could be the most momentous day of my life if I got through; but I was gripped by the thought of failure, of having to return to Berkhamsted with my tail between my legs, admit defeat to my family and friends and face the next few years of completing my apprenticeship at the printing factory. I so did not want that.

I found RADA in Gower Street, a twenty-minute walk from Euston Station, and to my surprise I was greeted outside the entrance by Donald Douglas who was in his first term.

'Good luck,' he said.

'I'm terrified,' I replied.

'Of course you are, but contain it. They'll probably send you to the Little Theatre for your audition. It's down in the basement.'

He wished me luck again and practically pushed me through the door.

Donald was right. I was directed down into the semi-darkness and sat in the wings to wait my turn. There were others there waiting to do their auditions, but through the dimness I focused on a very pretty girl who went on before me.

When I was called to the stage I was sweating. I couldn't see anybody – they were all sitting out there in the dark. I had no idea who they were, who would be judging me.

When I found out later who they were I was amazed, stunned and honoured. Apart from RADA principal John Fernald, there were two wonderful actresses who later became great Dames of the theatre, Athene Seyler and Sybil Thorndike; the actor Anthony Quayle (six years later I made a film with Anthony, *East of Sudan*); and (the phrase 'last but not least' is simply inadequate) Sir Laurence Olivier.

I didn't know then that this would be the first of two auditions.

I stood on the stage of the Little Theatre and I did my *Richard II*: 'What must the king do now? Must he submit?'

'Thank you. Have you got something else?'

I did my speech from *The Seagull*: 'She loves me, she loves me not.'

They said, 'Thank you very much.'

I said, 'Excuse me, I've just finished my National Service and I'm an apprentice printer and I've got to go back to work at the factory so you have to give me a scholarship and a grant otherwise I can't afford to come.'

A voice from the back said, 'Will you wait?'

I went into this room and waited for half an hour. A lady who turned out to be Miss Brown, the secretary to the principal, came up to me and said, 'They want you to come back on Thursday and will you bring two more pieces?'

I thought, do I have any more pieces?

I went back home to Berkhamsted and I phoned my English teacher, Mrs Watling.

'You remember,' she said, 'you learned that poem that you loved so much when you left school – *Gunga Din* by Rudyard Kipling. Do you still know it?'

I said, 'Yes, I do know it. I've done it lots of times.'

'And you played Bottom in *A Midsummer Night's Dream* at school,' she said. 'Do some of Bottom.'

'Which bit shall I do?' I asked.

'There's Pyramus's death speech from *Pyramus and Thisbe*, the play within the play. Do that.'

I went back to the same Little Theatre with a lot of people still sitting in darkness at the back.

A deep female voice said, 'Thank you very much for coming back. What are you going to do for us?'

'I'm going to do Bottom from *A Midsummer Night's Dream*.'

'All right. In your own time.'

The words came much more easily than I thought they would:

'Ay, that left pap

Where heart doth hop.

Thus die I, thus, thus, thus.

Now am I dead.

Now am I fled.

My soul is in the sky.

Tongue, lose thy light.

Moon, take thy flight.'

'Thank you, have you got something else?'

'I've got a poem called *Gunga Din* by Rudyard Kipling.'

There was silence, then, 'Okay, begin.'

'You may talk o' gin and beer

When you're quartered safe out 'ere,

An' you're sent to penny-fights an' Aldershot it;

But when it comes to slaughter

You will do your work on water …'

After two verses they said, 'Thank you so much.'

'Hang on,' I said, 'there are another five verses.'

'No, that's fine Derek, thank you for coming. We will let you know.'

I think I reminded them that I needed a scholarship and a grant.

Donald had been through all this, the same as me, and got a scholarship but not a grant. I saw him outside and over a cup of coffee he told me he had just started his first term.

He said, 'It's wonderful, wonderful.'

'I don't know if I'm in or not,' I said.

'You'll hear in about ten days.'

I walked back to Euston Station and got the train home. Mum was waiting on the doorstep as I arrived.

'How did it go?' she asked.

'I have no idea. It's important, I know it's important but if I don't get in, I don't get in.'

Her reply, which she repeated whenever disappointment came or beckoned: 'It's just one of those things.'

So I went back to the factory, back to the boss, Mr S. H. Smith, who was a sour old bugger really. When I was 14 I won a competition at Butlin's holiday camp. I think I did *Gunga Din* for that and I won the prize that qualified me to go back for the 'All Winners' show at the end of the season. Mr Smith wouldn't let me go, saying, you're an apprentice and I want you here. On the Monday morning when I was supposed to be at this Butlin's camp he phoned up my foreman, Arthur Lindsay, in the composing room asking if Fowlds was there. When Arthur told him I was, Mr Smith slammed the phone down.

This time when I went in he said, 'Fowlds, when are you coming back?'

'I don't know whether I am.'

'What do you mean? You've got four years' apprenticeship to do.'

'I've taken an audition at the Royal Academy of Dramatic Art.'

'You've done what?'

'If I get in I'm going to be an actor.'

'An actor! You!'

I told him that if I didn't get into RADA I'd love to come back.

'Just call me,' he sighed. 'Call me when you get the letter and I'll see how we're fixed.'

Ten days later my mother shouted upstairs, 'Derek, it's here.'

'Can you bring it up?'

And Mum, dear Mum, sat on the edge of my bed and said, 'Look, it's got "The Royal Academy of Dramatic Art" on the envelope.'

I said, 'Oh God! Open it for me.'

Then she opened the letter (I can see her now) and read aloud, 'You have won the Countess Leverhulme Scholarship and we are giving you a grant of £5 per week. We look forward to you coming to RADA on 2nd April 1958.'

I went to the factory and saw all the boys, telling them, 'I'm going to be an actor.'

The reply came, 'We'll see you back here in a few years' time.'

When I told Mr Smith I'd got in it was the first time he looked at me and I saw him smile. 'Good luck, Fowlds. I wish you good luck.'

I was thrilled. My mother was thrilled and worried; my dear sister was over the moon.

*

So began two years at drama school, an enormous challenge in my life.

Starting at RADA was a complete culture shock: this working-class boy from Berkhamsted, who had never been anywhere except Malta, suddenly in London at the Academy training to be an actor.

Life had changed for me. On the first day I looked around at the other students in my year. They included Edward Fox, Tom Courtenay, John Thaw, Sarah Miles, David Burke. All kids at the beginning of our new careers.

All the new people I had to get to know! It was quite daunting.

I used to commute from Berkhamsted. My home was very near the railway station, and for the first few weeks my mother would wave me off with whatever dishcloth or towel she happened to be using. The 7:30 train took me to Euston Station from where I would walk to Gower Street, arriving at 8:30, and put my named card in the cubby hole. I spent two years commuting up and down.

I was shy and withdrawn at the beginning but slowly I settled in. I didn't know then but my experiences in the RAF helped me to adjust to difficult challenges, small and large.

The first inspiring teacher I had (and I'm happy to say we remained in contact and became friends) was Peter Barkworth. He taught technique. I remember we were all sitting around in a circle waiting for our teacher to arrive and suddenly he burst in and said, 'Speak the speech I pray you as I pronounced it to you, trippingly on the tongue.'

He went through the whole of that speech from *Hamlet* and said, 'That is technique'.

I said, 'Really, I had no idea.'

He was very inspiring.

There were a lot of wonderful people there. Clifford Turner, who taught voice, made us laugh so much – we had to do these voice exercises sliding up and down the wall.

He used to repeat, 'Do you remember an inn, Miranda? Do you remember an inn? Red leather, yellow leather.'

What is all this about, I thought. Somebody said you can't teach anyone to act, it's a gift, but you can teach them technique; the background, the history of drama, fencing, movement, breathing, the voice and all the technical things you need as an actor.

Clifford Turner said to me, 'Derek, your voice is not that bad but you have terrible speech.'

He used to put his hand on my diaphragm and whisper, 'Breathe in, now leave your ribs out. Reserve, Derek. Leave your ribs out. Breathe out but leave your ribs there.'

I remember one particular tongue-twister which we had to repeat faster and faster: 'A tutor who tooted the flute, tried to tutor two tutors to toot. Said the two to the tutor, is it harder to toot or to tutor two tutors to toot?'

I had many influential teachers at RADA. As well as Peter Barkworth and Clifford Turner there was Amy Boath, Nelly Carter, Ellen Pollock and Denis Blakelock. Extraordinary people.

Coming from Hertfordshire I had these flat vowels; it was difficult to pronounce A-E-I-O-U as Clifford wanted. 'RP,' I was told. I had no idea what that meant. (I later discovered it meant 'Received

Pronunciation' – the form of spoken English in the educated south!) At RADA I got this little prop, like a bone with little grooves top and bottom, which I used to clip between my teeth; this supposedly put your mouth in the correct position to say the vowels correctly.

On a trip back home I called in at my old club, Sunnyside Working Men's Club, where I spent many happy hours playing snooker and darts and drinking with the boys. I used to put my bone prop in and put on these exaggerated vowel sounds: 'I'm gOO-ing tOO bEE AAn AAct-OOR.' A great bunch of lads who never believed that I would be successful and stick drama school for two years, they took the mickey and teased me; but it was always done with great affection. All of them remained close friends until one by one they passed away. Happy days.

When we were at RADA in 1958 I don't think any of us thought about film and television. We all wanted to have careers on the stage. We never thought about being famous or anything like that; we just wanted to earn a living as actors and actresses.

There were some very talented people in my class. My year was divided into two. In my group there was William Gaunt and Edward Fox and Sarah Miles. In the other group was Tom Courtenay and John Thaw. It was a very exciting time, and I got some really nice parts. Helen Ryan and David Burke were also in my year. We did a play the principal of RADA John Fernald directed called *Palace of Strangers*. People came to see it and I started getting letters from agents towards the end of my two years.

Like many things of that time tastes in music were changing and at a rate never seen before. Glenn Miller, Ted Heath: big, bold bands playing dance music had been the hits. Show music too, choirs, brass bands – they were sounds I was most comfortable with. I had limited knowledge of classical music – Mozart, Beethoven (the well-known pieces) – but I was a fan of the great musicals: *Oklahoma!*, *Carousel*, *West Side Story*, *My Fair Lady*.

The new sounds, the new songs, the new singers were everywhere. Everyone knew someone who had a record player. 'Pop', in all its guises, was here to stay: the Everly Brothers, Jim Reeves, Duane Eddy, Perry Como, Frankie Avalon, Frankie Laine, Elvis Presley, the Platters and Connie Francis. I think Cliff Richard and the Drifters (later called the Shadows) brought out 'Move It' about then.

I read the other day that on 19th July of that year the Beatles (at that time known as the Quarrymen) had paid 17 shillings and sixpence for their first recording session: 'That'll Be The Day' by Buddy Holly and 'In Spite of All the Danger' written by Paul McCartney and George Harrison. Quite an investment!

As a group of 20-somethings any excuse to party, to have fun, was seized upon. We worked hard and we played hard. An invitation to a party usually meant me staying in town overnight. Most of the students stayed in hostels or bed-and-breakfasts, spread far and wide in London. I remember waking up in some very strange flats or houses, trying to recall how I got there.

There were times I would tell my mother that I wouldn't be back that night. An inquest always followed.

'Where are you going, what are you doing?'

'I'm going to a party so don't cook me a meal, don't wait up and don't worry.'

She may not have cooked me a meal, may not have stayed up, but she always worried.

Some of the students became good friends, but such is the nature of show business that you remain close for a while then go separate ways, with paths that never cross. Even later, as your horizons widen, you do a play, a series, a film and for those few weeks you become part of a new family. Willingly, you become emotionally involved; then, when the production concludes, the relationship abruptly ends and never rekindles.

The curious thing is that if, after five or ten years, you do bump into an old friend, it is as if the intervening years never existed. I don't know if this happens in any other profession.

*

Every now and again money got very tight, so I applied to the Bourne Trust in Berkhamsted for a supplement to my RADA grant. Travelling by train cost quite a lot and I always gave my mother some money each week for my keep. The Bourne Trust were very generous and their grant enabled me to survive.

Donald Douglas was a term ahead of me, though we kept bumping into each other. Before he left RADA he did me another favour when he won a part on television in a series called *Red Gauntlet*. Taking the role meant that he had to abandon rehearsals for *The School for Scandal* in which he was playing the part of Charles Surface. Donald suggested to Hugh Millar, the director, that he offer the part to me instead, which he did. I owe Donald my thanks because it was a big success. I remember John Thaw played Snake and I kept thinking, God! he's a good actor. He was a very quiet, unassuming person.

I remember we went to Geneva. In the cast was a lovely girl called Suzanne. It was the same pretty girl I had seen through the darkness at my audition to RADA. Bizarrely, my second son, Jeremy, was taught decades later by Suzanne at the Academy of Live and Recorded Arts (ALRA). While I was at RADA I had three girl-friends called Susan or Susie or Suzanne. Or was it Susan, Suzanne and Susie. I might have called them Susie one, two and three. Susie Fuller was in *The School for Scandal* which was my last performance at RADA.

John Fernald, the principal, had his favourites. One day he sent Tom Courtenay and me down to the Old Vic because Michael Bentall wanted to find a Constantine in *The Seagull*. Tom and I went down and did our auditions. We didn't know who was going to get it.

We came back and John Fernald said, 'Neither of you got it. Derek, you're too young and Tom, you're not quite right.'

John was determined that one of us should play the part one day. He did ask me to stay on at RADA for another term and do *Doctor Faustus* for him. Tom would play Faustus and I was to play Mephistopheles.

31

During my last term at RADA when I was doing *Palace of Strangers* and *School for Scandal* I was written to by various agents. It was a wonderful dilemma to have, but in the end I chose to go to an agency called Al Parker Ltd in Mount Street, London. I had to sign a seven-year contract; can you believe that in 1960? I thought that I would be employed for seven years but it didn't quite work out like that.

Just before I left RADA the agency sent me to audition for a play called *A Piece of Silver* by N. C. Hunter, which was going on tour before hopefully coming into London. I got the part and had to go to John Fernald and say, 'I've got a job! I've got a job!'

He said, 'I'm very sorry, Derek, but I want you to stay on for another term and be in *Doctor Faustus*.'

I said, 'I'm sorry, I can't. I've got to start earning my living. My mother has told me I've got to get a job and pay my way through life.'

And he gave me his blessing.

I adored John Fernald. He cast John Thaw instead of me in the part of Mephistopheles. I saw the production and both John and Tom were fantastic. I just knew that something terrific would happen to both of them.

At the end of 1959 we did three performances at the Vanbrugh Theatre of a musical called *Shut Up and Sing*, one of the 'in house' RADA productions for students in their final term. It was loosely based on *West Side Story*, with two rival gangs in the East End. I narrated the story, singing songs and playing the guitar. Tom Courtenay played a leader of one of the gangs and stole the show. My regret was I didn't continue playing the guitar. Three of the songs I remember are 'Shut Up, the Boss Said', 'Live', and 'Where Do They Go to Make Love in a City'. There were noises made about a possible commercial production, but it never happened. Music was by Anthony Bowles, who later built a huge reputation as a musical director and conductor, and the lyrics by Caryl Brahms and a young Ned Sherrin who went on to be a giant in the world of stage and broadcasting.

My time at RADA was all-consuming. Events in the outside world, small and large; almost all passed me by. We really did work, sleep, eat, drink, cry and laugh our studies. Our spare time was taken up by going to theatres or cinemas. I do, however, remember the terrible race riots in Notting Hill and I did witness Bertrand Russell giving his anti-nuclear speech in Trafalgar Square. I joined his gathering again in 1960. For me and many of my friends the movement was a cause to follow.

Another huge happening in that time was the launch of the 'Mini' motor car. I recall this as my sister, Babs, was one of the first owners, of a bright red Mini. I complained about the colour, red being the colour of Arsenal football club's strip. I wanted blue to match my team, Chelsea. My sister was unmoved. Little did we know what an iconic motor car it would become.

The summer break was eight weeks. During my first 'holiday' I went to an agency called Vincent Shaw who, much to my surprise, sent me to Colwyn Bay to do weekly rep at the Prince of Wales Theatre. I had the job of assistant stage manager with small parts. This meant plenty of cleaning and sweeping floors, setting up props, making tea. There were days when a play was rehearsed in the morning and staged in the afternoon with a different, previously rehearsed, play in the evening.

I so enjoyed my time there, helped, I think, by a celebration of my 21st birthday. Most members of the cast and crew joined me for a party held in my digs. Wine and other booze flowed and someone took out a pack of cards and suggested strip poker. Everyone volunteered and it wasn't too long before a few were exposing more flesh than they were covering up.

Then came the moment when my lack of poker-playing skills was laid bare, along with other things. A knock on the door saved me and hushed the roars of laughter. It was my landlady. I pulled the door open a matter of inches, turning my head so she could see only part of my face.

'Derek,' she said, 'have you put the cat out?'

Smothered giggles came from behind me. 'No, I haven't. I haven't seen the cat.'

'Never mind,' she said, adding quickly, 'Oh, I see you have visitors.'

'One or two of the theatre company,' I said. 'We're playing cards.'

'Have a nice time, then.'

It seemed an age for my landlady's footsteps to fade away as everyone in my room stifled laughter.

The director of the Prince of Wales Theatre was Keith Andrews. He put on plays including *Black Chiffon* and *Sailor Beware*. There were many good actors in the productions but the only one I've seen around since is Sheila Hammond.

In the summer break of my second year I joined the Penguin Players, doing mostly Agatha Christie plays.

The films of the time threw up new actors, new heroes for us students to admire: Montgomery Clift, James Dean and Marlon Brando.

When I saw *A Place in the Sun* with Montgomery Clift, Elizabeth Taylor and Shelley Winters, I was so impressed, so moved; I wanted to be Montgomery. Others wanted to be James Dean. James Dean was very influential to actors of my generation, as was Marlon Brando in *On the Waterfront*. We started wearing T-shirts and jeans and perfecting the art of slouching. When we took it too far in class and added slurring to slouching we were pulled up, lectured and told never to repeat such unbecoming behaviour within these hallowed walls.

At the Old Vic Theatre I saw some wonderful performances by Michael Redgrave, Laurence Olivier, Ralph Richardson and John Gielgud.

It was quite rare for me to come across a television set and sit around long enough to become a fan so I never regularly watched any of the early productions. There was the US import *I Love Lucy*, and *Life with the Lyons* from the BBC. Everyone seemed to watch, and talk about, *Dixon of Dock Green*, *Quatermass* and *Maigret*. With the *Wednesday Play* the BBC had started a popular format that ITV later adopted with the weekly *Armchair Theatre*. Many writers became household names including Ted Willis and Harold Pinter. It seems bizarre and terrifying now that most of the early productions were 'live'. If an actor got it wrong tens of thousands witnessed it.

Radio, however, was something I did tune into regularly: *The Goon Show, Take it From Here* and *Paul Temple*.

At the end of one term I was playing Oberon in a short scene from *A Midsummer Night's Dream*. Although I had previously played Bottom I was having difficulty with the part. I asked Nelly Carter who taught us Shakespeare, 'What do I do with this?'

'Remember the poetry,' she said, 'remember the iambic pentameter.'

It didn't help; but what did was a visit to see the *Dream* with Oberon played by John Justin. He came on stage, dressed as Oberon, camouflaged with twigs and leaves.

'Ill met by moonlight, proud Titania,' was Oberon's opening line and at that moment I knew what I would do – I'd find my own twigs and leaves and take them into rehearsal.

Poor Nelly Carter had a fit. 'Derek! Derek! What are you doing?'

'Oberon is king of the fairies,' I said, the conviction of my explanation fading with every word. 'He lives in a wood. Twigs, branches, leaves, trees ...'

The look on Nelly's face told me to stop. 'Really, Derek! What are we going to do with you?'

I got through the scene minus foliage but relishing the role. *A Midsummer Night's Dream* remains a great favourite of mine amongst Shakespeare's comedies.

Early in 1958 there was a buzz around RADA, indeed there was a buzz around the whole theatre world, in Britain and elsewhere, when the Lord Chamberlain's office banned all public performances of *Cat on a Hot Tin Roof* due to its references to homosexuality, still a criminal offence in 1958. Peter Hall's production couldn't be publicly seen. Some got around the ban by staging the play in a private member's club, called the New Watergate. The club was established a year earlier with the express purpose of giving the censor, who had no powers over private performances, one in the eye.

When Arthur Miller's *A View from the Bridge*, which also dealt with homosexuality, was staged the club attracted 13,000 members; when *Cat on a Hot Tin Roof* premiered, that number had grown to 64,000.

Thank God, we (and the censor) have moved on.

I did have a great two years at RADA, met some terrific people and, strangely enough, while I was there I won four awards – can you believe it? I won the Fabia Drake prize for comedy for my Andrew Aguecheek, and the Beerbohm Tree prize for dramatic recital with a speech I did from *Our Wilderness*, a play by Thornton Wilder. And then I won (I'm showing off now) the Denis Blakelock prize, named after another inspiring teacher, for audition technique. I think I went way over the top in a speech from Terence Rattigan's *Flare Path*. I also won the RADA Diploma with Honours. And since I left drama school decades ago I haven't won anything. That's show business!

I went off to do *A Piece of Silver* with Esmond Knight and Joyce Heron. That was my very first job as a professional actor. I was 22 years old.

When I left the RAF for RADA I can remember people's reaction. My gran's relatives were strict Baptists. They were lovely people, very religious, and their reaction when I told them I was going to be an actor was horror. They couldn't accept that I was giving up my apprenticeship and going up to London and going on the stage. They couldn't believe it, and never mentioned me by name for a long time. I became the black sheep of the family in many respects. Rather sad, really. Not just my gran or my mum but all those relations in Potten End. The Baptist church looked on actors and entertainers as rogues and vagabonds – which, of course, we were.

Chapter 4

Silver in Sunderland – *Miracle* in the West End – Filming with
Kenneth More

THE ROUTE WAS A FAMILIAR ONE, a train from Berkhamsted to
Euston Station and a tube ride to Charing Cross. A short walk took
me to the Little Theatre to audition for the play *A Piece of Silver*,
written by N. C. Hunter. I got there early that morning (arriving
early became a lifelong habit) so I sat in a coffee shop opposite the
theatre where I could see people going in, hoping for a gesture, a
smile, a sign that would reveal that everything was perfectly normal
and that my anxiety was totally unfounded.

As it turned out my anxiety *was* unfounded. The company
couldn't have been more welcoming. Peter Powell, the director,
introduced me to everyone and showed me around backstage where
an actor was lying on the floor doing exercises. As we walked on I
asked who he was.

'Stamp,' he said. 'Terence Stamp.'

I had no idea who he was.

I told them that I was finishing my studies at RADA in three
weeks' time.

'That's fine,' said Peter. 'We start rehearsing in London on 2nd
April and open at the Everyman in Cheltenham. We go on a short
tour ending up in Sunderland. Then, we hope, a West End theatre.'

I got the call that said I had the part. I was over the moon. And
promised 12 pounds a week! Then 2nd April loomed and arrived –
the first rehearsal of *A Piece of Silver* was to take place, my first
rehearsal in my first professional play.

But it took my first steps on the professional stage to realise what a giant leap I had made. The nerves were still there but tempered by controlled excitement. It was both challenging and stimulating. Stage fright, nerves, fear of forgetting lines, timing and position. They were all with me at the start but, as the play progressed, the more relieved I was that all was going well. At the end I was positively effusive.

Members of the cast helped, of course they did; none more so than Esmond Knight. Esmond Knight and Joyce Heron played my parents. Among the cast was David Stewart, a Scottish actor, Irene Bradshaw and John Croft.

I didn't know at the start of the tour that Esmond was almost blind. I should have guessed, for at the read-through I observed he wasn't reading the script. He had learned the part, the whole play, by heart, before joining the cast. He and I got on so well we became good friends and later, when I auditioned at the National Theatre, Esmond helped me enormously.

The opening in Cheltenham got some excellent reviews. We toured for six weeks ending up in Sunderland when we heard that the play was not coming into London. Although the playwright, N. C. Hunter, had had successful plays staged in the West End, it wasn't to be for us. The tour, the play, was over – finished. For the first time in my fledgling acting career I found myself wondering what I was going to do next.

The apprehension I had about my future was made lighter by the reflection on my first few weeks as a proper actor. It had been wonderful to walk on the stage, pinching myself later with the realisation that this was to be the way I would earn my living. It would be my life. The world (even if the world didn't know it) was at my feet.

Naively, having secured a long contract with my agent, I had thought that a curtain fall for one job would immediately be followed by a curtain rise in another. I complained to my agent who quietly pointed out that this is how professional theatre works and that nothing – we mean nothing – is guaranteed. It was advice that haunted me for the rest of my career.

They did, however, send me up for an American play directed by Terence Kilburn called *Look Homeward Angel*.

After auditioning for Kilburn's play I got a call from a director called Basil Dean, a notorious and powerful director as it turned out. He was doing a tour of James Elroy Flecker's *Hassan*, and he wanted me to play Salim, the servant and a fountain ghost. As the ghost I had to stand on a plinth wearing just a loin cloth and recite. With nothing else on the horizon I signed a contract to do it.

It was while I was rehearsing for *Hassan* that I was offered the juvenile lead in *Look Homeward Angel* which they were going to do on tour and hoping to come into the West End. But of course, I'd already signed to do *Hassan*. I went to Basil Dean and told him I had the opportunity of playing the lead in this play. He would not release me.

I was really upset not being able to be in *Look Homeward Angel*. The part went to Peter McEnery, and the play came into the West End with Richard Pascoe and Andrew Cruickshank. I went on tour in a loin cloth as the fountain ghost!

But that's what happens in show business. In the end I had a lovely time on tour with actors such as Frank Thornton and Neville Jason.

On tour I got a call from Susie Fuller, who was my girlfriend at RADA. She had left me for a very famous director, the great Peter Coe, who had directed *Oliver!* in the West End and *The World of Suzy Wong*. Susie said he was going to do a play, a short tour, and bring it into London. It was called *The Miracle Worker*, the story of Annie Sullivan and Helen Keller, and she had suggested me to play James Keller. I met Peter who gave me the job.

Peter held the first rehearsal in his flat in Holland Park. In the play an illness has rendered the infant Helen Keller blind, deaf and mute. By the age of six she has grown into a wild and angry child. Her parents employ Annie Sullivan as governess. So it is a serious and heart-rending story.

To get the cast on board with his vision of the play, Peter arranged for the cast members to visit him at separate times. When I arrived other members were already there including Janina Faye, playing the little girl. Janina had been blindfolded for our arrival and she wasn't allowed to talk, just to 'feel' the room. As I entered Peter introduced me to my 'mother', my 'father' and my 'sister'. Immediately Janina (in the character of Helen) started to feel my face. She continued to play her part as Peter invited us to read the script. Over coffee and a bit of chat we all bonded, getting to know each other as family members. After a while Anna Massey (who played Annie) arrived. So a very real relationship was built up between us with the characters we played uppermost in our minds.

After rehearsing for two or three days in Peter's flat we moved to a hall where the roles continued to be built up slowly. Peter didn't want us to learn lines at home, he wanted any learning to take place with the cast around us. This was Peter's brilliant way of helping his actors to become the parts.

So, thanks to Susie, I made my West End debut. We toured for a few weeks before opening at the Royalty Theatre in Kingsway, and then we transferred to Wyndham's. I have always thought of Wyndham's as 'my' theatre; it supplied some of my fondest memories. The play ran for nine months, a huge success, with glowing reviews. Anna Massey was superb as Annie Sullivan. John Robinson played the father.

Most of my teachers came to see it. Denis Blakelock saw it and afterwards we went out for coffee. He said, 'Derek, I really hope this is the beginning of something special.'

I said, 'So do I. So do I.'

Funny old life, show biz. It was a wonderful start to my West End career, although the stage had to wait while I did my first television play in *Sunday Night Theatre* on the BBC, transmitted live! I played the son of a German (or Russian) family in *The Assassins*. It was directed by Gerard Glaister, a prolific TV producer and director, and starred Maurice Denham as my father and Anne Pichon as my mother. Gerard Glaister pointed out to me that I was not on a stage. 'Bring it down! Less is more! You are in front of a camera. You don't have to project to the stalls.'

As the action was transmitted live to people's homes it was very scary.

There was a scene where I had to play the piano, impossible for me as I never could play. This was overcome by having a piano-playing stand-in wearing the same shirt and signet ring, so as I sat down to play they cut cameras to the other fellow in a corner of the studio.

It did appear that I played and played well, so I never corrected praise I received for my suddenly acquired musical skills.

Gerard Glaister's insight into television acting was readily passed on and, later in my career, proved an invaluable asset.

Later I did a play for Associated-Rediffusion called *Breakthrough* in which my part was a young working-class boy climbing the social ladder in London. It was directed by Michael Currer-Briggs and Jeremy Lloyd was in the cast.

The Wedding of Smith Seven-Nine was another TV play. I went up for the lead role but was only offered the role of his mate. Rodney Bewes had the main part. It was set around the time before the hero's wedding. The bride-to-be was played by Julia Foster who later gave up acting and married veterinarian Bruce Fogle and is the mother of British television adventurer, Ben Fogle.

I played a junior army officer in *The Gaming Book*, directed by Eric Till. As an experiment, my character was allowed to join a club of high-ranking aristocrat officers, but quickly found himself out of his depth and humiliated.

After what everyone thought was a successful audition I was pencilled in to front *Dietrich Bonhoeffer* for the BBC. At the last moment they cast Michael York instead of me, though they did give me a part as a German officer. It wasn't the lead I'd hoped for but any disappointment subsided when I met Michael. He was a delight, talented and with no side to him. We got on famously.

Between 1962 and '64 everything kicked off. When I was in *The Miracle Worker* in '62 I met up with a RADA chum, George Pensotti. George and I always got on although we were from completely different backgrounds. George was public school and I was secondary modern, but I adored George and we decided to share a basement flat in Haverstock Hill, Belsize Park.

While I was in *The Miracle Worker* George was in repertory a lot. After we'd been living in the flat for three months he asked me, would I mind if his friend Ben came to stay with us. 'He's not working and has nowhere to live.'

Of course I agreed, and into the flat came the brilliant Benjamin Whitrow. We shared that flat for nearly two years. An amazing time. We used to stay up all night and do our various acting bits to each other. Like, 'Go on, George. Do your Richard II.' 'Go on, Ben. Do your Henry V.' 'Go on, Derek. Do your Hamlet.'

We were young and in love with what we were doing. They became very close friends. It was in 2011 that sadly George passed away and Ben and I were there to say goodbye. That period together was extraordinary. It was great fun, friendships were formed, and to this day I see Ben, phone him up. Treasured memories of that flat in Belsize Park.

When *The Miracle Worker* came to an end I was given my first film: the classic *The Loneliness of the Long Distance Runner* directed by the great Tony Richardson. I only had a small role but it was great to be a part of it. It starred, in my opinion, three of the greatest actors of my generation – Tom Courtenay, John Thaw and James Bolam. Tom played the lead and I was supposed to be one of his borstal mates.

It was filmed in a huge building near Chessington Zoo. I stayed nearby at my aunt Edie and uncle Harry's house.

Tony Richardson fascinated me. He had a reputation as a genius director. On the day he turned up on set saying to his camera operator, 'Well, boys, what shall we do today?' It was as if he was making it up as he went along, as if everything was improvised; but, of course, it wasn't so. He was a superb craftsman, a skill that was gloriously demonstrated through the whole film.

Being part of the film was great fun, but when I went to the premiere I couldn't see me. I think I ended up on the cutting room floor. It didn't matter.

While I was doing this film I screen-tested for a big part in a film based on John Winton's book, *We Joined the Navy*, starring Kenneth More, a hero of mine. I couldn't believe it. I went down to Elstree Studios and screen-tested. Kenneth was there and came over to say hello. I knew there were other actors up for this part. It's the story of three boys training at Dartmouth College, all very different roles. I was up for the part of Carson, the bespectacled, intelligent one who had the answer to everything. He was a bit naive in many respects. I went down to the set having learned this speech in which I had to describe a boat. I was terrified.

Wendy Toye, who directed me, said, 'Thank you very much Derek, that's lovely.'

Kenneth thanked me and wished me good luck. That was it.

Kenneth More had starred in huge films. He played the hero, Group Captain Sir Douglas Robert Steuart Bader CBE, who was a Royal Air Force fighter ace during the Second World War, in *Reach for the Sky*, a film which was as successful as it was important in the inspiration it gave to so many. Kenneth also starred alongside Dinah Sheridan, Kay Kendall and John Gregson in the 1953 British comedy film *Genevieve*, in which they played two couples comedically involved in a veteran automobile rally.

As I came to the end of filming *The Long Distance Runner* I got a phone call to say I'd got the part in *We Joined the Navy*. I was so excited. And £50 per week! The other boys were played by Dinsdale Landen and dear Jeremy Lloyd. Jeremy later co-wrote *'Allo 'Allo!* and *Are You Being Served*? They, I found out, earned £75 a week – a fortune, I thought, until someone revealed that Kenneth More was on a contract with Rank at £40,000 a film. I think it was then I discovered the term 'megabucks'.

I thought Kenneth was such a lovely man, very kind, generous and thoughtful. In fact, in 1964 he asked me if I would play his son in a television film he was doing in Teddington, called *Old Soldiers*. What a thrill it was to see him again and play that part. The gorgeous Francesca Annis played my sister. I kept in touch with Kenneth until he sadly passed away. The ten weeks of *We Joined the Navy* were among the happiest ten weeks I can remember, looking back at my career. As I write, in 2014, Kenneth More would have been one hundred years old.

Before I started filming I went down to Worthing. I used to go to Worthing quite a lot – weekly rep in those days. How did we do it, weekly rep! I played *Billy Liar*, the part that Tom Courtenay took over from Albert Finney in the West End. I remember when we were filming *The Long Distance Runner* I picked Tom's brains about various bits of business he did, which I pinched for the play in Worthing. I loved playing *Billy Liar*. We did a short tour after that.

Our first scenes for *We Joined the Navy* were filmed on location in Villefranche, near Cannes. We arrived in France, Jeremy, Dinsdale and I and all the crew, along with other members of the cast including Lloyd Nolan, the great American actor.

It was there that I met the leading lady, though I think she rather met me. She was an American actress named Joan O'Brien. What a gorgeous woman she was. She always used to be by my side. I was 24 and she was 29.

On the plane going back to England Joan was sitting up front with Jeremy Lloyd. Dinsdale and I were sitting a few rows back and Jeremy came to join us.

'Joan wants your telephone number,' Jeremy said to Dinsdale.

Jeremy took the number to Joan then returned to us. 'She wants your number as well, Derek,' he said.

I had a few days' break and went to see my mum in Berkhamsted. At teatime one day the telephone rang and Mum answered it.

'There's a Joan O'Brien on the phone,' Mum said.

I tried to hide my excitement. 'Hello, Joan. How nice of you to call.'

Her voice and accent were unmistakable. 'Derek,' she said, 'are you available to have cocktails with me at the Savoy?'

'I can't,' I said. 'I'm at home with my mother eating cucumber sandwiches.'

'Where?'

'Berkhamsted.'

'Is that far away?'

'Too far away for cocktails.'

'That's a pity,' she said. 'Okay, it's nice to talk to you.'

'Wait!' I pleaded. 'I've got a week off and then we're shooting the dance sequence on board ship.'

'Perhaps we'll meet,' she said. 'Goodbye.'

The next few days seemed endless. My unease lasted until I found myself on set sitting next to Joan. I apologised about the phone call and told her that sharing cocktails with her would normally take first place in my priorities.

A few days later we were filming in Torquay. One evening, at a party – a get-together with everyone in the hotel – Joan came up to me and said, 'I want you.'

'What?'

'I want you.'

I said, 'That's very nice.'

We circulated a bit before it was time for bed – we were due to rise at dawn for early filming. As I approached the lift Joan joined me, followed by Kenneth. I ignored the fact that the lift had sped past my floor and stopped to let Kenneth get out. We said our goodbyes and as the doors closed Joan invited me to see where she lived.

What room, what floor – I have no idea but Joan's wish came true that night.

So began a relationship I cherished. Joan was an amazing woman. When the film had finished we stayed on together for two months and then she got a film with Elvis Presley, *It Happened at the World's Fair*, which meant she had to go back to the States.

I wore a ring, which I really cherished as it had been my father's. It was given to me by my mother when I was 18 and engraved on the back were the words, FROM MOTHER TO JIM – 1927. Before Joan left she asked if she could keep a photograph of me in *Billy Liar*. So I gave her the photo and I also gave her the ring, and I went to Heathrow Airport to say goodbye. It was very hard to say goodbye to Joan. I adored her.

After filming I went back to Worthing to what I thought was a great play called *How Are You, Johnny?* by Philip King who also wrote *Sailor Beware*. In the play I would be working alongside Ian McShane. He was younger than me and so good-looking that all the girls adored him.

It was terrific working with him but the play wasn't too successful, although we did have two months in the West End. It was the story of two drivers, removal men; and Johnny, played by Ian, hated his stepfather and killed him. He rolled him up in a blanket and hid him in the back of the van. Les, my character, was gay and totally in love with Johnny. On one of the trips he discovered the body in the back of the van, and started to blackmail Johnny for his love.

The last line of the first act was: 'I am holding your life, Johnny, your sanity, in my two hands.'

Curtain!

We both enjoyed doing the play. Ian had just done the film *The Wild and the Willing*. Although he was only 18, I thought there were great things ahead for him. Of course, that's how it turned out. *Lovejoy*, Hollywood, success. I've not seen him since. I've seen him on the screen and being interviewed and I always think back to our play and the running joke we had about the play's subject, suggesting it should be called *The Loneliness of the Long Distance Homosexual Lorry Driver*.

After *We Joined the Navy*, Kenneth More got me another part in a film. He saw the director, Philip Leacock, who was casting for the comedy film *Tamahine,* and suggested me for a part. *Tamahine* is a film about a Polynesian woman who believes she can change the culture of Hallow School, a British boys' boarding school. It starred the gorgeous Nancy Kwan, Dennis Price as the headmaster, James Fox (known to all of us as Willy) and Derek Nimmo – this was my first meeting with my dear friend, Derek.

The lead public schoolboy was played by John Fraser. John was amazing. We were all playing teenagers. John, I think, was too old for 'teenage years' but when he came out of make-up he looked terrific.

It was a really fun time. The film was shot at Wellington School, and we stayed at (what was then) a swanky hotel in Maidenhead, called Skindles. Derek Nimmo constantly brought young women back to the hotel and we would party until the early hours – sometimes a matter of minutes before the car arrived at dawn to take us to Wellington to start work. I've never seen the film; I was told that one of the big scenes I played with James and John was cut.

So that's the business – cut from *Long Distance Runner,* cut from *Tamahine!*

Chapter 5

ONE DAY IN 1962 I WAS WALKING IN LONDON thinking, what direction
shall I take? Shall I walk down Park Lane – because that's where my
agent was, just off Park Lane – or should I stroll down Oxford
Street? I went for Oxford Street and who should I bump into
walking toward me but an old RADA colleague, Peter Tory. I asked
him where he'd been.

'I went to Sheffield,' he said. 'After that I went back home to sail
my boat.'

'Where's home?' I asked.

'Bermuda.'

'That's not a bad place to be.'

Peter had been a year ahead of me, but we did bump into each
other and I always tried to see him at work. He was a very good actor
and most handsome. On leaving RADA he went to the Sheffield
Playhouse for a season along with Geoffrey Whitehead and Sheila
Hammond. I remember being envious of them, starting out on a
career so soon after finishing studies. I had heard that after two
seasons Peter had packed it in and left the country.

'I'm back,' he said. 'I'm going to try the acting business again and
get an agent.'

He then asked what I was doing. I told him I was in a play at the
Vaudeville. 'Well,' he said, 'on Saturday my sister is coming over
from Bermuda to do a secretarial course and I'm giving her a party.
Come along after the show.'

He gave me the address and I asked his sister's name.

'Wendy.'

'Wendy. Will I fancy her?'

'No, but you'll fancy her friend.'

'That's all right then.'

After the show on the Saturday I found Pete's address in West Hampstead. It was a great party but I had to ask Pete where his sister was.

'She's out on a date,' said Peter. 'She'll be here later.'

Just before midnight Wendy walked in. I was totally knocked out. She seemed six foot tall, very thin and stunningly beautiful. And 17 years old!

Wow!

Dear, oh dear, I thought, where will this lead to?

Wendy had a beautiful face, a lovely laugh and warm personality. She was young, exciting and enthusiastic. She told me about her secretarial course at a college in South Kensington; I told her about my play and that she must come and see it. And so began a year-long relationship.

I got very cross with Wendy at times because I thought she was very spoilt. She had a £50-a-month allowance which was a lot of money in those days. She used to go through it in less than two weeks so I used to lend her money. I was, however, completely besotted with her and I was very upset when she went back to Bermuda.

Looking back through the sixties, so much went on. An incredible period.

In 1962 Peter Tory and I moved into a flat together at 43b Lonsdale Road, just over Hammersmith Bridge. We had the top flat and underneath was the brilliant theatre director John Dexter and his partner, Riggs O'Hara. We really enjoyed their friendship.

The house was owned by a wonderful family, the Lynches: Professor Benny Lynch, his wife Irene and the two children Adrian and Yvonne.

Peter had found an agent and played one-off appearances in TV series, *It Happened Like This* and *R3*. He had previously done Shakespeare and toured the Soviet Union and Eastern Europe as a spear-carrier but few doors were now opening for him.

However, through his father, Sir Geofroy Tory, a high-flying diplomat who achieved High Commissioner status in various postings, Peter was introduced to the *Daily Express* newspaper, doing a regular Saturday report. His writing skills and his sense of humour were increasingly valued by his editor who took him on the full-time staff. His career rocketed: a journalist and raconteur who worked at the *Daily Mirror*, *Daily Star*, *Daily Express* and *Sunday Express*. He wrote a diary column, where he irreverently documented both trifling and important matters – with a sharp eye for the odd and comical. In his column he wrote as William Hickey.

We had many parties and great times at 43b. John Dexter was about to direct *Chips with Everything*, the play by Arnold Wesker, at the Royal Court and wanted me to play Charlie, the working-class boy. The play was about twenty conscripts and in many ways it was the story of my life: my upbringing, my years as a National Serviceman. I auditioned twice and I remember John ringing me up suggesting we meet on the steps of the Royal Court.

'It's between you and Colin Campbell,' he said. 'Just do what you did before. I want you to play it; Arnold wants Colin, and Bob Swash, the producer, has the casting vote.'

I went in, did my bit, then went back to Worthing where I was doing a play and John phoned me to say it was Colin. Colin was very good in it. Woodfall Films later bought him out to make the film *The Leather Boys*, with Rita Tushingham. Colin seemed destined to have a huge career, but I don't know what happened – it never seemed to take off. I worked with him again in 1968 when we took over from Ian McShane and Ian McKellen in the Russian play by Alexei Arbuzov called *The Promise*; Prunella Scales took over from Judi Dench.

When Colin left *Chips* John Dexter said to me, 'At last. You're going to do Charlie.'

'But I can't! I've just been offered a film.'

John was aghast. 'What film?' he asked without really wanting an answer.

The film I was about to start was called *Tower of Evil*, directed by Jim O'Connelly. It turned out to be a terrible film, though I enjoyed making it. While I was doing that John looked for someone to take over from Colin. I unexpectedly saw him one morning and asked if he'd found anyone.

'Yes,' he said, 'he looks a bit like you but he's much better.'

'What's his name?'

'John Hurt.'

'Never heard of him,' I replied, but of course I had. He'd done the film *The Wild and the Willing* with Ian McShane before I'd worked with Ian in *How Are You, Johnny?*

So that was it. John Hurt took over from Colin but he didn't go to America with the play.

*

At the end of 1962 we had a very harsh winter.

When I didn't get the job in *Chips* the following year John Dexter asked if I was auditioning for the National Theatre. Practically every actor in London was auditioning at the Old Vic. It was to be run by the great Sir Laurence Olivier.

'Yes,' I said, 'I'm going to audition. We all are.'

'What speech are you doing?'

'I don't know yet.'

'We'll all be there,' he said. 'I know because I'm involved.'

So it was John Dexter, Bill Gaskill, Laurence Olivier and Pieter Rogers. I remember they were all out there in the auditorium and when it was my turn I walked on to the stage thinking, oh God! Help!

I said, 'I'm going to do *Henry V*.'

There was a stunned silence. It was one of Sir Laurence's famous roles in one of his greatest films.

'And I'm going to do the St Crispin's Day speech.'

This famous speech is a rallying call to the troops before the battle, but I did it as a prayer. I knelt down (I had Joan of Arc in my mind) and said, 'This day is called, the Feast of Crispin.'

Anyway – 'Yes, thank you. Have you got anything else?'

Then I fell back on my favourite speech by Constantine in *The Seagull*: 'She loves me, she loves me not.'

'Thank you so much.'

And I left and went back to Worthing. I got a phone call from John Dexter saying, 'You're in. You're going to play the National Theatre. Larry loved you and we all thought you were great.'

'What am I going to play?'

'Don't know yet. I'll let you know.'

Weeks later he did let me know, saying that my first part was Laertes.

'What?'

'That's right.'

'Who's going to play Hamlet?'

'Peter O'Toole.'

'That is fantastic. I'm such a fan of Peter O'Toole's.'

I recalled O'Toole's Shylock. To this day I think it the best Shylock I've ever seen. After the film *Lawrence of Arabia* success followed success for Peter. I met him again when I filmed in Paris.

'What about the other plays?' I asked John Dexter.

'We don't know yet. I'll be in touch and behave yourself down in Worthing.'

I was thrilled and excited to join the National Theatre and to play Laertes in *Hamlet* and to work with the great Sir Laurence Olivier.

I was in Worthing when I got a call from John Dexter asking when I was back in London.

'At the weekend,' I told him.

He said, 'Meet me in the pub we use in Seven Dials, Cambridge Circus.'

When I arrived there was John.

'Is it good news or bad news?' I asked.

'I've got both. Sit down. The bad news is that you can't join the National Theatre.'

'Why?'

'Because you're too young. And they can't cast you in the other two plays which are *Armstrong's Last Goodnight* and *The Recruiting Officer*. You could join but you'll have to carry a spear. Nothing else.'

Sometimes I wished I'd done that. Michael Gambon joined that company and did just that, as did other well-known actors of today.

I asked John Dexter who he'd got to play Laertes, *The Recruiting Officer* and *Armstrong's*.

'We've got to find someone to play all three,' he said.

'Who have you got?'

'Some actor from Birmingham. Apparently he's very, very good. He looks more mature than you.'

'What's his name?'

'He's another Derek. Derek Jacobi.'

'I don't know him.'

Derek Jacobi stayed with the National Theatre for ten years and played great parts. I sometimes think, what a wonderful career to have had, Derek's career.

'But I've got good news for you,' said John. 'I've always wanted you to play Charlie in *Chips with Everything*.'

'I know.'

'Well, we're going to revive it at the Royal Court and we're going to take it to Broadway in the autumn. And you're going to play Charlie at last.'

I was so thrilled. I was going to America.

I found out that it would cost me only $90 to fly from New York to Bermuda so I wrote to Wendy telling her of my plans and hopes of seeing her.

I left John and went back to Worthing where I got a phone call. The stage door man said, 'Derek – Dirk Bogarde is on the phone.'

'Dirk Bogarde!'

Earlier in 1963 I had appeared with the wonderful Dirk Bogarde in one of the 'Doctor' films. He was Simon Sparrow in *Doctor in Distress* and my part was a student doctor, Gillibrand. We filmed in a hospital in Surrey and at Pinewood Studios with James Robertson Justice and Barbara Murray. I was so in awe of Dirk Bogarde I couldn't believe I was standing on the same set as he was. I went into his caravan to run lines and talked to him. He was a total delight and very kind. But I never thought I would hear from him again.

I took the phone and said hello.

'Derek? It's Dirk.'

'How wonderful to hear you.'

'Look, I hear you're going to do *Chips* in America. When?'

'In September.'

'Well, would you like a holiday? I'm doing a film called *Hot Enough for June* in Florence and there's this one scene where I'm escaping; I have to change clothes because I'm on the run, and I go to a swimming pool, I lie down by this guy and pinch his clothes tag so I can put his clothes on. It's a very short quick scene. You don't have any lines except "Oi!" or something like that. I thought it would be nice to fly you out, give you a holiday before you go to America.'

'I don't know what to say; I would love it.'

I had a week in Florence. I played the scene with Dirk, and we said goodbye. Betty Box and Ralph Thomas were the producers.

I've never forgotten Dirk's kindness and generosity toward me. That film is never off the telly! People say, you didn't have much to do in that. But I tell them I had a wonderful holiday with Dirk Bogarde.

In September we started to rehearse *Chips with Everything* in the Barracks in the King's Road. RSM Brittain drilled us and trained us. He was terrifying and had the loudest voice I've ever heard. My service days came back quickly. I'd done it all before. Admittedly that was 1956 and this was 1963, but the experience helped me enormously. I was really playing me in the time I was doing my own National Service. We got so good at the drill that at the end of *Chips* we had our own passing out parade. That really was an amazing moment.

Alan Dobie played the sergeant brilliantly. Also in the cast were Gary Bond, Frank Wiley, Michael Standing, Barry Evans, Corin Redgrave and the great, late Ronnie Lacey. We opened at the Royal Court. It was a revival but they all loved it. We were ready for the 'Great White Way' in New York.

I can remember being so excited at the airport when we said goodbye to our families. On board were Christopher Timothy and George Layton, who played RAF policemen and were also understudying me and Gary Bond. We were about to embark on an amazing adventure – Broadway!

I shared a dressing room at the Plymouth Theatre with Corin Redgrave; although he was funny and friendly, we never got that close. I'm not sure if he was active in politics by then; I know that later, with his sister Vanessa, he became a leading light within the Workers' Revolutionary Party. He went on to be an incredible classical actor.

Years later I worked with Corin's second wife, Kika Markham, when I appeared in two episodes of the television series *Van der Valk*, set in Amsterdam and starring Barry Foster as the cynical Dutch detective.

It was quite an experience to take *Chips with Everything* to Broadway. On the opening night we had about twelve curtain calls. Wonderful reviews followed. Gary Bond (who was playing one of the leading parts) and I walked into Sardi's, which was the big restaurant on Broadway, after the first night and we got a standing ovation. It was so enthusiastic that we were tempted to go back onto the street and make our entrance again.

Then all the other members of the cast came in; people just stood up. It was an extraordinary time. It turned out to be a massive hit. We were all very young and knocked out by the reception. We went to parties and met so many famous people. At one party I was at, I wanted to go to the loo and it was locked so I waited outside. When the door opened I couldn't believe it. I think I said, 'Gosh! You're Shelley Winters.'

She said, 'Hello. I am Shelley Winters,' and stuck her tongue right down my throat. I was totally stunned. But I can always say I've been kissed by Shelley Winters. I've already mentioned that *A Place in the Sun*, starring Shelley along with Elizabeth Taylor and Montgomery Clift, was one of my favourite films. In the film George (Montgomery) plans to murder Alice (Shelley) by throwing her from the side of a small boat on a lake but changes his mind. During a heated exchange Alice stands up, causing the boat to capsize. George survives but Alice drowns. Later Alice's body is discovered and her death is treated as a murder. George is found guilty and sentenced to death in the electric chair. A great film.

I also met Tony Perkins, Kirk Douglas and many other incredible people.

At that time there seemed to be so many Brits on Broadway. Albert Finney was appearing in *Luther*. The production of *Oliver!* was on. And Peter Cook, Dudley Moore, Alan Bennett and Jonathan Miller were in *Beyond the Fringe*. I had previously met Dudley Moore when my (then) girlfriend, Susie, had a flat in Holland Park. Often, when we there, with Susie's brother-in-law, the three of us used to record funny voices, do funny things. One evening Dudley was there and I asked him what his next job was.

'I'm going to do a show at the Edinburgh Festival with three other guys from Oxford and Cambridge.'

'What's it called?' I asked.

'We're going to call it *Beyond the Fringe*.'

And now here they were on Broadway.

One evening while we were in *Chips* I had a tap on my shoulder at the stage door. It was Alan Bennett.

'I've seen the play,' said Alan. 'You were wonderful.'

I couldn't help saying, 'I think you're terrific too.'

There were so many actors we got to know that we formed a bowling league, with two teams – 'Chips One' and 'Chips Two'. We played against many famous people. In one match we played against George Peppard and Maureen O'Sullivan who were in the play *Barefoot in the Park*. Maureen O'Sullivan had been Jane in Johnny Weismuller's *Tarzan* films. It was a great thrill to meet her.

One of my agents was a lovely lady called Monti Mackie who, along with Ronnie Waters and James Sharkey, made up the Al Parker Agency. While I was in New York, Monti phoned me and told me she was coming to the show that night and was bringing a friend. We met after the show at a very famous restaurant called Downey's, which was a haunt where all the actors went after the show. A bit like Joe Allen's. In Downey's was Monti with a very dapper man in his sixties. I was introduced to him as Lehmann Byck. Monti and Mr Byck said they enjoyed the show. Mr Byck fascinated me. I asked him what he did.

'I'm a manager,' he said. 'I manage people. I'm also a voice and singing coach.'

'Well, I sing,' I said.

'Really!'

'Yes, I do.'

'Well, I'd like to hear your voice.'

We had a lovely meal and I was very attracted to his charm and personality. He gave me his card and told me to call him at his studio.

I was staying at the Claridge Hotel on Broadway, which was later made famous in the film *Midnight Cowboy* with Dustin Hoffman and Jon Voight. It only survived for a couple of years after that before they pulled it down; I'm not sure what was built in its place. The actors in *Chips* were put up at the Claridge when we arrived in New York, but most moved out after a while and got apartments, and digs. However, the hotel was just a stone's throw from Broadway and a ten-minute walk to the theatre, so I opted to stay there all through my time in America.

A week or so after the meal at Downey's, Mr Byck came on the phone. 'Derek? You haven't called me.'

'I'm sorry, I will.'

'Come on. Come and see me next Wednesday.'

On that Wednesday I found his apartment at 19 West 56th Street. I've never forgotten that because underneath there was a jewellery shop; I can remember that, some time later on in our stay, Wendy and I were looking in the window when she said, I really like that ring. At $20,000 I dragged her away from that window pretty sharpish.

I arrived at Byck's apartment building, went up in the lift and was ushered into a small room. I could hear this beautiful voice singing some sort of aria. I thought, blimey! I'm not that kind of a singer.

The lesson ended and this guy came out.

I said, 'Hello, I'm Derek Fowlds.'

He said, 'I know, you're expected.'

'What a fabulous voice you've got.'

'Thank you very much. My name is David Daniels.'

I didn't know it then, but he was one of the wealthiest people in America. He had property and artworks, and he did possess the most fabulous voice.

He left and I walked into Byck's studio for the first time. He sat at the piano and asked how I was.

'The play's going very well, I'm really enjoying it.'

'Derek,' Byck said, 'let me hear your voice.'

'What do you want me to sing?'

'I don't want you to sing. I want to hear you do scales. "Aaah" and so on.'

Aaaaaaeeeee. Aaaaaaeeee. I did these scales while he pounded the piano. He kept me at it until I was exhausted. Eventually he said, 'Stop. Listen. You can't sing.'

'What do you mean?'

'You can't sing but you have a voice.'

'What does that mean?'

'It means you have to work on it. Come and study with me three times a week.'

'I can't afford three times a week.'

'What can you afford?'

I think it was $3 an hour in 1963, so I said that I thought I could afford two classes.

'I'll throw in a free lesson, so you'll come to me three times a week but I'll only charge you for two.'

So began the most wonderful friendship that lasted until he died aged 99 in 2010. Byck became my mentor in America. We never lost touch.

I did go to him three times a week. We had lunches in Connecticut. Socially we had a great time and I think he was a very good teacher. I got quite a lot of fun out of his classes.

*

On 22nd November 1963 President John F. Kennedy was assassinated. I was with Jane, a friend from drama school, watching the film *Cleopatra* in the afternoon. In the interval she went to the loo and when she got back she said that Kennedy had been shot.

I said, 'What do you mean?'

'Just that. He's been shot.'

'Where?'

'I don't know. I just heard a woman saying he'd been shot.'

'Is he dead?'

'I don't know.'

They carried on with the film. In the second half of *Cleopatra* Mark Antony is chasing the murderers of Julius Caesar. We sat through it thinking, what are we going to find out when we leave the cinema?

It was dark outside except for the lights of camera crews. The lights of Broadway had gone out. There were people being interviewed on the street. I said goodbye to Jane and set off down to my theatre. Although it was in darkness, the stage door man was there.

'Derek,' he said. 'The show's cancelled. Most of the shows on Broadway are cancelled.'

'Where can I find the boys?' I asked.

'You might find them in the Open Kitchen cafe around the corner on 45th Street.'

It didn't take me long to get there. The boys were sitting, mostly silent.

'What's going to happen?' I asked.

'We don't know.'

We all went back to our hotels or bedsits or wherever we were staying to watch television and saw what had happened in Dallas. Extraordinary scenes. I managed to get through to Wendy in Bermuda and she suggested I went down if the play was delayed.

'It's not expensive. I'll meet you,' she said.

My great friend, Byck, took me out to the airport. While I was waiting to go through to board I was watching television and there, in front of my eyes – live – I saw Lee Harvey Oswald being escorted out and a man, Jack Ruby, step out and shoot him. I couldn't believe what I was watching. I saw that murder live!

I flew down to Bermuda, and Wendy and her stepfather met me. We travelled from the airport to her home by boat. Bermuda's shaped like a horseshoe, with the airport on one tip and Wendy's home on the other. We sailed across and moored the boat.

The house was like a huge hotel – I'd never seen anything like it. Flagpole in the front garden. I met her mother and the staff and Wendy said, 'You're in the blue suite. The gong will go at six o'clock and we'll gather for drinks.'

They had a wonderful cook called Moselle. I was knocked out by it all. But they were very kind to me in those few days. It was the first time Wendy and I had been able to be together in many months.

I stayed for three days before going back to New York. After a week we reopened the play, but it was never the same. I remember when we were on parade Alan Dobie, as the sergeant, had a speech about a bullet and how the bullet travelled and what it did. Before the assassination Alan played it brilliantly: carefully timed, effective and very dramatic. Afterwards, he was so clever, he took it at a rate – he just went straight through it without pausing – because he did not want to dwell on that particular speech.

I wrote to Wendy's mother and thanked her for her hospitality, and I said I wondered if Wendy could come up to New York and spend New Year's Eve with me.

She wrote back, 'Take very good care of her.'

I replied that of course I would.

Wendy had just had her 19ᵗʰ birthday. We had a wonderful time in New York together. She met my friends, she met Byck and we had New Year's Eve in Times Square.

We were very much in love with each other.

After one performance of *Chips* Wendy and I were in Downey's and a guy came over and spoke to us. He said his name was Alan and he was a writer who lived in Hollywood.

'What are you doing here?' I asked.

'I've come over to see some plays on Broadway. I really loved *Chips with Everything*.'

We got talking, and I don't know why but I said: 'Do you know an actress called Joan O'Brien?'

'Joanie! Of course I know Joanie.'

I told him the story of how we met on the film *We Joined the Navy*, about our three-month relationship and how I totally, totally fell in love with her. 'She kept my picture of me as Billy Liar, and a family ring. I tried so hard to get in touch.'

He said, 'I'm going back to Hollywood and if I see her, I'll tell her.'

'If you do, that would be wonderful. Will you give her my number at the Claridge Hotel?'

'I will do my very best.'

We had a nice evening, and before saying goodbye he made Wendy and me a little dog out of matchsticks, which Wendy called Twoshows.

'Why call it that?' asked Alan.

Wendy replied, 'If Derek has two shows he has to conserve his energy, so we can't make love on matinee days.'

So he left us with Twoshows.

I wondered if Alan would get in touch with Joanie. I hoped he would.

Shortly before Wendy went back home I said that once the play was over (and because of Kennedy's assassination we didn't expect it to run much longer) I'd come down to Bermuda and we could spend more time together, and maybe get engaged.

Wendy left. The play limped on; nothing at that time was successful on Broadway, it was all very muted.

We had the notice to say that *Chips with Everything* would be closing.

And then I got a phone call from a friend of mine in England, a film producer called Charles Schneer.

'Derek,' he said. 'When are you free? Do you want to make a movie? Come back. We're doing a film called *East of Sudan* with Anthony Quayle and Sylvia Syms and there's a very good part for you if you want it.'

I said, 'Yes. Wonderful. When do we start?'

'We start in two weeks. So just come straight back when you've finished the play.'

Charles – what a fantastic man. I met him through Peter Coe, who directed me in *The Miracle Worker*; Peter knew that I played tennis, so being a member of the Queen's Club he used to call me to make up a foursome. We played on grass during the summer and a wooden court in the winter months. Often Charles played opposite us with Jesse Lasky Jr, the great American screenplay-writer whose films included *The Ten Commandments*. Whenever possible over eight years or more we played Sunday mornings at Queen's.

After the last performance of *Chips* I was packing my bag in my hotel room. We were all ready to go to the airport when the phone rang and a voice said, 'Derek, hello, it's Joan.'

I couldn't believe it.

'This is amazing,' I said. 'I can't believe I'm talking to you. Do you realise I've been on Broadway for the last six months?'

'I'm so sorry. I've just heard.'

'How are you?' I asked.

'I'm fine. I'm working.'

'The funny thing is, I'm leaving tomorrow. I'm going back to England to make a picture.'

'That's wonderful.'

'I'm also thinking about getting engaged.'

'Derek, that's fabulous news. I've never forgotten you and never will forget you.'

I said, 'Will you do me a favour? Do you still have my ring?'

'I certainly do.'

'Can you send it back to me because it was my father's and had great sentimental value to me. I would love to have it back.'

'I'll pack it up and send it to you, but can I keep that picture of you with the penny in your eye when you played the character Billy Liar?'

I said, 'Joannie, please keep it. I must tell you how wonderful it was spending that time together. And I'll never forget you.'

'Derek, I wish you well and I love you very much.'

I phoned Wendy and told her I couldn't go down to Bermuda as I had the film part to do.

'Fine,' she said. 'I'm coming back to England.'

I said, 'It's a six-week shoot and I start in two weeks' time.'

I said goodbye to all the cast and to Lehmann Byck and Frederick Koch.* It was very hard for me to say goodbye to Byck. He gave me a big hug.

He said, 'Derek, it's so wonderful to know you, and I'm so grateful that you are leaving.'

'Why?'

---

* See page 97

'I don't have to listen to that voice any more.'

'Tell me you're kidding.'

He just laughed. He was a great man and I visited him many times over the next thirty years.

I came back home to my flat in England, 43b Lonsdale Road, and started filming *East of Sudan* at Shepperton Studios. It was February 1964.

Chapter 6

A co-star with Sylvia Syms and Anthony Quayle – A wedding –
A birth – The gleam that was Jo

WITH THE EXOTIC TITLE *EAST OF SUDAN* echoing in my mind I asked Charlie Schneer when we were going to the Sudan.

'We're not,' said Charlie. 'You won't be moving outside the studio.'

'How can that happen?' I asked in protest.

'Derek,' said Charlie, 'after this film your education will be complete.'

I know that some of the 'wild African' scenes were borrowed from other movies. They stole a jungle scene from a film with Victor Mature. They projected it on to a large screen and I waited for Victor to go out of shot. 'Action,' they shouted as the cue for me to jump across the jungle background behind me. I think, I hope, it looked as if I was really there.

Sylvia Syms, who starred in *East of Sudan*, was a great actress and one of the most beautiful women I'd ever met. I couldn't stop looking at her and found myself in daily awe, no more so than when she picked me up on her way from Barnes to travel to Shepperton Studios together. I had seen Sylvia in *Ice Cold in Alex* with John Mills and Anthony Quayle; and she had also been in *No Trams to Lime Street*, *Victim* and *Ferry to Hong Kong*. She was a real star.

Jenny Agutter was only 11 years old and I had to carry her through the mock-up jungle. Anthony Quayle – what a fabulous, kind man. He knew what he was doing. He ran the Royal Shakespeare Theatre for years. A black actor was also in the film, Johnny Sekka, whom I got to know very well. Directed by Nathan Juran and produced by the marvellous Charlie Schneer. It was a terrific six weeks making that film, a joy; but it was to be interrupted by an alarming phone call.

After I'd been filming for three weeks, Wendy's mother called from Bermuda to tell me that Wendy was pregnant. I was thrilled in one way but really frightened in another. Wendy was 19, I was 26. I didn't know what this entailed and how my life might change. I loved Wendy very much and I knew she was coming over to England; but her mother said that we could get out of this. I guessed what she meant.

'What do you mean? Certainly not. I love Wendy very much.'

'Well, she loves you too.'

I simply said no, she must have the child.

'All right, Derek,' her mother said. 'We shall be coming over to make arrangements. We will be staying at the Kensington Close Hotel and we must fix a date for the wedding.'

It all happened so quickly.

I went down to my neighbours, Irene and Benny Lynch, and told them my life was going to change again.

On the set the next day with Anthony and Sylvia, I told them that I was going to get married at the end of the picture.

Charlie Schneer gave a big party and it all snowballed.

I had to visit my mother and tell her the news. That was quite an emotional day. I told her that Wendy was coming back and we were going to be married. She seemed surprised but she knew how we felt about each other. Then I told my mother that we were going to have a child. Mum was upset and happy at the same time, for she was very fond of Wendy.

At the end of shooting on the film, on 30th March 1964, Wendy and I got married at the Holy Trinity Church at the Brompton Oratory. Dear Peter, Wendy's brother, was on the road with the RSC so he couldn't be my best man. Another friend of mine, Robin Hawdon, who I was with at RADA and a good mate, took over the best man duties. We both wore grey top hats and morning suits.

So there we were on the big day, with all my country cousins from Berkhamsted and Wendy's lot who were all posh. It was like two tribes meeting. It felt as though I was in a play; certainly a part worth playing. The leading man to Wendy's leading lady.

Robin drove me to the church and looked at me. 'Well, Derek,' he said, 'this is it.'

'What do you mean? Is this the end? Or is it just the beginning?'

It was a wonderful wedding. We had the reception at the Kensington Close Hotel after which we were driven to the Hindshead Hotel in Bray where we spent our first night, and then we flew off to Spain for three weeks' honeymoon. A place called Almuñécar. Never been back since. The hotel on that unspoilt beach was called Hotel Sexi, which made us laugh. But there was nothing to do. At the Spanish bookshop the only English-language books they had were the *Whiteoak Chronicles* series, written by Mazo de la Roche. We just sat and read and enjoyed them enormously, wondering why they were never made into a TV series.

Wendy was pregnant and continually being sick. There were days when she wasn't well at all which affected her greatly.

At the end of the first week she packed her bag and stood at the bus stop.

'Where are you going?' I asked.

'I'm leaving.'

'There isn't another bus for two weeks. You'd better come back.'

Of course, she did; and at the end of the honeymoon we came back to England and moved into 43b Lonsdale Road. My mother and sister had been at the flat and spruced it up and were there to welcome us when we got back. That was April.

The flat opposite was where James Bolam lived. He always seemed to be cleaning his car. He and I had been in *The Loneliness of the Long Distance Runner*. It was always great to see him.

So there we were, married and about to have a baby.

Wendy said, let's have a party. Like most of our parties we held it in the ground-floor flat owned by the Lynch family. Benny Lynch played the violin, the Lynch children played guitar. Another guitarist was Paco Peña, by then a famous musician. All kinds of people came. Robin Hawdon with his girlfriend and mother; Ian Lindsay from RADA who was a great friend of Pete's. That night, at that party, looking across the room I saw the most stunning girl and I said, 'Who's that?!'

Somebody said, 'That's Ian's wife, Jo.'

I couldn't resist it. I walked over and said, 'Hello.'

It turned out that Jo had two children. She looked about 12 – and a very beautiful 12. Little did I know at that time that she would play such a huge part in my life. Jo became Wendy's best friend. I was always saying, get Jo around, she makes me laugh. I adored Jo from the moment I met her but had no idea that she would become the love of my life.

1964 was an incredible year. So much seemed to happen: the events after Kennedy's death when nearly all the plays on Broadway closed, then the return to film *East of Sudan,* Wendy's mother's phone call and the wedding.

After the honeymoon I did manage to do a couple of jobs. I did *Spring Awakening* at the Royal Court. That was an extraordinary play and everyone was hoping it was going to be a commercial success and transfer to the West End. It was directed by a very strange man called Desmond O'Donovan. I think he became a monk and went slightly bonkers, or so I've heard. He's no longer with us now.

There was a very controversial scene in *Spring Awakening*, when the boys were put in prison. I played a 15-year-old boy (although I was 27) teaching my friends the facts of life and demonstrating to my friend Moritz, played by Richard O'Callaghan, what life and sex were all about. We were put into prison for some misdemeanour, leading to a scene that we referred to as 'the masturbating scene' where we played this game and all masturbated. It was cut from our production because of the Lord Chamberlain. We were told that if the scene was cut we had a better chance of being transferred to the

West End. Around the time of the final performance we heard that the production was not going to transfer. Desmond O'Donovan was very upset, as we all were. He said, 'Let's have a rehearsal before the last performance and let's put back the wanking scene.'

It was electric. I do remember it vividly. The silence in the Royal Court Theatre was deafening. It's a wonderful play, *Spring Awakening*, and has enjoyed some splendid revivals.

There was a lovely girl in the play I was quite attracted to. I don't know why. I'd only been married a few months, but these things happened. I always regretted it because I wanted my marriage to work. A weakness in me, I suppose. A desire to be loved by as many people as possible. That's not fair, is it?

I also did an *Armchair Theatre* with Kenneth More. He had asked for me to play his son in the play *Old Soldiers*. A very beautiful 17-year-old, Francesca Annis, played my sister.

Francesca used to pick me up and drive us to the studio. She was such a fast driver. She frightened me to death.

Wendy and I prepared ourselves for the birth of our first child. I was lucky enough to have saved some money and I met with an accountant, Harvey Jacobs, who became a friend who looked after me for forty years. He told me I had enough money for a house.

Wendy and I had spent time in Pinner because my sister, Babs, was the district nurse there. Wendy had said she really liked Pinner, so with Babs' help we looked at properties. We found a house in Dawlish Drive, Whittington Way. It was on a corner, had a garage, three up, two down, kitchen, bathroom, French windows onto the lawn and we fell in love with it. In 1964 that house cost me £5,250. It must now be worth a million.

We moved in in the September and Jamie was born on 14th October, 10lb 11oz. He was enormous. Babs delivered Jamie at Wendy's request and he was born at home. I was the assistant midwife. Poor Wendy was in labour for thirty-six hours. Babs gave me a running commentary: 'Oh, the waters have gone.' And, 'There's the afterbirth. Go and burn it in the garden.'

It was extraordinary seeing Jamie born. It was just the most wonderful experience, with Babs, Wendy and I together. Funnily enough, when Jamie popped out, the cord was around his neck. It was rather worrying, but it was sorted out. The doctor came over and Jamie had his first bath. He was huge – nothing's changed there. It was a very happy time.

Mum arrived soon after, Wendy's mother came over from Bermuda and we all enjoyed the new arrival, James Laurence Fowlds.

We called our house 'Pooh Corner'. It was on a corner and down the road was the Le Bon family. Ann and John Le Bon often called in with the boys, Jonathan, David and Simon. Ann told me that Simon was going in for a poetry competition and asked, would I listen to him. I think he was 12 when he stood in our sitting room and read.

'That's terrific,' I said.

He had so much natural talent. I didn't know then he was going to be a singer, a pop star. I often name-drop Simon Le Bon. At the time, the Le Bon family were great friends.

About this time I decided that I had to buy a car and learn to drive. I found an instructor who agreed to teach Wendy as well. It got quite competitive. I took my test and failed; Wendy took hers and passed. Passed! First time! It took another three months of training for me to pass. A huge blow to my ego! Nevertheless, we were very proud of our first car: a Morris 1000 Traveller, a wood-framed estate car with bright blue paintwork. At my request the same model was used in *Heartbeat*.

I was a guest villain in *The Man in Room 17*, a crime series about a secret government department, 'Room 17', dealing with crimes that baffled police and security agencies. It was headed by veteran WW2 agent Oldenshaw, played by Richard Vernon; in the second series he was partnered by Denholm Elliott. The two men solved crimes without ever leaving their office. I'd met Richard Vernon in the film *We Joined the Navy* in 1962. An eccentric man, full of fun, who later did a couple of episodes of *Yes Minister* as Sir Desmond.

Denholm Elliot was also eccentric. He carried all his worldly goods in a carrier bag. One day I suggested that a posh briefcase would suit him better.

'No, Derek,' he replied, 'you can accommodate everything you need in a carrier bag.'

In 1965 I went for another TV job and got it. It was a boy detective. Peter O'Donnell, who created *Modesty Blaise*, had written this six-part serial about a detective and his French wife known as Frog. *Take a Pair of Private Eyes* – a great title, a wonderful script. I think we would have gone on to make more, but the film rights were sold and it never happened. Jeanne Roland, who played Frog, was just lovely. Henry McGee and John Sharp were in it, and my dear friend Sam Kydd played my father. He and I were friends for many years.

I did hear that they hoped to make the film with David McCallum; then Mick Jagger's name was mentioned? I don't think it was ever made.

While we were making the series I was very attracted to this beautiful girl who was a make-up artiste. I was very happily married to Wendy, but this girl got to me. I thought she was stunning but nothing really happened. We parted after a brief relationship. I went back to Pinner after *Private Eyes* had finished.

Chapter 7

IN 1965 I SCREEN-TESTED FOR THE PART of Maxim in a big picture
which was going to star Alec Guinness and Gina Lollobrigida. The
play, *Hotel Paradiso*, had been a big hit with Alec in the West End;
Peter Glenville had adapted it for the screen. I remember looking at
the boys being tested with me and thinking I didn't have a cat in
hell's chance. You can imagine I was so thrilled and surprised to be
offered the part. We went out to Paris to film for eight weeks.

What an amazing cast: Alec, Gina, Robert Morley, Peggy Mount,
the fantastic Douglas Byng, Leonard Rossiter, Mary Bell, Kenneth
Griffith. It was very nerve-wracking being one of the three juveniles
(David Battley played the bootman and Ann Beach was the maid). I
played Maxim, the virgin, and we all ended up staying at the same
hotel.

On and off the set I was in awe of almost everyone, especially
Alec.

When I was a young boy I was taken with a friend and his
mother to the local cinema to see *Great Expectations*. I'm not sure
what I thought would happen, what I thought I would see, but I
didn't expect to be terrified. When the Scottish actor Finlay Currie,
playing Abel Magwitch, jumped from behind a gravestone in a
foggy, dark, threatening graveyard, I screamed. It was the first time I
had experienced such terror.

Although there have been a few television adaptations and
several films (including one in 1998 and another in 2012 with

Helena Bonham Carter and Ralph Fiennes), the 1946 version is the one that made the biggest impression, helped, of course, by being the first film I saw. With John Mills, who played Pip, were Martita Hunt as Miss Havisham; the gorgeous Jean Simmons as Estella; and a young actor cast as Herbert Pocket, called Alec Guinness.

Alec went on to star in the Ealing comedies *The Man in the White Suit* and *The Lavender Hill Mob*; *Tunes of Glory*, a 1960 film directed by Ronald Neame; and, in 1967, the epic *The Bridge on the River Kwai*. Ten years later, in 1977, he became a hero to a whole new generation when he created the role of Obi-Wan Kenobi in the first of George Lucas's *Star Wars* films.

I was also fortunate enough to see him on stage in *Wise Child* by Simon Gray. Simon Ward acted with him. I was so envious of Simon acting with Alec.

So the news that I was actually going to Paris to act with the great man came with a huge dose of rapture.

As it turned out Alec was not at all intimidating. He was so kind and generous in the scenes I had with him. On the first set, in a garden, standing opposite Alec, I couldn't take my eyes off him. I was almost dumbstruck.

There was one scene where I had to rush in from the garden and announce forcibly that I had important news to tell the group inside. It's a miracle I didn't fluff my lines for, as I got inside, standing in a semi-circle staring at me were living legends of British drama: Alec, Robert, Peggy, Leonard and Douglas. We rehearsed it four or five times, each time as daunting as the last. If I ever catch the film I still get nervous as this scene approaches.

For some reason (perhaps a French reason) we didn't work British hours. We started at noon and filmed until seven in the evening with the odd eating break. So evenings were mostly free. The Café de Flore was nearby so we often wined and dined there.

Thirty-five years later with my darling partner, Jo, I went back to the Café and ordered exactly what I used to order; and, after a toast to dear Alec, gave my best Alec impression as I said to the waiter,

'Could I have a black coffee and a cognac,' Alec's favourite tipple. Much to Jo's surprise I pocketed a Café de Flore ashtray as a souvenir. It still sits on my kitchen table.

On Sundays Alec used to ring the hotel in Saint-Germain-des-Prés and ask who was there. Inevitably we were – David, Ann and myself – and Alec would invite us out for dinner in various restaurants with his lovely wife Merula.

On one occasion I hadn't eaten and wasn't feeling very well. I had to be excused, and Alec followed me down to the toilet saying, 'What have you been up to?'

'I just haven't eaten.'

We walked outside in the fresh air and I suppose I was a bit drunk. I said, 'Do you mind if I tell you a story?'

'Go ahead, Derek.'

'When I left drama school, John Fernald, the principal, said, "Derek, I want you to become another Alec Guinness."'

I can't believe I told that story to Alec as we walked arm in arm to get me sobered up. I cherish that moment, thinking, how dare I. It was a ridiculous thing to say. He responded in good faith saying, 'The original is in good shape at the moment.'

Another lovely thing he did was when Wendy joined us in Paris. After filming one Sunday, Wendy, Alec and I were strolling around looking in shops when Wendy saw a little prayer book. 'That's lovely,' she said.

Alec looked at it and agreed. We walked on and noticed that Alec had disappeared. A few minutes later he came back and pressed the prayer book into Wendy's hands saying, 'There you are.'

I thought that was a wonderful thing to do.

Wendy and I did the tourist bit and relished every moment visiting places and seeing things we had only read about: the Louvre, the Tuileries, up the Eiffel Tower, the Bateaux Mouches on the River Seine, restaurants and galleries.

Robert Morley was bigger than life itself, on screen and off screen – a giant of theatre and cinema, with an appearance in *The African*

Queen with Katharine Hepburn and Humphrey Bogart on his CV along with many other great films: *Beau Brummell, Beat the Devil, Around the World in Eighty Days, Those Magnificent Men in Their Flying Machines.*

Before Wendy arrived he used to take me out to local restaurants and to clubs. Trailing in his wake we waited at seemingly closed clubs where he knocked loudly, shouting, 'Morley!'

The door would always open, and we followed Robert in.

On one such occasion who should be sitting there but Peter O'Toole and Audrey Hepburn. They were filming *How to Steal a Million.*

I said few words to Peter and none to Audrey. I was agog at just seeing her in the flesh.

I did see Peter O'Toole again many years later. My son, Jeremy, was in a production in Hampstead and when we were in a restaurant after the show he spotted Peter at a distant table. Jeremy knew what a fan I was of Peter's and encouraged me to go over and say hello. I did, but afterwards I wished I hadn't. Through a mist of cigarette smoke I said hello, said who I was, effused my career-long admiration of his work and thanked him for the enduring joy he had given me over the years. Peter took a deep suck of his cigarette, stared at me briefly and said nothing. I slowly eased away.

One evening Robert Morley took me aback with an unexpected question: 'Derek, who do you think is the better actor, me or Alec?'

I couldn't believe that Robert Morley, one of my heroes, was asking me who was the better actor between him and Alec Guinness.

'Come on, Derek,' he said. 'You can be honest.'

'I don't know what to say. You're both magnificent.'

'You must have an opinion,' he insisted.

'Alec is a great actor and you are a great personality.'

There was a silence until he said, 'You got away with that awfully well.'

Also in the cast of *Hotel Paradiso* was the extraordinary Italian actress, Gina Lollobrigida. I remember standing next to Gina when we were being lit for a scene. I looked into her eyes and said, 'You have the most beautiful eyes I've ever seen in my life.'

She looked me up and down and then called for her stand-in. She never spoke to me again.

I know that Alec never enjoyed working with Gina. She used to arrive on set with her entourage – secretaries, make-up artists, hairdressers and goodness knows what. Sir Alec used to mutter under his breath, 'Here comes the Mafia.'

The police inspector was played by a young Leonard Rossiter, a cracking fellow who went on to huge success on British television playing Rigsby in *Rising Damp* and Reggie in *The Fall and Rise of Reginald Perrin*. A very funny man with immaculate comic timing. I swear that had Leonard not become an actor he would have been a (Rigsby type) landlord.

Then there was dear Peggy Mount, whose ear-splitting voice belied her gentle demeanour. Her performance as Emma Hornett in *Sailor Beware* on stage and on film was masterful and made the part her own.

Douglas Byng played Mr Martin. He, I heard, was the first drag act to entertain the Prince of Wales. In an act that was billed as 'Bawdy but British', he was famous for his female impersonations with songs full of sexual innuendo and double entendres.

It was a very happy film on and off the set. Alec and Robert made it so easy for all of us, no more so than when we dined out. There were times when, after that extra glass of wine over dinner, Sir Alec was willing to answer all our questions and talk about all the films he had made. It was fascinating. He and his wife were wonderful company. We were thoroughly spoilt. I was totally in awe and loved his company as I did Robert's.

One of Robert's favourite restaurants was actually called the Hors D'oeuvre. All we had was hors d'oeuvres which were thoroughly enjoyable. We chatted about everything.

He did such a generous thing for Wendy and me. Wendy and I have the same birthday, 2nd September, and that year it was her 21st.

I happened to mention this to Robert during the morning when we were prevented from filming due to heavy rain and were huddled together waiting for it to stop.

'How wonderful,' he said. 'And what are you kiddies going to do this evening?'

'A quiet dinner on the Left Bank, we think.'

It was still raining in the afternoon and so we were told we were not going to be used.

Robert said, 'My family are over here, and we are all meeting tonight at the George V Hotel; if you can join us we would love to buy you a birthday drink. If it doesn't suit your plans, don't worry.'

I asked Wendy what she thought. 'I'd love to go,' she replied.

At the hotel we met Robert's family, Annabel and Sheridan, and while we were enjoying our drinks Robert asked if we had planned our restaurant.

'We think we have.'

'Well,' said Robert, 'we're all going to a very nice bistro around the corner and we would love to have you with us. But don't let us change your mind. If you want to be on your own then please be on your own, but if you join us you would make us very happy.'

I took Wendy aside and asked her what she wanted to do.

'They're such a wonderful group of people. Let's go with them.'

'Okay,' I said, and to Robert, 'We'd be delighted to join you.'

And when we arrived at the bistro around the corner there was music, gifts and balloons which had all been arranged during the lunch hour. Robert had done it for us hoping we would come. He did say, 'It was always my intention that you would come in the end.' He wanted us to decide for ourselves but he had arranged the whole birthday supper. It was an amazingly generous gesture, full of love and bonhomie and great company.

Wendy and I enjoyed a very happy six weeks in Paris. All too soon the film was over and we came back home to Pinner.

In the year 2000 I felt compelled to write to Sir Alec, hoping that he would remember me and the times we spent together and reminding him of the hours spent in the Café de Flore. I confess I was not that confident he would reply but he did, three days later. He was as generous in his words as he had been on the film set, telling me that he had kept an eye on my career, had admired my work and was envious of my recent visit to the Café. He ended his letter by writing, 'I do hope work will continue to flood your way and that you can pick and choose what you do. Yours ever, Alec.'

It is a letter I treasure.

Chapter 8

A second son, but hard times at home – *Basil Brush* –
Hamlet – Royal Command

I GOT ANOTHER FILM IN 1966, a Hammer Horror called *Frankenstein Created Woman*. I had a really nice part and met the lovely Peter Cushing. I've been so lucky in meeting great actors, people I have loved and admired for many years; and Peter Cushing was such a gentle man, extremely kind and generous. Also in the film were Thorley Walters, Peter Blythe and Barry Warren, and this beautiful Austrian girl called Susan Denberg.

I was quite taken with Susan and one evening she said, 'I would like you to come to dinner.'

I said, 'I can't. I live in Pinner.'

'No,' she said, 'you must come to dinner. I have an apartment in St James's Street in London.'

I made some excuse to Wendy and drove up to St James's Street for dinner with Susan. I remember it vividly as the streets were totally empty. There was no one around; they were all indoors watching the football. It was the World Cup year and England were playing Portugal in the semi-final, which of course they eventually won, going on to beat West Germany in the final 4-2.

I knocked on the door of Susan's apartment and she opened it with almost nothing on at all. Just a nightie.

She said, 'Come in, would you like a drink?'

I said, 'Thank you very much.'

She was a stunning girl. I heard subsequently that she'd had personal problems.

So I remember the film chiefly for two things: working with Peter Cushing, and my dinner with Susan Denberg.

Years later I received a letter from Peter saying how splendid he thought I was in the *Yes Minister* series. 'I send my deep thanks,' he wrote, 'for one of the very few special treats on television.' He then went on to write (and this is so humbling and embarrassing but amazing at the same time): 'It's an awfully nice feeling of basking in reflected glory, to smile somewhat smugly and say, "I worked with him."'

This from the masterful actor that Peter was. It was truly over-whelming.

It was around this time when Jamie, my son, was coming up to two that I realised that things between Wendy and me were not quite right. She was very frustrated in Pinner and I was all over the place working. She hadn't really got a job except for looking after the house and Jamie and going to Tupperware parties. I think this got to Wendy, who was a tremendous personality but hadn't really found what she wanted to do in life. Eventually at the beginning of 1967 she left me. She went off to Bermuda, back to her mother.

I was really quite shattered and I went up to Manchester to do a play directed by Braham Murray, *Waiting for Godot* with Anton Rodgers, Trevor Peacock and Wolfe Morris. Anton and Trevor became really great mates. When I talked about Wendy going back to Bermuda they said, 'You've got to go there and bring her back. You've only been married a short time. You have a two-year-old son! Get out there.'

And that's what I did. At the end of the play the boys made me get my ticket and I flew to Bermuda and, I must say, when I arrived it was so lovely to see her and Jamie and I think she was pleased that I had flown out. We were very happy to see each other. It was then that Jeremy, our second son, was conceived.

I returned to Manchester to do Eugene O'Neill's *A Long Day's Journey into Night,* again directed by Braham Murray. It is my favourite American play. It runs for four hours and it really is

Eugene O'Neill's autobiographical play. It was tremendous to be in and very successful.

While we were in rehearsal I had a call from my agent asking when my birthday was.

I said, 'September.'

'You're going to have an early birthday present and you're going to have to look after her. Go down to Manchester Piccadilly station and meet a young lady who is going to play the Irish maid. I've told her you're one of my clients and that you will look after her.'

So I went down to Piccadilly Station to meet the three o'clock train and there was this gorgeous girl. 'Hello,' she said, 'I'm Helen Mirren.'

I said, 'Hello, I'm Derek Fowlds.'

Helen was incredible as the Irish maid, Cathleen. She was also great company and I just knew this girl had something special. She had begun her career playing Cleopatra with the National Youth Theatre, and was very confident and extremely talented. I found her a very funny girl, still only 20 years old, but with an acting maturity that was simply mind-blowing. She was also one of the most exciting women I've met.

We went to the movies together, had meals and a few drinks – never as a date (my loss, I think) but as good friends, still relative novices in our profession.

I only saw Helen once after the play in Manchester. I remember the long hug. But, as I write, I haven't seen her for many years. I've been thrilled to watch her success and remember that time when we were together rehearsing and doing that wonderful play. She is truly a great actress. Helen is now a Dame and has won many (unquestionably deserved) awards.

Helen is the only 'Dame' I've worked with. I missed out on Dame Maggie Smith, Dame Eileen Atkins and, of course, Dame Judi Dench. I had met Michael Williams, Judi's late husband, at drama school and we socialised every now and again, so I did spend some wonderful moments with Judi. Her generous spirit is second to none and her sense of humour can be summed up by her comment, years later, on working with Billy Connolly: 'Working with him was heaven. We share the same sense of humour – very blue!'

We were established back in Pinner when Wendy realised that she was pregnant. Our second son, Jeremy, was born on 7th January 1968. Wendy's mother owned a house in Kent near Paddock Wood, called Bainden Farmhouse, a beautiful home. Wendy was staying there when she had Jeremy in Pembury Hospital.

So we now had two children, two lovely boys. We should have been happy; but still, I felt, there was something not quite right between the two of us. We were having problems, and it was soon after Jeremy was born that she said she wanted the end of the marriage.

Within days she had left. I was devastated and really didn't know what to do.

Eventually I decided to sell the house and rented a flat in West Hill, London. It was a really nice flat in Colebrook Close. I found out that Wendy had moved to the bottom of West Hill in Hurlingham. Jeremy was now one year old, and Wendy had placed Jamie into a private school nearby. I didn't really know how Wendy was getting on or who she was with. I guessed that she was with another man at that point.

In 1968 I was cast in Colin Spencer's play *Spitting Image* which was the story of a gay marriage. In the play my character gives birth. I found the rehearsal period difficult because of my recent split from Wendy and it was affecting my performance.

The play's director, James Roose-Evans, said to Julian Holloway who was playing my husband, 'I don't think Derek will manage this.'

Julian's reply was firm. 'Stay with him.'

I must admit it was tough getting into the mind of a woman, actually being a female. So I called Prunella Scales who I'd worked with earlier in *The Promise*. She agreed to help and proceeded to direct me in various skills: how to iron as a woman, how to argue as a woman, how to knit as a woman. She was brilliant.

At rehearsals the next day James asked, 'What happened to you last night? It's wonderful. It's really coming together.'

Giving 'birth' was rather tricky. It was a caesarean birth! To get as close as I (a mere man) could get to that kind of pain I wrapped my bare belly with chicken wire for the entire scene.

The play was a huge hit in Hampstead and moved to the Duke of York's in London. On opening night we were booed by the 'gallery first-nighters' and cheered by the stalls. It was as if they had watched two different plays.

The next night on my way to the theatre I was confronted by the 'gallery first-nighters' shouting abuse. 'How dare you be in this terrible play? It's disgusting. You should be ashamed of yourself.'

I loved the play and working with the great Lally Bowers and Frank Middlemass. Sadly it only ran for two months.

To this day Julian, who now lives in America, often sends a message saying, 'Give my love to the wife.' And I always send love back to 'my husband'.

*

One day in 1969 I was in Scotland filming *Dr Finlay's Casebook* with Andrew Cruickshank and Bill Simpson when I had a call from my agent saying, would you like to work with a puppet? I'd been an actor for years and puppets to me were Sooty and Pinky and Perky.

My agent said, 'No, no, no. There's another puppet called Basil Brush.'

I said, 'I think I've seen him on television with David Nixon – very clever.'

'Well,' said my agent, 'they've given Basil his own show. They've already done the pilot series with Rodney Bewes. Rodney isn't going to go back for another series and they're looking for someone to take over. Your name came up and I thought you might be interested to go and meet them.'

Do I really want to work with a puppet, I thought?

Anyway, I went down to the BBC and walked in to meet the producer, Johnny Downes. He asked me if I knew Basil, and I said I didn't although I had seen him on the David Nixon show. Suddenly this fox popped over my shoulder saying, 'Hello, Mr Derek.'

Blimey! I thought. This is extraordinary, talking to a puppet over my shoulder. In the end Ivan Owen, who was Basil, or worked him, came out and said hello. They said they were going to do another series of eight shows and were trying to find someone to replace Rodney. They were seeing a few people, and would I be interested? I said yes although I really didn't know what to say.

When I got back home later on that afternoon the phone rang saying they wanted me to do it. I said, good grief, what do I do? My agent at the time, a lovely guy called James Sharkey, encouraged me to do it. So I agreed to do eight shows of *Basil Brush*. I kept thinking of my boys, knowing that they would love me to do it.

The first series was quite hard really. I remember the first rehearsal when I asked Johnny Downes, what do I do.

He said, 'You say, hello, welcome to the show.'

'Yes,' I said, 'but how do I do that?'

'Just be you,' he said.

I didn't know how to be me. 'I'm an actor. I don't know how to be myself.'

Anyway, I did find a way of doing it.

Basil was a glove puppet, an anthropomorphic fox, who spoke in a 'posh' accent and had a valued and over-praised tail – his 'brush'. His jokes, which came thick and fast, were always followed by his catchphrase: 'Ha! Ha! Ha! Boom! Boom!'

Peter Firmin had designed the puppet in 1962 so he was already seven years old when I met him. Basil, as a character, was much older, cultivated and sophisticated with humour that appealed to all ages.

Ivan Owen shunned publicity. He was never seen, allowing Basil all the limelight. I think Terry-Thomas was the inspiration for Basil's voice.

The show ran for 25 minutes with a studio audience. The running format hardly ever changed. Basil and I would start, tell a few jokes, and that was followed by a comedy sketch. Then came a guest singer or group. Because of the large audience we had big stars queuing to appear. There were times when the guest would sing a song with Basil and me joining in.

The show would end with my delivery of a story about a relative of Basil's: Blast-Off Basil and his journey to the stars (a spoof of TV's *Star Trek*) or Basil de Farmer, the knight (a spoof of Robin Hood). At least, I tried to tell a story, for I was continually interrupted by Basil's jokes and comments.

In that first series I enjoyed working with Ivan; the scripts by George Martin were terrific. But I did feel slightly uncomfortable. I thought, here I am, a classically trained straight actor, with my arm around a bit of fur looking into a couple of button eyes, doing sketches. Anyway, I did it; and somehow I continued for the next five years!

I must confess I was relieved when the first *Basil Brush* series had come to an end, but it was followed by a period of unemployment. I was in my flat, alone, thinking: I must get some money.

There was a job advertised in the paper for a mini-cab driver. I went for it and got it. I became a mini-cab driver based in Earl's Court. I did that for six months. I did earn quite a lot of money during the Wimbledon tennis fortnight. My passengers were mostly Americans, mostly rich, who gave large tips.

I spent one extraordinary day with Winston Churchill's daughter, Sarah. Sarah Churchill called the cab office, I went to pick her up and spent the whole day with her. She was drinking solidly all day. She was charming, funny and she wouldn't let me go.

I recalled that, as a boy, I used to listen to *Variety Bandbox* on the radio with a comic, Vic Oliver. Sarah claimed that she married Vic Oliver. I was intrigued by the many aspects of her life. We went shopping in Knightsbridge, went for drinks, then back to her flat in Earl's Court.

I never saw her again but I've never forgotten the day I spent with Winston Churchill's daughter. She died in 1982. I remember she was delightful company.

Also, one day, I had to go and pick up Hattie Jacques. I had met her briefly when we filmed *We Joined the Navy* in 1962. She was married to John Le Mesurier. My cab rolled up at Hattie's door as she came out.

'Derek! What are you doing here?'

'I'm your mini-cab driver.'

'How lovely, how lovely.'

Hattie was diabetic and wanted to be taken to her doctor for an injection.

We chatted and laughed during the journey and when she got out she said, 'It's so lovely to see you. Hope you get a job soon, Derek. But please tell me why you're wearing dark sunglasses when you're driving?'

It was a very dark day and the sun was certainly not shining.

I said, 'Well, I do hate signing autographs in the rush hour. It makes everything a lot easier.'

I never saw Hattie again but did follow her career on the telly. I was quite a fan of Hattie's. She had great talent.

During that summer I had a phone call from Wendy saying, please, please will you come and see me. At her request I picked up Jamie from his prep school which was a place I didn't like. Four- and five-year-olds regimented behind their desks in their grey uniforms. When I walked in they all had to stand up and be polite and I couldn't help thinking that this was wrong for a five-year-old. He should be allowed to be a kid. When we arrived at Wendy's flat in Hurlingham, Jeremy was in his high chair making a loud noise with a spoon.

'Will you stay and have a drink and give Jamie a bath?' Wendy asked.

'Of course.'

I bathed Jamie, told him a story and put him to bed.

Wendy and I were in the kitchen when Wendy broke down. She said, 'I really can't cope. I really, really, want to come back to you.'

It was a shock to me, and part of me was thrilled at the prospect of getting my family back after such a long time. She came back, although I had a gut feeling this was not the best thing for either of us. I should have listened to my gut.

Then came another shock. Although we thought we had taken precautions, Wendy discovered she was pregnant. Being away from me for such a long time and having just finished another relationship she was unprepared, unable and unwilling to go through another pregnancy. I agreed that she wasn't stable enough to handle it. We sought the advice of our doctor who thought the best course was for Wendy to have a termination. 'Wendy is not mentally or physically fit to go through a birth,' the doctor said.

It was an awful time for both of us, particularly for Wendy, but we both knew the right decision had been made. It also brought clarity to the rocky nature of our relationship.

Although neither of us would admit it, we both knew our marriage had no future; but for the sake of the boys I was determined to establish a routine. Wendy never stood in my way in bonding with the boys. I was always grateful to her for that.

Wendy's brother, Pete, had taken over her flat so she settled into my flat at the top of West Hill.

And then I was offered *Hamlet* at Exeter University Theatre. I thought *Hamlet*! Grief!

Tony Church, who was running Exeter, wanted someone to play Hamlet and it was Prunella Scales, who I'd worked with in *The Promise* in 1968, who suggested me. I hummed and hahed and Wendy said, you've got to do it.

'You're an actor,' she said. 'These opportunities don't come round that often.'

So, I agreed to do *Hamlet* and knew it was going to be the whole of October and November – a month of rehearsal followed by a month of performances. I endlessly practised soliloquies when walking across Wimbledon Common. It's the way I work, absorbing the words, feeling the words, being the part.

I met up with some of the *Basil Brush* crew and told them I was going off to play Hamlet, that I was going to go legitimate again.

Basil sent me a telegram asking, how legitimate can you get?

Playing *Hamlet* in Exeter was such a rewarding couple of months. Tony Church, who directed it, had played Polonius in the play with the Royal Shakespeare Company. In the evenings he and I would just rehearse one to one in a gymnasium. I can remember leaning up against the wall and Tony leaning up against the other saying, 'Derek, tonight we'll do "To be or not to be".'

'What am I going to do with that?' I asked.

'Just think about it,' he replied. 'Think of the words. Think of the text. What would you do?'

And that was the way we worked on all the soliloquies: 'Oh what a rogue,' 'How all occasions do inform against me,' 'Speak the speech I pray you as I pronounced it to you, trippingly on the tongue.'

Tony and I worked very hard together or on our own, and during the day we were rehearsing all the ensemble bits.

There was one rehearsal when we were coming up to 'Oh, what a rogue, a peasant slave am I,' where Tony usually stopped me, but on this occasion he didn't – he just let me go on. There were people sitting around in the rehearsal room, some knitting, some doing crosswords, when I began, 'Oh, what a rogue'. As I went through the soliloquy people stopped what they were doing. It was the first time they'd heard me do one of the great soliloquies. It was a moment I'll never forget because at the end of it the company applauded. I felt so close to them all. From then on we ran all the soliloquies in the play.

I loved playing Hamlet and Wendy actually came up to Exeter and helped me through the lines. For a while, we became very close.

I had quite a few good luck messages before we opened, including a telegram from my friend and acting colleague, Ian McKellen. It read: 'Much love and luck and envy'.

I don't recall the moment Ian and I first got together, but for a few short years we became good friends, Ian helping me move house once. His back-to-back performances of Shakespeare's *Richard II* and Marlowe's *Edward II* were roundly acclaimed at the 1969 Edinburgh Festival and sold out for two seasons in London. And now of course (apart from his knighthood) he is famous for his role of Gandalf, the wizard, in *Lord of the Rings*.

The first night of my *Hamlet* was quite scary. Wendy, family and friends came. I did get some good reviews, but the one that worried me the most was B. A. Young in the *Financial Times* who wrote, 'Derek is the funniest Hamlet I've seen in twenty-five years.'

John Bardon, who played the gravedigger, became a great friend and years later was the best man at my second marriage.

I did get lots and lots of fan letters from girls and kept them in a box. I expect they're all grandmothers now.

*

Around about that time I appeared in *Crown Court*, a lunchtime drama filmed in Manchester. Each story was broadcast over three episodes with the verdict coming right at the end.

Bill Simons (later my colleague in *Heartbeat*) played a barrister, though we didn't get to talk much. I played a young factory boy who accused three women of raping me – it was a bizarre script but very funny.

The prosecuting counsel was played by the brilliant Judy Parfitt. Judy, like me, was a giggler and there was one line I had to say that really got us going. I said, 'Well, Miss, they got this lipstick and drew a circle around my navel.'

Judy's face cracked and we both went into hysterics. Eventually they placed a camera between us so our eyes couldn't meet.

It was time to decide if I was going to do a second series of *Basil Brush*. It wasn't an easy decision but in the end I agreed. It was a bit more money, with the possibility of a third series.

It was also a time when it became increasingly clear that my marriage was not going well. Although it was lovely having the boys with me, the reconciliation with Wendy wasn't working. But we limped on.

It was in the second series of *Basil* that something really magical happened.

One day, when I was rehearsing early on in the series, I looked at Basil – and he was alive. The eyes, the furry tail. He became my best friend. It was a very happy period work-wise.

I just adored Ivan who played Basil. I always got on with him. He was an actor with tremendous timing and a wonderful sense of humour; we did laugh a lot and George Martin's scripts were very, very funny. George was an old musical comic who was regularly on television shows with his pipe and newspaper, telling gags. There was Johnny Downes, the producer, and another producer, Robin Nash: big face, huge teeth, wonderful smile. A great team to work with.

I used to warm up the studio audience, mostly children, with simple 'Knock, knock, who's there?' jokes. It certainly gave me a more relaxed approach to the recording.

Basil and I would do a bit to camera, talking about silly things that we had been doing. And then in the middle section of the show we would do our sketch, dressing up to do silly parts.

My favourite was when I played Romeo climbing up to the balcony where Basil, as Juliet, waited. As I climbed I said, 'But soft – what light through yonder window breaks? It is the east, Juliet is the sun.'

When I reached the top Juliet said, 'Oh, hello, Mr Derek. I think you're overacting.'

Hysterical!

I've always wanted to be in a Western so we got George to write a sketch with me dressed in black, with a stetson and guns, and Basil was the saloon barman. I kicked open the swing doors and stood there shouting, 'This is it.'

I'd practised twirling the guns and tried a deactivated real gun but could hardly lift it. So I resorted back to the toy gun.

Another time I played Marco Polo.

And there was always the story at the end: the adventures of Basil de Farmer, or Des P. Rado (a pun on 'desperado').

Ivan and I shared a filthy sense of humour. Under the table, working Basil, Ivan was quite naughty and mucked about a lot. That's why I often grabbed him by the snout and did not let him move.

The guests included the Tremeloes, Freddie and the Dreamers, Herman's Hermits, Gerry and the Pacemakers. Lulu appeared; so did the Bachelors – they all came on the show. Neither Ivan nor I had much contact with the singers; they were still in the early days of their careers. They were all, in a sense, newcomers. Often there was a novelty act – a ventriloquist, a contortionist or a dancer. They did their stint and by the time the show ended, they had left.

Ivan and I had our favourites. Standing out (then) was the song 'Little Arrows', written by Albert Hammond and Mike Hazelwood and sung by Leapy Lee. It peaked at number two in the charts. I heard later that Leapy was jailed after a violent fracas in a bar, an event that must have put back his career. I also heard he was earning a living singing in Majorcan bars.

Even to this day (it was after all 1969 to '73) I'm often asked to sing the *Basil Brush* song. 'Basil de Farmer, the knight in shining armour, fought against injustice, with his sword held high; and all his enemies used to tremble at the knees, and everywhere he went they heard his battle cry. He's a brave, brave man …' and all the kids used to shout, 'Who's that?'

Even when I was doing *Heartbeat* years later all the crew called me Mr Derek.

We were asked to go down to Luton Hoo, a grand English country house set in acres and acres of land. Every year the Queen and Prince Philip celebrated their wedding anniversary at the home of Lord and Lady Wernher. They had a cabaret and this particular year they asked Basil, myself and the late, great Roy Castle.

When we arrived we were shown backstage in one half of the beautiful ballroom. There was so much food there for the entertainers – cakes, sandwiches, sausage rolls. Every drink imaginable. It was only us three. We drank rather a lot before the show. We looked through the curtains as the Royal Family sat in the front row with the staff.

Roy went out first and banged his piano and said, 'I suppose you're wondering why I've sent for you.'

Not a titter. Blimey, I thought, we're not going to get any laughs.

Roy, who was a great showman, did his bit and there was a ripple of applause and then we went on.

I wheeled Basil down on his desk and he said, 'Hey, Mr Derek, this is wonderful.'

I said, 'Yes, what an amazing place. Look at that chandelier.'

'Yes,' said Basil. 'My cousin Cyril was here last year and when he bit into a Crunchie bar the whole bloody lot fell down.'

Not a laugh!

'That made me laugh,' I said.

'I'm glad somebody did,' said Basil.

After the show we were ushered in to meet the Royal Family. I did feel honoured and privileged. It was a great fun night.

In 1970 there was a Royal Gala in Shepherd's Bush. It was packed. The Queen and Duke were in attendance.

It was quite a bill. People like Frankie Howerd, Dave Allen, Morecambe and Wise, Rod McKuen, Cilla Black, the cast of *Dad's Army* and us.

As we were in the second half, Ivan and I sat on a bench outside to watch the arrivals at the doors of the Shepherd's Bush Empire.

I saw Wendy arrive and my mother and sister, followed later by the Royal party.

I thought, crikey! We're going to do it.

We were both very nervous but it did go down well.

When we met the Queen and the Duke afterwards I think we all remembered the performance at Luton Hoo the previous year.

The Queen said, 'And what have you been doing since I saw you last?'

'Looking after this one,' I said, pointing to Ivan.

I've no idea if the Queen knew Ivan was Basil Brush.

It was quite a wrench to leave the *Basil* programme but I knew I had to return to my acting. They found Roy North as a replacement, who I thought looked a bit like me. He was very good, very Northern, and they went on to be a great success together.

Throughout my career I've never sought publicity or fame but it was during my time in *Basil Brush* that public recognition started to happen. I found I had an enormous following from young girls – and quite a few of their mothers. They followed me everywhere. When I did my first schools matinee of my *Hamlet* I had to walk down towards the audience and all the kids shouted out, 'Where's Basil?'

I slowly took out my dagger and looked in the empty scabbard to signify that Basil wasn't with me.

I have never felt that I was famous; quite a few people know me, but the level of fame achieved by other actors passed me by. Doing good work was always my priority.

About ten years ago a journalist rang me to say that Basil was coming back to the screen.

'They're bringing Basil back,' he said.

'They can't bring Basil back,' I replied. 'Basil is dead. He died. And whoever this one is, is an impostor.'

Basil was my best friend. They can't replicate him, can they?

Sadly, they did.

Chapter 9

Shaking Sinatra's hand – Saved from drowning by
Laurence Harvey – Separation

IN A GAP BETWEEN *BASIL BRUSH* SERIES I was cast in a new play in London called *Child's Play*. Written by Robert Marasco, it was directed by Joseph Hardy, an American director, and starred Laurence Harvey and Rupert Davies.

The production was due to begin with a brief tour before going into the West End. Before the tour we rehearsed for three weeks, during which we all had to get into character – finding a voice, finding a walk, discovering particulars and making them work.

Laurence kept himself to himself during that time and no one was tempted to intrude. We were all in awe of him. He had already done so much in his career, with films such as *The Good Die Young*, *Cairo Road*, *The Alamo*, *The Manchurian Candidate*, and *Room at the Top* for which he was nominated for an Oscar for Best Actor in a Leading Role.

The fact that we were all rehearsing in the same room was rather daunting, and acting with dear Rupert Davies (famous for his TV portrayal of Inspector Maigret) was just as dazzling.

Rehearsals, in those days, were both challenging and joyous, the opportunities for triumph or disaster only too available. But we always spent time doing it together, unlike a lot of modern day television drama where you learn lines at home, alone, and then go to the studio and speak them to camera.

I just adored Laurence Harvey. He was very funny, very cynical. I remember the final dress rehearsal before our opening night in

Brighton went on and on and on. Laurence's dressing room was near mine and I could hear him swearing and cursing as it went on until late evening. It became a technical rehearsal and I asked why we weren't getting any laughs, knowing there wasn't an audience. After the rehearsal he came into my dressing room and asked what I was doing.

'It's eleven o'clock at night,' I replied. 'When are we going to finish?'

'Not for another hour,' he said. 'We've got to have a meal.'

He picked up the phone and called Wheeler's, a famous restaurant in Brighton, and came back to me saying, 'They're staying open.'

So after that awful rehearsal we went off to Wheeler's and had a lovely meal. Laurence ate Dover sole, off the bone; I later discovered that was the only meal Laurence ordered, always washed down with a bottle of Chablis and a whole packet of Lark cigarettes.

After Brighton we did Bath and then Cambridge before moving into the Queen's Theatre in London where we got reasonable reviews. The play ran for six months, and Laurence and I became good pals.

We often talked about the demands of performing in *Child's Play*. In the play there is a rivalry between two faculty members at an exclusive Roman Catholic boarding school for boys. Joe Dobbs is an easy-going, well-liked English teacher. Jerome Malley (played by Laurence) is hated by his students for his strict disciplinary methods. Malley's mother is dying and he receives threatening phone calls and letters. He's certain Dobbs is behind it. There is a growing realisation that the school may be possessed by the Devil.

One day Laurence asked me if I thought he was any good in it.

I replied passionately, 'You're great!' Then I added, 'But please tell me: in the play, when you receive news of your mother's death, why do you break the line up? You should say, "I should have been with her for that." You say, "I should – have been – with her – for that."'

95

'Right,' he said. 'Just after I say that you come on.'

'I do. I come on, grab the statue of Jesus and I say, "What's a nice boy like you doing in a place like this?"'

'Okay,' said Laurence. 'If you ever hear me say that line without a break, that's a cue for you to say, "What's a nice *Jewish* boy like you doing in a place like this?"'

Mindful of the Catholic School setting of the play I didn't immediately take up his challenge; but one night on tour Laurence delivered his line without a break and scampered over to me waiting to go on stage. 'Go on,' he laughed. 'Go on!'

I grabbed the statue, reeled around the stage and said, 'What's a nice Jewish boy like you doing in a place like this?'

A howl of laughter came from the audience; but the company manager reported us and we were entered in the 'black book' that recorded all performance detail. No doubt it read, 'Laurence Harvey and Derek Fowlds were naughty boys.'

When we were in London Laurence often picked me up in a souped-up Mini or his chauffeur-driven Rolls Royce and we would go clubbing, to Annabel's and Tramps. Sometimes we used to go back to his flat in Grosvenor House to smoke some really good dope. I'm not proud of that but we did have a good time together. So good that the rest of the cast couldn't resist showing their concern for me. Jimmy Berwick, Richard Heffer and Philip Brack called me into the dressing room one evening during the interval, telling me they were worried about me.

'Why?' I asked.

'We all think your performance has changed,' someone said, 'and we've got to ask – are you on anything? Have you and Laurence been burning the wrong sort of candle?'

I tried to convince them that nothing was amiss and, if my performance had changed, it was nothing to do with my social life. I don't think they were persuaded but I know they meant well. My performances and the play went on without mishap.

*

Before I met him, Laurence was married to Joan, the ex-wife of film magnate Harry Cohn, the president and production director of Columbia Pictures. Laurence told me that the lady with the torch, Columbia's ever present logo, was Joan.

When we met, Laurence was divorced from Joan and married to the beautiful model, Pauline Stone. They lived in Hampstead with their baby daughter, Domino.

When visiting the Harvey house you had no idea who was going to answer the door. On one visit I was greeted by George Hamilton, and on another by John Ireland who played Cherry Valance in the film *Red River* with John Wayne and Montgomery Clift.

On one occasion Laurence and Pauline had a lunch party and I was invited. It was during a break from shooting on a film in which Laurence was starring with Elizabeth Taylor, and she was there. There were exotic snacks and plenty of fine wine, but my attention was entirely on the gorgeous Elizabeth. She was enchanting, kind and seemed interested in what I was doing. It was two hours of bliss in her company.

I introduced Laurence to Wendy at a time that Wendy and I were growing apart; I knew that and, I think, Wendy knew that. However, we decided, when the play was over, to go on holiday to Italy.

When we were in New York doing *Chips with Everything* we met a lovely bloke called Frederick Koch who was very wealthy. He used to take a villa in Florence every summer and he invited Wendy and me to spend time there with him and his family. We decided to take him up on his kind offer, knowing we would enjoy Fred's company and at the same time it would give us an inexpensive vacation.

When I told Laurence we were going to Florence he suggested we break the journey as he would be in Cannes for the film festival.

He said, 'Why not go early, fly to Nice, and I'll meet up with you there?'

Wendy and I thought that was fantastic.

Child's Play came to an end and we flew to Nice where a telegram from Laurence awaited, telling us to get a taxi to Cannes and that he would be waiting at this famous hotel called the Carlton. The Hotel Carlton in Cannes! How much will that cost, I thought?

Laurence was on the hotel terrace when we arrived. He came running out, took our bags, paid the taxi and invited us to join them on the terrace.

We were introduced to a man; I missed his name, but he was very entertaining. When I told him we were going on to Florence, Laurence said, 'That yacht over there belongs to a friend of mine, John Mills – not the actor, the entrepreneur who owns restaurants and the London club Les Ambassadeurs. He's giving a party tonight and we would love you two to come. I've booked you into the hotel.'

Laurence did all of this. An amazing thing to do. He showed us around the hotel, and in the evening we went down to the boat. It was a lovely party and I got talking to the man Laurence had introduced us to on the terrace at the Carlton. I almost said, I'm sorry I didn't catch your name.

He said, 'I'm Loewe – Fritz Loewe.'

Crikey! I thought. Then: 'You're Fritz Loewe! But you're a genius'.

And there were Wendy and I on this boat talking to Fritz Loewe, the composer of *My Fair Lady* and all those wonderful musicals. I couldn't believe it.

I think I asked him which comes first, the music or the lyrics.

'How I work is,' he said, 'I would look at the book – *Pygmalion*, for example. There is a line: "I could have danced all night." I took that one line and composed around it. I sang "I could have danced all night" over and over again until I got the music.'

I couldn't believe it.

Laurence had yet another plan. 'Why don't you come on board tomorrow?' he said. 'We're sailing to Monte Carlo. Please come.'

I was so staggered. 'We've got to get to Florence,' I said.

'Don't worry. We'll get you to Florence.'

So Wendy and I spent the night at the hotel and the next day we went aboard the boat heading for Monte Carlo. At lunchtime we dropped anchor and something happened that was quite scary. I dived in, not realising the tide was very strong. I was soon in difficulty. I'm a swimmer, but not a strong swimmer. I kept waving and waving. Realising I was getting further and further from the boat, Laurence and one of the crew dived over the side and helped me back. I was really shaken and told Laurence he had saved my life.

'Well,' he said, 'you owe me.'

'I owe you for a lot,' I replied.

It had been a very frightening moment.

We sailed into Monte Carlo harbour which was the most incredible sight with the Palace on top of the hill, home of Grace Kelly and Prince Rainier. Laurence booked us into another hotel saying, 'You can catch the train to Florence tomorrow, but tonight you're having dinner with us in the Hôtel de Paris.'

Dressed up, we left our hotel and arrived at the Hôtel de Paris which blew our minds. We went up to the restaurant at the top, almost on the roof, where Wendy and I dined with Laurence and Pauline. Then began a firework display. I'd never seen anything like it. Fireworks over Monte Carlo harbour!

Another extraordinary thing happened. Wendy was facing the door and she looked at me saying, 'Don't look round, don't look round. I can't believe this.'

Larry got up and waved to somebody and Wendy said, 'He's coming over. He's coming over.'

The man came over, saying hi to Laurence.

Laurence said, 'You know Pauline, my wife; and this is Wendy Fowlds, and this is Derek Fowlds.'

I turned around and there was Frank Sinatra. Did I say I admired his work? I can't remember. My mouth was open wide and he shook my hand saying hello. What an evening. Laurence was generosity itself.

The next morning we got on the wrong train so had to come back to Monte Carlo and start again.

Finally we got to the Villa Caponi, Fred's villa, in the early hours of the morning. Fred and his guests had stayed up to greet us. It was wonderful to be there, and in the morning when we woke up we could see all of Florence below us.

But that was almost the end of our marriage. I think Wendy knew that and, when we got back from Florence, we decided to separate. Wendy and the boys stayed in the flat in Colebrook Close and I moved out to stay with friends. It was 1971.

It broke my heart but I knew it was the right thing to do. It was the break-up of the family that upset me, knowing there would be difficult times ahead.

I never got to see Laurence Harvey again. He was always a heavy smoker and a tireless drinker. He got very ill, shrank to only six stone and died from stomach cancer in 1973 at the age of 45. His daughter, Domino, was only four when he died. She became a bounty hunter and was 35 when she died tragically, in 2005. The Los Angeles coroner determined that she had overdosed on a painkiller drug. Father and daughter are buried together in Santa Barbara. In recent years a film, starring Keira Knightley, was based (I suspect loosely) on the 'bounty hunter' part of Domino's life.

*

I had met an actor in *Child's Play* called James Berwick and his wife Belita. She was a famous ice-dancer who had danced in the Olympics in 1936 and made a few Hollywood films, although she had now retired from the business. She and Jimmy ran a garden centre. I stayed with them for six months, not knowing that they were both alcoholics.

There were many good times with James and Belita but their drinking often got out of hand. I had never had any experience of living with alcoholics. Good times and bad times, but they were good pals. It was sad to see their demise and the way they died but I won't forget them. They were very kind to me during a difficult time.

From my *Basil Brush* earnings I had saved enough money to put down a deposit on a house in Barnes, very near to our old flat. It was in Lillian Road and cost £11,500. The same house today could be worth up to two million!

Some time later I met John, Wendy's new lover who, she suggested, was the love of her life. He reminded me of Demis Roussos, the singer from Greece; a huge man, huge stomach, long beard and hair. John could have been Demis' double.

She was obviously happy with John and they decided to move to Yorkshire, to Bingley. Of course they were going to take James and Jeremy. That upset me, knowing I wouldn't be seeing them very often as establishing regular visits to Yorkshire would be very difficult. They moved, and I bought a house in the spring of 1972.

Chapter 10

IN 1972 I MOVED ON FROM AL PARKER to another agent: a friend from RADA, David White, who had abandoned acting to establish his own agency. On one occasion I was sitting in reception when out of his office came the brilliant Eleanor Bron. I'd never met Eleanor but I certainly loved her work. We said hello to each other.

'I'm such a fan of yours,' I said.

'Thank you very much,' she replied and off she went.

I'd been talking to David for half an hour when his phone rang. He picked it up, said, 'Yes,' looked at me and added, 'I don't know. I'll ask him.'

David covered the mouthpiece and said, 'Can you sing?'

'Sing! Of course I can sing.'

Into the phone David said, 'Yes, he can sing. Okay, I'll talk to him about it. I'll call you back.'

'That was Eleanor,' he said. 'They're doing a series, a satirical sketch show, for the BBC, written by Eleanor, John Fortune and John Bird. John Fortune's had a heart attack and they want someone to replace him. Eleanor saw you and wondered if you could do it.'

The series – which was called *After That, This* – was produced by Robert Chetwyn, with music written by the prolific composer Carl Davis. I was sent over to Carl's house in Clapham where he sat at his piano and took me through all the scales. A lot of the sketches were parodies on classical music composers, set in modern times.

I passed the singing test and got the part. We did eight episodes with vastly differing themes: an opera; an operetta; and a massage parlour sketch with Eleanor and me, in which she pummelled me while I sang, 'I have always gone for older women – women who are older seem to be much bolder,' and so on.

We recorded the series in Scotland. It was an absolute joy to work with such talented people. All were educated at top universities, and on occasions I felt out of my depth, but that was entirely my fault. Eleanor, the two Johns and the crew were generosity itself.

Regrettably we didn't make a second series and the original tapes have been erased.

I see Eleanor from time to time and the two Johns went on to make the successful series *Bremner, Bird and Fortune.* Alas, John Fortune passed away in December 2013, aged 74.

*

The same year I did a play called *A Life of the General* by Ronald Mavor who was James Bridie's son. We were trying the play out in Nottingham with my old friend Donald Douglas as my brother and the superb Robin Bailey as the visiting professor.

Binkie Beaumont Management then decided to bring the play to the West End; it was going to be a starring vehicle for the great genius, Alastair Sim. Robin Bailey had been superb in that part but Alastair Sim, playing the role, changed the dimension of the play.

Sadly, Donald Douglas left the production. Peter Cellier played my brother and, I believe, Ian McKellen was asked to play my part. He said no, but he would like to direct it. I think he stood up for me by saying I should play his original part.

It was a big hit, and I enjoyed the play very much. As part of my performance I was required to do a full frontal strip.

The play is the story of an Oxford don who visits the Black family in order to research a book he is writing about the late General Black. The general's two sons have their own versions of what their father did and, of course, their mother has her version. The professor comes to talk to all three of us, to gather how we really felt about the general and what he was like. He was a famous military man who fought some tough and difficult battles and hated bureaucracy. Having returned from the front line he was told he had to parade the troops, but he declined. When he was ordered to do so by the powers that be, he walked out to inspect the troops with just his hat on.

My version, as the youngest son, was that he was my hero; during the course of the play, I had to re-enact what he did. My brother knocks me out and I'm carried naked to lay on my mother's lap. Alastair Sim had to cover me with a blanket.

The title of the play was changed from *A Life of the General* to *A Private Matter* and I remember my mother sending me a telegram asking me to keep it as private as possible.

It was wonderful working in the West End again, especially with the great Alastair Sim. It was quite a masterclass watching him every evening. On the first night in London we were on the stage together before the show; I was chuntering away doing my vocal exercises when he asked if I was nervous.

'Nervous? I'm terrified!'

'Who are you going on the stage for?' he asked.

'I'm going on the stage for my family, the audience and the critics.'

'No, no, no,' he said. 'You've got it so wrong, Derek. You only go on the stage for one person and that's yourself. Except when you're working with me.'

On one occasion I woke up with a terrible bout of hay fever. My eyes were puffed up, I kept sneezing and I could hardly speak, but I managed to get a telephone call to the company manager to tell him I couldn't go on stage. However, I did offer to attend the rehearsal with my understudy to help if I could.

I was not much use to anyone but I thought I'd better talk to Alastair to explain personally. I was sitting in my dressing room collecting myself when a knock on the door was followed by a rapid entrance by Alastair.

'Alastair!'

'Derek, Derek, I hear you've not been well today.'

'Look at me, Alastair. I've been sneezing since seven o'clock this morning.'

'Please listen, Derek. I don't want to play with the understudy. You'll have to go on tonight.'

'I can't! I really can't!'

'Take the day in with you, Derek.'

'What do you mean?'

'We are playing human beings; we all have our idiosyncrasies, we all have our frailties, we can be ill with laryngitis. We are human. Take the day in, Derek. Have a cold shower, and on stage take your hay fever in with you. Do this for me, Derek.'

'I'll try, Alastair.'

'You're a good boy, Derek.'

I had a shower and, still feeling rotten, went on stage carrying a handkerchief.

At the opening of the play I'm laying on a sofa, the bell rings, and I get up to open the door. Alastair bounces in.

'Come in,' I say, 'you must be Professor Dakyn. My mother won't be long. Have a drink?'

'That would be lovely,' said Alastair. 'You must be Anthony, the youngest son.'

'Yes,' I replied.

Then Alastair came out with a line that wasn't in the script, 'Oh you're the one that suffers from hay fever.'

I said, 'Yes,' without thinking.

Alastair continued, 'Has it been a bad day for hay fever?'

'Yes, it has.'

What I didn't realise at the time was that Alastair had given me my performance.

Later, as we watched the curtain fall on the play Alastair walked up to me and said, 'You've never been better.'

Dear Alastair. What a wonderful, wonderful man.

*

Meanwhile at the end of 1972 I was still doing *Basil Brush*, and one day when I was in the television studios at BBC TV Centre I went to see my old friend John Noakes who was in the popular children's programme, *Blue Peter*. John had been in *Chips with Everything* with me in America all those years before. I asked him for some *Blue Peter* badges for my sons. When I went down to the dressing room to meet him he introduced me to Lesley Judd. I'd spotted Lesley as a dancer with The Young Generation and I said to her, 'I've seen you before, when we did the Royal Variety. I was with Basil Brush and you were dancing.'

'I was,' she said.

John suggested I come back after the recording and he'd get the badges. When I went back Lesley asked what I was doing.

'I'm going home,' I said.

'No, no. Come and have a drink.'

So I went to the bar with Lesley and told her the full story of being separated from my children who were in Yorkshire. I said I was very unhappy. When I told her of my new house in Barnes she said she'd like to see it.

'Okay,' I said.

We had another drink and went off to Barnes.

'It's so bare,' she said of my home. 'There's nothing in it.'

'I rather like it that way,' I said.

'Well, come and see my flat.'

We got into the car, had something to eat on the way and went to Lesley's flat which was the complete opposite to my house. It was full of plants and ferns, a four-poster bed and packed with tasteful furniture. It was very Victorian but very cosy.

I stayed the night. My first meeting with Lesley. We got on so well. I so enjoyed her company. Within three months she had moved into my house. I always describe Lesley as picking up the strings of a puppet; I was the puppet on the floor after the separation from Wendy and the boys. Lesley just picked up the strings and taught me to dance again.

For the whole of 1973, Lesley and I were together. She phoned Wendy, who was living in Bingley, and said that she was now living with me and that I needed to see the boys. It was because of Lesley that the two boys flew down every other weekend from Leeds Airport. We met them at Heathrow. It was wonderful to have them with me and very hard when they went back. We also had them in the holidays. It was a very happy time.

That summer, I gave up *Basil Brush*. It was then that Lesley said, you must get back into the theatre.

I had thought that Ivan (as Basil) and I could become a double act; building on the successful TV show, we could do variety shows and pantomime. But Ivan had no wish to become part of a double act so we parted amicably, fully understanding each other's ambitions.

After the Alastair Sim play, Lesley and I went on holiday to Spain and took my boys. While we were there we met the most wonderful family.

We were around the communal pool one afternoon. Lesley said, 'Look at those three boys.'

They were swimming up and down, up and down, and their father was walking around the pool not letting them get out. I thought, what is going on here?

We stopped the man and I asked him what was happening.

'They're all going to be champion swimmers one day,' he said. 'They're training and they can't get out of the pool until they've done twenty-five lengths.'

Or was it five miles?

'Anyway,' he said, 'they're showing off. They've heard that the girl from *Blue Peter* and the boy from *Basil Brush* are staying in one of the apartments. The same apartments as us.'

We got to know that family so well. The parents were Basil and Ann Weissand; the boys were Paul, Simon and Adam. And today, over forty years later, they are still among my closest friends. At times they feel like my family. They have been such consistent support and I love them very much.

I said to them, I hope you don't live in Ireland, Scotland or up North. They told me they lived in Bushey, which is about five miles from Pinner and twelve miles from my home town of Berkhamsted. How lucky was that?

It was during our holiday in Spain that we got a telephone call from Wendy saying that she and John, her partner, had decided to move to Northern Ireland. John had a friend there who was teaching and working with children of the two denominations, Catholic and Protestant. Wendy said that she and John wanted to go over there and help, and to live there. And – the big bombshell – could Lesley and I take over the boys?

I couldn't believe what I was hearing – that Wendy would hand over the boys to Lesley and me. I told Wendy I would have to get back to her on this; I needed time to think. I remember sitting on the balcony with dear Ann and Basil and Lesley, talking it over.

Lesley suggested she could have one boy.

'We can't really separate them,' I said.

'Well,' said Lesley, 'Jeremy is almost six and Jamie is nine and at big school. Why don't we take Jeremy on?'

It was a very difficult decision for me, and when we got back I contacted Wendy and discussed it with her.

'That's okay,' she said. 'You have Jeremy and my mother and I will put Jamie into prep school.'

So the four of us went down to Seaford to see the headmaster of the school. That was very hard. But that's what happened. Jeremy came to live with us and Jamie went to prep school. I think to this day that it was a big, big mistake by all of us.

So Lesley and I had a whole year together, and when my divorce from Wendy came through Lesley suggested we get married.

'Please,' I said, 'I don't want to get married; let's just stay the way we are.'

Lesley really wanted the security of marriage – I understood that – so in December we decided to name the day.

On 5th January 1974 Lesley and I were married in East Sheen Registry Office. We were surrounded by some dear friends. Mum was there, as was my dear sister Babs, and Jamie came down. We had the reception in a restaurant we used to go to in London, but we never managed to get away on honeymoon. Lesley was tied up with *Blue Peter* and I was out of work. I wasn't sure what was in store for me in 1974.

News came from Wendy that wasn't good. One day, in their friend Sean's house in Northern Ireland, there was a knock at the door. Sean opened the door and was shot and bled to death in Wendy's arms. It was a single tragedy in a country and at a time when there were many, many, tragedies, but for the family and loving friends of the victim it was devastating; the most awful thing to happen, resulting in great suffering. The event took its toll on both Wendy and John, so much so that John left and returned to his home town, Grimsby, and – as far as Wendy was concerned – disappeared completely off the radar. Wendy moved back to their house in Bingley.

Six weeks after we were married Lesley came home to say she'd been asked by *Blue Peter* to go to Ethiopia. She and Peter Purves, her co-presenter, were to go. At first she said she didn't want to but I told her she must. It's wonderful to have the opportunity to travel. She said she'd be away for two weeks; I said, fine. At that stage we had Jeremy living with us and I had to take him to school.

Lesley went off to Ethiopia. She was away for nearly three weeks and when she came back it was as if she was a different person.

Jeremy was asleep, it was late in the evening and I asked if she was okay.

'No,' she said. 'I've just had the most extraordinary experience.'

'Have you had an affair out there?' I asked.

'Yes,' she said, 'an affair with life. I realised you were right, that we should never have married. I cannot take the responsibility on for you and Jeremy.'

I'm afraid I lost it and she didn't even stay that night. She got a taxi and went back to Peter Purves and his wife and stayed there.

So that was the end of the marriage. I saw Lesley only once after that. It was obviously all over with no chance of a reconciliation. That was the end of my second marriage. It was all very strange and sudden. Very sad.

Out of the blue Wendy called to say that John had left her. She was in a terrible state, saying she didn't know what to do, where to go, who to turn to.

I said that John was the love of her life. 'That love doesn't go away overnight. He'll be back.'

'He won't. I know he won't.'

'Listen, give him time.'

'I haven't got time,' she said.

I was taken aback. 'What do you mean?'

'I'm pregnant,' she said.

I cannot recall my exact words but I tried to express my deep concern for her well-being and said that she should find a stable place to live, face each day as it came and stay as healthy as she could for her and her baby's sake. 'John will come back,' I insisted.

Bless her. She took my advice and found the strength she didn't feel she had. In a matter of weeks she had left Bingley, bought a caravan, and parked it in her mother's orchard in Kent. In March 1974, now living in her mother's farmhouse, she gave birth to dear Fletcher.

After Lesley's departure I knew I had to make some decisions. I felt I had no alternative but to take Jeremy back to Wendy. I was an actor, working all over the place, I couldn't bring up Jeremy on my own. I only wish I had done but I took him back. It was Easter.

As Jamie was very unhappy at prep school we decided to bring him out. So poor Wendy was in a caravan with baby Fletcher, Jeremy back in her life and Jamie arriving imminently.

Jeremy was aged six and he kept asking when he was going to see Lesley again. (I knew in my heart that he never would.)

One afternoon I was driving my two sons somewhere and out of the blue Jamie asked why his second name was Laurence.

'You're named after the best actor in the world,' I said. 'Laurence Olivier. Your first name, James, after my father, then Laurence, your second name.'

Jeremy piped in and I love him for it. 'My second name is after the second best actor in the world,' he said in triumph. 'It's Derek, after Dad.'

Wendy had enormous responsibilities. It was very tough for her. I remember, when I left them, asking Wendy to call me when everything was settled and arrange for me to see the boys. 'When it's the right moment for you,' I said.

I said goodbye and drove away. I parked the car after a few miles and my heart just broke. I didn't see the boys for about six months.

I remained in the flat that Lesley and I bought together. It wasn't a good time at all. And I wasn't working.

One day Darrol Blake, the director, knocked on the door and said, 'Would you like to do a play at the Institute of Contemporary Arts? It's called *The Importance of Being Neutral*.'

I read the play, written by Royce Ryton, and jumped at it. It was very original, innovative and extremely funny with a great cast. I was attracted to the piece as it was a series of parodies of different plays with different acting styles. There were scenes from John Osborne, Joe Orton, Chekhov and the Brontës. It was sometimes bizarre, sometimes complex but always enjoyable to act. At the end I came out in a smoking jacket and said in my best David Frost voice, 'Hello, good evening and welcome.' It was as if the play was starting all over again.

It was good to be working again. Darrol Blake was great. I liked his company and got very close to him and his family. I enjoyed working again, but my heart was down there in Kent with my boys and Wendy.

While I was rehearsing the play I was probably drinking too much, taking drugs, pills and so on; and one night when I got home from rehearsal I called a girlfriend and said, why don't you come over, I can't sleep?

She said, 'Do you realise what time it is?'

'I've got no idea,' I said. 'I've been rehearsing. I just called up to say goodbye.'

She put the phone down.

It seems that I made other phone calls before I passed out totally naked.

Suddenly there was an almighty crash. I opened my eyes and there were two policemen peering at me alongside an ambulance driver.

I said, 'What are you doing in my flat?'

'Come on, sir,' they said. 'We had a telephone call saying you were not well.'

'I'm fine,' I said. 'I've been working. I've been rehearsing a play. I just couldn't sleep.'

They told me to put some clothes on and took me to Charing Cross Hospital. They said, bring a pound so you can get a taxi back.

This is a bit bizarre, I thought; but when I got to Charing Cross Hospital they put me into bed and gave me a tablet and I woke up the next morning with my director, Darrol, and his wife Anne gazing down on me.

'What have you been up to?' they asked.

I said, 'I've no idea. All I remember is, I was on the phone then I went to sleep. Am I late for the rehearsal?'

'They said they're not letting you out.'

'What? They have to.'

'You have to go to see a psychiatrist,' they said.

So I went to see a lovely black guy who was a psychiatrist. He quizzed me with all these different questions and in the end he said, 'I'm not going to let you go home.'

'Why not?' I asked.

He said, 'I don't think you're capable of looking after yourself.'

'Look,' I said, 'I'm rehearsing a play and it opens in three weeks' time. I have to go to work.'

He thought for a moment and then said, 'I'll send you to rehearsals with a nurse. They will sit with you while you work and they will bring you back here, and you will stay here until I feel you are capable of looking after yourself.'

I suppose I was committed. What a thing to happen to me! I was committed, and, much to the amusement of the whole cast, went to rehearsals with a nurse who sat in the stalls and watched the play come to life.

After ten days I went to the psychiatrist and pleaded with him to let me go home. 'I can't stand it here.'

He said, 'I'll let you go home but you'll have to report to me on a regular basis.'

I saw him twice a week, and at the opening night of the play all the nursing staff of the hospital were in the audience and they gave me a standing ovation. It was a really funny period in my life. It was December 1974.

What next, I wondered? What next?

Chapter 11

Hits, near hits and pilots – Commercials – The radiance of Jo

I FELT I HAD TO LEAVE THE FLAT IN BARNES that Lesley Judd and I lived in and start afresh. It was then that my dear friend, the impresario Peter Bridge, knew someone about to rent out his house in Clapham. I went over and met Bob Howe who was a choreographer and dancer. It was a very nice house.

'I'm having a party tonight,' he said. 'Why don't you come and meet some of my friends?'

It was there that I met David Kernan and his partner Basil Poole. I'd known David from *That Was the Week That Was* and lots of other things and thought he was extremely talented. He said he adored *Basil Brush* and Mr Derek.

They lived in a big property in Fentiman Road. I said I was going to take over Bob Howe's house while he was away but he would be coming back eventually.

David said, 'The whole of the ground floor of our house is a flat and it's empty. If you feel you would like to come over and look at it, please do.'

I did. I went over there in early 1975. After seeing it I said I'd like to take it. It was going to be for a few weeks but I ended up staying for five years, and dear David and Basil became like my brothers. They're like family members now and I will always be grateful for their love, their kindness and their support. I so enjoyed my time there. We had great fun.

Being on my own again was hard. 1975 was a strange year, but I was slowly getting back on my feet when I got a call from Frank

Dunlop, the director, asking what I was doing.

'Nothing.'

'Get down to the Young Vic. I want to talk to you.'

I walked into Frank's office. He was sitting behind a desk and in front of him was what looked a Polo mint.

'Do you know what this is?' he asked.

'It looks like a mint.'

'No. This is the rim of a cauldron. I'm doing a production of *Macbeth* and I want you to be in it.'

'What am I going to play?'

'You're going to play a witch, Macbeth, a murderer and Duncan.'

'How do I do all that?'

'At the opening of the play thirteen witches come out of the cauldron, because in a coven of witches there are thirteen. And there are masks at the back of the stage. You put on these masks and become these different characters. You come out of the cauldron going, "Hee, hee, hee. Let's do a play. We'll do *Macbeth*." I've got three Macbeths. One Duncan, two Lady Macbeths.'

I said, 'Frank, it sounds amazing.'

'It will be,' he said. 'Are you on board?'

'Yes, please!' I replied.

We did this incredible production. It was very exciting. Alfred Lynch was 'Macbeth One', James Bolam was the all-powerful 'Macbeth Two' and I played 'Macbeth Three' who slowly disintegrates and is executed. He was killed with a stake through his heart. That's how you kill witches. It had some unbelievable reviews, one of which by Jack Tinker of the *Daily Mail* asked, why did these three meet at all? This made us laugh so much we cut the paper out and stuck it on the dressing room mirror.

It was a good time at the Young Vic. Not only did we do *Macbeth* in London, we toured Mexico: Guadalajara, Guanajuato and Mexico City. It was an exciting tour in these huge theatres. I'm sure half of the audience didn't know what we were talking about. With masks and multiple Macbeths, I think it must have been very confusing.

I did, however, meet the Mexican actress Dolores del Río, at a reception in our honour. Dolores was a hugely successful Hollywood star of the 1920s and 1930s.

I stayed on at the Young Vic and did a production of *Two Gentlemen of Verona* playing the servant, Speed. I had quite a few scenes with Alfred Lynch: a lovely guy, a lovely actor. Sadly no longer with us – like so many.

At Christmas 1975 I was asked to do *Aladdin* in Leatherhead – my first pantomime! Gerry Flood, Linda Thorson and Carmen Silvera were in it. We had a lot of fun, but it wasn't really my cup of tea. I played Wishee Washee. I thought at the time that this was probably my debut and my swansong in panto. It was enjoyable for a couple of weeks but I didn't feel I wanted to do it again.

At the beginning of '76 I had a call from the director Alan Strachan who said, 'I'm doing a production of an Alan Ayckbourn play which is transferring from Scarborough.'

I adored Alan Ayckbourn's work. I thought he was a genius. They were bringing his play *Confusions* into London and I was offered a part.

It was a short five-act play and we ran for nine months at the Apollo. In the company were the lovely Pauline Collins and her husband, dear old John Alderton; and the great James Cossins. There was also the gorgeous Sheila Gish – another one sadly no longer with us and much missed. I loved working with all those talented people. It was a very happy time and we were a big hit.

Above my flat in Fentiman Road I could hear much activity in David and Basil's rooms. There was music and singing, long pauses, animated language, endless laughing and more music and singing. I was all ears! David Kernan had a wonderful tenor voice and sang in shows such as *1776* (the musical by Sherman Edwards set around the signing of the Declaration of Independence), *Robert and Elizabeth* and *A Little Night Music*. It turned out that he was putting together a show as a tribute to the great American composer, Stephen Sondheim, so the wonderful sounds I could hear were rehearsals. Ned Sherrin

Mum and Dad on their wedding day

Mum in our back garden in Berkhamsted

My Nan with me and sister Babs

My Gran with me and sister Babs

In my back garden with tin baths in background

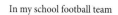

In my school football team

Me aged 18

SAC Fowlds, Wireless Operator in the RAF

Midshipman Carson in *We Joined the Navy*, 1962

We Joined the Navy with me, Dinsdale Landen and Jeremy Lloyd

Joan O'Brien

My wedding day to Wendy, 1964

East of Sudan (1962) with Sylvia Syms, Anthony Quayle and Jenny Agutter aged 11

With Sylvia Syms in *East of Sudan*

Hotel Paradiso with Alec Guiness, 1966

BBC series *Take a Pair of Private Eyes* with Jeanne Roland

Frankenstein Created Woman with Susan Denberg

With Helen Mirren in *The Ortolan*, Manchester 1967

With Prunella Scales in *The Promise*, 1968

My name in lights! My mother's wish came true

Hamlet, Exeter 1969

Mr Derek and Basil Brush

Meeting the Queen Mother with
Ivan Owen and George Martin

Royal Gala 1972: meeting the Queen

Macbeth at the Young Vic, 1975

Two Gentlemen of Verona with
Alfred Lynch, Young Vic 1975

Lehman Byck, my American mentor
and friend

Hamlet with John Bardon as the Gravedigger

My son Jeremy aged two

My son Jamie aged five

Jo and I when we first got together, 1976

Fletcher and Jeremy

Jeremy grown up

Jamie grown up

Mentor and friend Bruce Wansbury and his wife, Pat

A favourite photo of my Mum

My English teacher, Enid Watling

Yes Minister 1980-87. My dear friends Nigel Hawthorne, Paul Eddington and me

My boys in *Heartbeat*, 1991-2009. Me with Bill Simons, Nick Berry and Mark Jordon

Meeting the Princess Royal

Sporting hair extensions for *Over the Hill*, filmed in
Australia in 1991

Olympia Dukakis and me, singing at
the wrap party for *Over the Hill*

I love this photo of Jo and me

Grandson Marlon with Jo's granddaughter, Alice

Jo's son Laurence and granddaughter, Alice

My grandson Jacob

Sister Babs with her husband, Alfred

My favourite cartoon from Jo

The way we were

was going to narrate the show, and the cast would include Millicent Martin and Julia McKenzie. Some of the songs were so clear, so vivid, I might have been in the same room.

When David and I spoke one morning he told me of his hopes and plans. Mischievously, I suggested the title *Send in the Clowns.* I believe David considered that, but he eventually told me it would be called *Side by Side by Sondheim.*

I went to the Stables Theatre in Wavendon, Cleo Laine and Johnny Dankworth's place, to attend the first night of the show. It moved on to London's Mermaid Theatre, then Wyndham's and then the Garrick for a grand total of 806 performances. It even made Broadway where the American Actors' Equity Association famously allowed the original British cast to transfer with the show.

Side by Side by Sondheim was a huge hit and I felt privileged to have heard the very first musical notes descending through my ceiling.

*

By this time Wendy had moved to a cottage in East Sussex, and I used to go down every other Sunday and take the boys out. We would go to nearby Eastbourne to visit the seaside and play the slot machines. It was always lovely to be with them and the hours passed so quickly.

One particular Sunday I drove down and when I arrived the boys were playing. It was a very warm day and Wendy asked if I would like a drink.

I said, 'That would be nice.'

'Oh,' she added, 'Jo is here.'

'Where?'

'She's sunbathing in the garden.'

I walked outside trying not to break into a gallop.

When I first met Jo, twelve years earlier, I thought she was a stunning girl with a terrific sense of humour. She was staying with Wendy that weekend.

Out of Wendy's earshot, I said, 'Hello, Jo.'

She replied by saying, 'Derek! Why do you marry all these weird women?'

'Well, I suppose that's the type I'm attracted to. Anyway, you've never been available.'

'Well, I am now,' she said.

She told me about a disastrous affair. I caught up with news of her children; three of them: Amanda, Gemma and Laurence, who was going into prep school. His grandfather, Donald Lindsay, was headmaster of Malvern College and through him Jo managed to get Laurence a place. Gemma was living with Jo, and Amanda had absconded somewhere. Nobody quite knew where she was.

Jo and I chatted and laughed and Wendy suggested that I stay, that we could all have lunch together. So off we went to a pub called The Kicking Donkey. We had a lovely meal in the sunshine and I kept looking at Jo thinking, you really are the most gorgeous girl.

Before I left I said goodbye to the boys telling them that I would see them again in two weeks. I turned to Jo and suggested that she came to see my play. I said, 'If you want tickets just call me and I'll arrange it for you.'

I felt sorry leaving everybody and I couldn't stop thinking about Jo and wondering whether she would call me. For some stupid reason I hadn't asked for her telephone number and felt I couldn't ask Wendy for it.

My patience was rewarded for, at the end of the show on the Monday night, there was a knock on my dressing room door and there was Jo standing there. I said, 'You didn't pay, did you?'

'Yes,' she said. 'I just felt I wanted to see you again, and I certainly wanted to see the play. I thought you were very good.'

Jo was never one to over-enthuse. She had this amazing, cynical, laid-back sense of humour; I've never met anyone so naturally comical.

We went out to dinner and chatted about what we'd both been up to over the past few years.

'What I remember about you,' she said, 'was that you loved Sunday lunch.'

I said, 'Sunday is not a Sunday without a proper Sunday lunch and a nice bottle of red wine.'

'Come and have lunch with me on Sunday,' she said.

'I'd love to.'

Jo and I had met in 1964 so we'd known each other for nearly twelve years. It was lovely to see her again and spend time with her. I was flattered that she came to see the play.

That Sunday she cooked a lovely roast, we had a couple of bottles of red wine and we just talked and giggled. We laughed for hours and hours. When I left I thanked her and suggested that we do this again. She said she would like that very much.

We both knew, I think, that we would start a relationship. I was so attracted to her and I loved her company. I think she felt the same. A magical Sunday in 1976.

A magical year, as it turned out. My relationship with Jo grew closer and closer, although it would be four years before we started living together in a house Jo had bought in Wimbledon.

I'm not certain how much I pushed for this arrangement. In the end David and Basil sold their house which meant I had to move too; so I had to go somewhere but couldn't ask Jo outright.

One Sunday at Jo's house, I said, 'Listen, I've got to move out of my flat as the house has been sold. I've got to find somewhere to live.'

'Where do you think you'll go?' Jo asked.

'I've no idea.'

I think I paused dramatically here. I shouldn't have, for my following words came out in a squeak like a cornered mouse. I said, 'Have you got a spare room?'

Jo smiled and said, 'We'll give it a try.'

I borrowed £10,000 to gut and replan Jo's house. The work was done in stages over a few months and it seemed that, each time the builder came, I got a job and had to go away.

There was no way of knowing then that Jo and I would be together for thirty-six years. We were soulmates, best friends, lovers. I loved her dearly. She was the love of my life.

*

I'd met the producer John Gale years ago when I left drama school and he was with Peter Bridge. They both took me under their wing and were so good to me and very supportive. I had lost contact with John over the years, but one day I got a call from him. He was producing the farce *No Sex Please, We're British*, which had been a great success and was now in its fourth year at the Strand Theatre.

'I would love you to take over the role of Brian,' John said. 'I'm offering a year's contract.'

'Are you serious?' I asked. This was the part that had made a West End star of the young Michael Crawford.

'Yes,' he said.

Over lunch I asked him if his play would really take a 'straight' performance. 'I do not want to do funny walks and funny voices, and I certainly don't want to try and follow the genius of Michael.'

'I know,' he said. 'The play will stand if you play it the way you want it.'

So I agreed. I signed for a year. We only had two weeks' rehearsal. It was directed by Alan Davis and in the cast were Peter Graves, Helen Christie and the great Hugh Lloyd.

When we opened I found it a very difficult play. Michael Crawford had largely repeated his performance in that role when he created the character of Frank Spencer in *Some Mothers Do 'Ave 'Em*, and I kept hearing him speak those lines. I wasn't that type of actor. I wanted to play it for real.

After Michael left, David Jason had done it, then Andrew Sachs. Both had done it in their own way, but I initially found it tough.

The play is about a porn dealer who awaits a new delivery from his supplier, Niko, but Niko mixes up the address with that of the local bank. Newly-weds David and Penny (who live above the bank) are shocked when porn photos arrive followed by films and two porno girls. They and fellow bank worker Brian have to get rid of the porn without anyone knowing. The bank manager is anti-porn and would contact the police if he knew. Brian gets the porn material muddled up.

In one performance, about twenty minutes into the play, I was in David and Penny's flat above the bank and took delivery of a parcel for them. This parcel was supposed to contain the first batch of porno photos. I had done it so many times: a doorbell rang, I used to go off stage to where the props were on a table, pick up the parcel and come back to continue the scene.

On this night I went out, picked up the parcel, and started walking back on stage. As I walked I shook the parcel and realised they were not the photos – they were the films which were to be disclosed later. I'd picked up the wrong prop. As the scene progressed I tried to think what to do next. Should I improvise and pretend I heard another ring of the bell? I realised that wasn't going to work so, to the amazement of my fellow actors, I suddenly came out of character and said, 'Stop!'

I turned to the audience and said, 'I'm sorry but I've got the wrong prop. This is the wrong parcel. So I'm going to take this one out and bring back the correct one. So we may have to lower the curtain and we'll start the scene again.'

Chaos and uproar!

I was in such trouble with the management; but what I liked about it was that, when the curtain rose again, I came in and said, 'Oh! You've seen this bit before,' and roars of laughter came from the audience. They went along with it. When I brought the right prop in saying, 'This is it,' more laughs and hearty applause.

We then got on with the plot.

But I didn't enjoy being in the play and it may have showed.

One day the director, Alan Davis, said, 'Derek, I'm not going to give you notes here. I want you to come to the Garrick club because I want to talk to you.'

'Okay,' I said.

So I went to the Garrick and sat with Alan.

'Derek,' he said, 'I want to tell you that you're one of the best actors to play this part, but you are the least funny.'

I said, 'Oh, thanks.'

'It really is not working.'

'Why do you think that is?' I asked.

'The central performance really needs the Frank Spencer touch. You've got all the physical business – you climb the walls, you do the backflips, you dive through the kitchen hatchway – you do all those things, but the character is so real it's not funny. So will you bear that in mind?'

I knew I had to do a year in this play, and slowly as the year went by I suppose I became camper and camper and the voice went up a couple of octaves. I played a silly sod and people started laughing a lot and Alan seemed happy, but I probably should never have done it.

The year's contract with eight performances a week was tough.

There was a stage in my career when, I suppose, I became king of the pilots. It began at the BBC's *Comedy Playhouse* where they would try out new situation comedies. I did one called *Captive Audience* (written by Dick Clement and Ian La Frenais of *Likely Lads* and *Porridge* fame) where a suburban family kidnap their landlord and won't let him out until he agrees to reduce their rent significantly. I enjoyed doing it and thought it was very funny, but it wasn't picked up.

I spent a wonderful ten days doing another show with the great comic actor, Terry-Thomas. I had been a fan of Terry's since childhood. All those black-and-white comedy films he made. I was so thrilled to be cast in this pilot, *The Old Campaigner*, where I played Terry's secretary and assistant and I had to escort him to Paris. Terry's character was having an illicit affair and my job was to keep it from his wife.

I laughed every single day I was in Terry's company. I even laughed during the take. In one scene I told him that one of my relatives had died having been run over by a steam-roller. Terry's reaction to that, and the way he repeated the line, had me in fits every time. I even laughed before he delivered the line. Terry was a comedy genius. I had a wonderful time with him and was really hurt when the series was made and I didn't play the part. I know Terry was upset I didn't do it. The part went to another actor, Jonathan Cecil. It was a huge disappointment to me not to make that programme. It only ran for one more series and I often regretted the fact that Terry and I didn't get to work together again.

I did a pilot for the series *Agony* which starred the brilliant Maureen Lipman. I loved working with Maureen and playing the part of her husband. It was a huge success and Maureen went on to do many series. Unfortunately for me, before the series started I was recast and Simon Williams played it. I have to admit it was better casting. He was taller than Maureen and I wasn't.

I'd met the great TV writer Richard Waring when he was writing *Marriage Lines* in the sixties for Richard Briers and Prunella Scales. I played the part of Richard Briers' friend during his wife's pregnancy. I remember the episode with great fondness.

Out of the blue Richard Waring phoned me and said he would like me to meet Michael Mills who was then head of comedy at Thames Television. He invited me over to his house where he told me he wanted me for a pilot called *The Last of the Best Men*.

'How wonderful,' I said.

'We think you'd be right for the lead. It's the story of a man who is always the best man, never gets married himself, and the adventures that happen subsequently.'

We had a great time doing it and thought it was very funny. It had Geoffrey Whitehead and Prunella Gee. Sadly, it wasn't picked up. So that was another pilot that never led to anything.

The wonderful actress Lynn Farleigh and I did a pilot together called *Running Wild*. It's about a middle-aged man who leaves his wife and daughter, sets up his own flat and tries to recapture his lost youth, starting to play the drums and forming a band. John Reardon directed it. When it came to do the series John Reardon, Lynn and myself were replaced. We never understood that. We all enjoyed doing the pilot, we thought it worked and was full of potential. However, the powers that be decided they would recast almost everyone. The only member they retained was Michelle Collins who played my young daughter in the pilot. Michelle grew up into a very talented actress but she is best known for her roles in the soap operas *EastEnders* and *Coronation Street*.

I think the show lasted two series. To this day I have never understood why we were discarded. Perhaps they thought we were not very good.

I was beginning to think that nothing would happen but then I was offered yet another pilot, *Affairs of the Heart*. The actor Paul Daneman had a heart attack and wrote the series based on his experiences: he couldn't manage the stairs at home and had to sleep downstairs, he couldn't make love to his wife, and all the things that come about when you do have a big heart attack and your life changes dramatically. People liked the pilot but we only did one series. It would have been great to carry on but it wasn't to be. It was not recommissioned. I had Sarah Badel as my wife and the lovely Holly Aird as my daughter. I think Holly was only 14 then. She went on to do *The Flame Trees of Thika*, *Scenes of a Sexual Nature*, *Soldier Soldier* and *Waking the Dead*.

Richard Waring called me and said, 'I've written another series and you're going to do this. I've written it for you.'

When it came down to it the powers that be at the BBC said they didn't think Derek Fowlds was sexy enough.

'They say you look too young,' Richard explained. 'They don't believe that you can carry it.'

I said I thought that was silly.

'I know, I know,' said Richard, but I knew there was nothing he could do.

The series was called *Rings on Their Fingers* and was very successful. Martin Jarvis and Diane Keen played the leads. I had a guest role in one episode but I never told Martin that Richard had written his part for me.

I was cast as Esmond in 'The Season of Heavenly Gifts: Part 1', an episode of *The Darling Buds of May* which starred David Jason, Pam Ferris, my old friend Michael Cochrane, and Catherine Zeta-Jones. Yes, 'the' Catherine, who went off and married some American film star. (There was a 'The Season of Heavenly Gifts: Part 2', but I don't recall being in that.)

My part was a drunk ventriloquist so I called on an old friend, Ray Allen who 'worked' with Lord Charles. I'd met Ray on a number of occasions, socially and on the golf course. I'd been given a doll to work. Its name was Desmond. Esmond and Desmond!

Over the phone I asked Ray, 'Can you teach me to be a ventriloquist in a day?'

'That's easy,' he said. 'Come on over.'

I visited his house in Reigate and after lunch we sat together, me with my new doll and Ray. Lord Charles was rudely absent.

For two hours he went through simple routines, offering basic tips that, barring a disaster, would be enough to see me through. I did complete my scene but I knew I wasn't very good at it. I managed to persuade the studio to sell me the doll (£50, I recall) and changed his name to Eric, thereby creating the possibility of a new variety act – Eric and Derek! Alas, no offers came our way, although I did bring him out during our *Heartbeat* party days. For some reason Eric was rude to many people and flirted unashamedly with the girls of the cast and crew. He was very naughty, was Eric; uncontrollable.

He stares at me now from a small chair in the corner of my office and, yes, there are times that we do chat, with me doing both voices.

So how many was that? *The Old Campaigner*, *Agony*, *Last of the Best Men*, *Walk on the Wild Side*, *Affairs of the Heart*. Probably more.

But I did do one pilot that went on to be the best of all: *Yes Minister*.

Hey, ho! It's all fate, isn't it?

I did a series for the telly in 1989 called *Rules of Engagement* which helped to change my image from comedy actor to dramatic actor, and I really enjoyed that switch. It starred Anna Calder-Marshall, Kenneth Cranham and Amanda Fawcett. I played an MI5 agent. It was a story of political intrigue and murder when Portsmouth is sealed off by the military on the eve of World War III.

Joining my fellow RADA student John Thaw, I did an episode of *Inspector Morse* called 'The Settling of the Sun'. I played Kurt Friedman, aka Michael Robson. When Morse is a speaker at a university dinner a Japanese man becomes ill and is later found murdered. Morse himself becomes an alibi for all the suspects.

Another series was *Chancer* in 1989 with the brilliant Clive Owen – I think it was Clive's first job. I thoroughly enjoyed working with him and relished his success that followed. Also in the cast was the lovely Simon Shepherd. I always enjoy meeting up with Simon who lives near me in Bath.

*

In the 1960s and '70s it was frowned upon for a serious actor to do commercials. Producers and the like considered it *infra dig*. There were, however, times when 'needs must' or, as sometimes happened, the pay was so good it couldn't be refused.

My first commercial was for Wall's ice cream. I played the husband of a pregnant wife who was addicted to ice cream. I discovered the ice-cream shop was closed (it was at night) and began throwing pebbles at the window above the store. Eventually, triumphantly, my wife got her treat.

Maxwell House coffee was my second. I had to audition as part of a family with Marty Cruickshank. I got the job as Marty's husband with two children. It was an interesting two days and the name of the director was Ridley Scott. I was quite impressed with his work and, as it turned out, so were plenty of other people. He went on to make many feature films including *Alien*, *Blade Runner*, *Thelma & Louise*, *Gladiator*, *Black Hawk Down*, *American Gangster*, *Robin Hood* and *Prometheus*. I think I caught Ridley too early in his career.

Years later, after *Yes Minister* and before *Heartbeat*, I got my second coffee commercial. I thought I might be on a roll and started counting how many companies made coffee. But it was just the one who wanted me – Nescafé – and wonderfully, they wanted Paul Eddington as well. Without mentioning our characters (Jim Hacker and Bernard Woolley) we had to sit in an office shaking coffee beans. It still staggers me that my fee was £60,000. I saw the money briefly as it swept through my bank account on its way to being paid as a deposit for our house in Colerne. It wasn't long before I got over the rapid disappearance of the money, as Nescafé came back to Paul and me asking us to do a second commercial.

I would have done an 'icing on the cake' advert for free!

Chapter 12

IN 1979 WHEN I WAS DOING *NO SEX PLEASE*, I was waiting outside my agent's office to see him when out came the actor, Jonathan Lynn.

I said, 'Hello, Jonathan.'

He said, 'Hello, Derek.' And that was it. I went in to see my agent and asked what Jonathan was doing there.

'He's very excited. He's casting for his new TV series and has just cast Nigel Hawthorne.'

I asked if there was anything for me in it.

'Don't be silly,' said my agent.

When I got home that evening my agent phoned me. 'When you came in today,' he said, 'Jonathan saw you and wants to send you a script because there may be a part for you in this new series.'

'What's it called?' I asked.

'*Yes Minister*,' he said.

'Is it about vicars?' I asked. 'Is it religious?'

'No,' said my agent, 'it's about politics. Read it and see what you think.'

I read it from start to finish. I just couldn't put the script down. It was different, innovative with great characters. I was being offered the part of the Principal Private Secretary (the PPS) to the Minister. I thought, I'd love to do this.

I didn't know at the time that other actors had been approached to play the part of Bernard. I have no idea who they were, but I think some considered the role as too secondary – a supporting character lacking in potential. Fortunately for me, they decided not to go for it.

Apparently, it took the reading of four complete scripts for Paul and Nigel to commit to the series.

The script had two main characters: Jim Hacker, the Minister of Administrative Affairs, and his Permanent Secretary, Sir Humphrey. A lesser role in terms of screen time was the Principal Private Secretary, Bernard. To my delight Paul Eddington had been cast as the Minister and Nigel Hawthorne as the Permanent Secretary.

Paul told me that John Howard Davies had offered him both parts, the Minister or Sir Humphrey. Paul saw that the Minister was the main part, the title role, and chose that one. Some time later when Nigel got his first comedy award Paul said to me (tongue in cheek, I think), 'Perhaps I chose the wrong part.'

I assured him that he had not. Paul never got the accolades he deserved. He was unquestionably one of the best (if not *the* best) light comedy actors of his time.

Paul Eddington had been an actor all his working life – stage, film and television – but he was in his forties before he became a household name after appearing with Richard Briers, Penelope Keith and Felicity Kendal in the hit TV comedy series *The Good Life*, first screened by the BBC in 1975.

Ten years before, I almost worked with Paul in Enid Bagnold's play, *Call Me Jacky*. I did a read-through and went to the first rehearsal but uppermost in my mind was that my wife Wendy was about to give birth to our second child. My need to be with my family overcame everything else so I went to the director, Frank Hauser, and asked to be let go. Frank acceded. I did regret that I lost the opportunity to work with Paul and with Sybil Thorndike, who starred in the production. Edward Fox played my part.

Nigel Hawthorne had appeared in *The Knowledge*, Jack Rosenthal's TV play about four men attempting to gain 'the Knowledge' required to qualify as London taxi drivers. I had known him for some years by then so I valued the opportunity of celebrating his success in the play. He was brilliant.

Yes Minister's humour hinged around the friction between

Minister Jim Hacker and Sir Humphrey with the loyalties of my character, Bernard, often split between the two. I also had the annoying habit of correcting Sir Humphrey's or Hacker's mixed metaphors, in a way that was nothing short of pedantry. Occasionally I made animal noises and gestures in an attempt to stress a particular point. These attempts were always treated with contempt by Hacker. As PPS I swung between guileless loyalty towards my Minister (my boss) and the realisation that (as I was reminded constantly by Sir Humphrey) my future was with the Civil Service and that Ministers rarely stayed in their jobs for long.

Armando Iannucci, the Oscar- and Emmy-nominated Scottish satirist, writer and television director, once said that I (as Bernard) had a difficult task because I had to 'spend most of [my] time saying nothing but looking interested in everyone else's total and utter guff' but '[my] one line frequently had to be the funniest of the lot'.

Sydney Lotterby, who later directed the series, told me that my role was, ' Pivotal, Derek, pivotal.'

I did ask, 'What does that mean? They can't do it without me?'

Sydney smiled.

The Minister's wife, Annie Hacker, was played by the extra-ordinary actress Diana Hoddinott. I first met Diana in the early sixties when we were both in an episode of the ITV series *The Villains* called 'Victim'; she played Marj and I played Johnny. I remember the transmission was scheduled for July 1964 but postponed until January 1965 because of a one-night strike by technicians demanding more pay (the ITV network enjoying large profits at the time). She had also worked with Paul Eddington for a season at the Bristol Old Vic.

Diana was a stunning-looking girl; when we first met she took my breath away. My voice returned, Diana tells me (I cannot remember this), when I suggested that if I hadn't been married she would begin to fancy me. She points out that she never did. Diana was married to Harry Towb, a wonderful and versatile actor who made many TV appearances including *The Avengers, Dr Finlay's*

Casebook, *Doctor Who*, *Minder* and *Heartbeat* as well as film comedies like *Doctor at Sea* and *The Fenn Street Gang*. They had three children, Joshua, Emily and Daniel.

Since Harry and my Jo died Diana and I have seen a little more of each other, taking parts in short films. When the chance came to make one of these films, *Kindred Spirits*, I suggested to Diana that this would be a wonderful way of commemorating the closest of human beings: Diana's Harry, my Jo and my sister, Babs. This we did in 2014.

Diana is a loyal, trusting and endearing friend. She is a kind and gentle family person, a very talented actress and a rare beauty.

None of us knew, when we first met up for rehearsals for *Yes Minister*, that it would be the huge success it turned out to be. I think Diana and I saw ourselves as minnows to the bigger fish of Paul and Nigel. It wasn't long before a friendly and professional bond was established between us and proved to be a valuable one that showed, I think, in all our performances.

The Cabinet Secretary, Sir Arnold Robinson, was played by John Nettleton. John had an impressive acting CV: *A Man for All Seasons*, *Please Sir*, *Elizabeth R* and *Upstairs, Downstairs*. John's character appeared in the pilot episode but then for some reason didn't reappear until the second series.

Sir Humphrey (who was promoted to Sir Arnold's position in *Yes, Prime Minister*) often discussed matters with Sir Arnold, seeking advice as to how to out-manoeuvre just about anyone outside the Service. Both were jaded, cynical, haughty and conspiratorial.

*

The two writers of the series were actor, director and producer Jonathan Lynn and writer, broadcaster and director Antony Jay. A full description of their experience and achievements in television, stage and the written word would run into pages long.

Jonathan Lynn played Motel, the tailor, in the original West End production of *Fiddler on the Roof*. He wrote episodes for the *Doctor* TV series and *On the Buses*, and later directed the comedy films *Nuns on the Run* and *My Cousin Vinny*.

Antony Jay wrote the BBC TV documentaries *Royal Family* and *Elizabeth R: A Year in the Life of the Queen*. He was appointed a Commander of the Royal Victorian Order for personal services to the Royal Family.

Because Lynn was short and Jay was tall the cast and crew of *Yes Minister* referred to them as 'Little and Large'. They were two incredibly talented writers with remarkable insight into human behaviour.

For the opening titles Gerald Scarfe drew caricatures of Paul, Nigel and myself, cleverly distorting our facial characteristics but keeping the images recognisable. I tried to buy mine but couldn't afford it at the time. I think it was £5,000!

Gerald's cartoons replaced an original set that seemed to us all poorly drawn. John Howard Davies, the BBC's Head of Comedy, had quickly rejected them.

Ronnie Hazlehurst wrote the theme tune. He described the composition, which echoed the chimes of Big Ben, as the easiest thing he'd ever done. This was also a replacement for an earlier commissioned theme tune written by Max Harris, who had penned themes for *Porridge*, *Open all Hours* and for the film, *On the Buses*. But Max's tune for *Yes Minister* wasn't right. It didn't fit.

Whenever Ronnie's tune comes on it reminds me of the grandfather clock in the house of my nan – my father's mother. Every hour was ratified by the clock's Westminster Chimes.

The question that was regularly asked (but, at the time, never completely answered) was, from whom did the writers get their inside information? Years later, in a programme screened by the BBC in 2004, it was unveiled that Jay and Lynn had gathered information provided by two 'background staff' from the governments of Harold Wilson and James Callaghan: Marcia Williams and Bernard Donoughue. I believe the diaries of Richard Crossman also provided inspiration. I remember a discussion that revealed that the writers would show their initial ideas to the 'deep throats' who would inevitably give extra information which, because it was true, was often funnier than anything the writers had first thought up.

I know that many people speculated on the 'real' people that the characters were based on, but I believed then and I still believe they were 'made-up' people. The brilliance of the writers was that the behaviour, the mannerisms, the language and the bearing all had echoes of truth that convinced the audience that each and every character 'probably' existed.

*

There was always a tight schedule in rehearsal. We would do a read-through on Monday and spend the following day learning lines. On Thursdays and Fridays there would be a full rehearsal. A technical session was held on the Saturday for most participants, the camera, sound and lighting crew, wardrobe, make-up – everyone including the writers. On Sunday we went on set to try our costumes on and rehearse non-stop until the supper break when the audience came in. Paul, Nigel and I used to wander around in different directions, umming and ahing, before we went on. Nearly always one of us would dry up which would break the nervous strain we were all under.

There were times when Paul would sidle up to one of us whispering, 'Are we getting laughs? Has anyone laughed yet?'

Nigel would reply, 'They're writing notes! Some are writing notes! Why are they doing that?'

Some of the script was difficult to learn. Nigel, especially, had very long speeches and he did them brilliantly without crib boards or aids. He demanded that scripts were made available well in advance so that the long speeches he had to do were well practised rather than learned only days before recording. I tried to imagine learning these lines by heart: 'Well Minister, if you ask me for a straight answer, then I shall say that, as far as we can see, looking at it by and large, taking one thing with another in terms of the average of departments, then in the final analysis it is probably true to say that, at the end of the day, in general terms, you would probably find that, not to put too fine a point on it, there probably wasn't very much in it one way or the other. As far as one can see, at this stage.'

I took a leaf out of Nigel's book by acquiring scripts in advance so that I could be word perfect in Latin or complex gobbledegook. Sometimes reading lines from a script and firming it up in my mind could take days. In one scene Sir Humphrey tells me: 'I need to know everything. How else can I judge whether or not I need to know it?'

My reply was: 'So that means you need to know things even when you don't need to know them. You need to know them not because you need to know them but because you need to know whether or not you need to know. If you don't need to know, you still need to know so that you know that there is no need to know.'

Sir Humphrey: 'Yes!'

Me: 'Good. That's very clear!'

Paul's part was very different. He had the more difficult acting job with his part demanding diverse emotions, from assertive (sometimes Churchillian) pontificating to snivelling contrition.

One of my most memorable scenes was in a later episode when the Minister complained about the press. It was also a triumph for me; after some of the best-written lines in British comedy, I got the biggest laugh.

'Don't tell me about the press,' said Jim Hacker. 'I know exactly who reads the papers. The *Daily Mirror* is read by people who think they run the country; the *Guardian* is read by people who think they ought to run the country; *The Times* is read by people who actually do run the country; the *Daily Mail* is read by the wives of the people who run the country; the *Financial Times* is read by people who own the country; the *Morning Star* is read by people who think the country ought to be run by another country; and the *Daily Telegraph* is read by people who think it is.'

Sir Humphrey piped in, 'Prime Minister, what about the people who read the *Sun*?'

Then me as Bernard: '*Sun* readers don't care who runs the country, as long as she's got big tits.'

The 'big tits' version was one of two takes; the other was 'big boobs'. I told Sydney Lotterby, our director, that I thought 'tits' was funnier. He shot both to compare the response. 'Tits' won.

When we began shooting the first series, Paul was appearing in Alan Ayckbourn's play *Ten Times Table* and I was working on the stage in *No Sex Please* every evening.

I can remember playing my very first scene with Paul outside number 10 Downing Street. I wasn't quite sure what I was going to do with my character. Initially I thought I would try a terribly pukka voice and wear a pair of glasses.

We were in a taxi going through our lines and Paul said, 'Why are you talking in that funny voice?'

'I thought it was rather good for the character,' I said.

'Don't be silly. And you're not going to wear those glasses are you?'

'Don't you think they suit the part?' I asked.

'No,' Paul replied, 'just be you.'

'That's the problem. I don't know how to be me. I've never known how to be me.'

'You remember how you used to talk to Basil Brush? Well, do it like that.'

Anyway, thanks to Paul, Bernard Woolley was the closest part I've ever played to me. This was in spite of the fact that Bernard was a high flier, scholarly and classically educated and I was none of those things.

Throughout the first series, Jim Hacker had a political advisor, a character called Frank Weisel, played by Neil Fitzwiliam. His surname was correctly pronounced '*why*-zel' but, of course, Sir Humphrey and my character, Bernard, always called him 'weasel' (as in the little mammal). In the second series Weisel had gone; I think he was sent off to a remote quango.

The pilot was directed by Stuart Allen who had a long and successful record of producing and directing situation comedies such as *On the Buses*. It soon became evident that Stuart was not impressed with the first *Yes Minister* script; he didn't find it funny. I think he wanted a touch of slapstick. He tried to encourage Diana (the Minister's wife) to up the sexiness by sticking out her bum for the camera to focus on.

I can remember Diana pointing out that the writers never intended the programme to be a 'domestic' sitcom. 'The bar is set higher,' she said.

Stuart even wanted to write new dialogue which, to say the least, upset Jonathan, the co-writer. Jonathan threatened that the show would not go out unless it was filmed as written. This, of course, was how Paul, Nigel and myself saw it. It was funny, and got funnier the straighter we played it. We felt the only way to do it was with total truth. We looked at it through an actor's eyes and trusted the script and the characterisation. The more real we could make it, the more convincing (and funnier) it was. Many of the cast started putting their foot down, arguing their point of view but growing frustrated at having to do so.

The dispute had nothing to do with personalities; it was simply 'the' interpretation of the words written. We really believed that there were such characters in Whitehall and Westminster. And time did prove us right.

In 2013, six new episodes of *Yes, Prime Minister* were broadcast on the television channel UKTV Gold. If I compare the detailed attention to characterisation in our version with the new series I have to say that, although I did try to like it, they lacked credence. I didn't believe them. They did cast two wonderful actors as Hacker and Appleby but the execution lacked conviction. I wasn't alone in my reservations. The *Independent* said the show was 'a beat or two off', and that 'further consultation' was required. And the *Radio Times*, in a detailed comparison of the original series against the new, concluded the remake was 'not even close' to the 'untouchable classic'.

*

The storyline of *Yes Minister*'s pilot episode starts after a general election when a new government is swept to power. Which party has won the election is never mentioned. A new Cabinet post is created, Minister of Administrative Affairs, with a department that includes a Permanent Secretary and a Principal Private Secretary. The new Prime Minister offers this position to Jim Hacker.

Hacker's Permanent Secretary, Sir Humphrey Appleby, believes that it is the Civil Service, rather than the politicians, that knows what is best for the country. He therefore provides a restrictive and conservative foil to his Minister's desire to improve matters (and thereby gain promotion and re-election). He confuses his perceived opponents with long-winded circumlocution, and supplies enough red tape to strangle the Minister.

As most of the storylines revolved around the inner machinations of central government, few scenes were set outside the offices of Whitehall and exclusive members' clubs. Jonathan Lynn explained, 'There was not a single scene set in the House of Commons because government does not take place in the House of Commons. Some politics and much theatre takes place there. Government happens in private. As in all public performances, the real work is done in rehearsal, behind closed doors. Then the public and the House are shown what the government wishes them to see.'

We had a studio audience, normal for BBC situation comedies at the time. There were some who felt an audience wasn't right. The production was full of interruptions, camera and lighting changes and so on, so the actors were unable to flow as they would in a theatre. Jonathan Lynn wanted an audience so that real laughter could be recorded as the scene progressed. It would, he thought, expose failings and encourage success. Initially the studio audience didn't warm to the in-jokes, so in the end we canvassed political affiliations and government offices and invited them along so the audience was made up of people who knew what we were talking about.

The glimpses of Jim Hacker's domestic life featured his wife Annie and, briefly, his rebellious daughter Lucy. Annie's feet were planted firmly on the ground; she never hid her frustrations and often displayed a cynical attitude to her husband's politics.

The pilot of *Yes Minister* was made in a general election year when no one was quite sure who the next government would be. So it was decided that we couldn't do the series until the following year after the real political dust had settled.

During this time there was a great deal of uncertainty over whether or not the *Yes Minister* series would be made. Political sensitivity was rife and, for a while, rumours were our only source of information.

Eventually Margaret Thatcher and the Conservative party won the 1979 election, with a 5.2% swing from Labour, the largest swing since the 1945 election. Mrs Thatcher became the United Kingdom's (and Europe's) first female head of government.

In the months of *Yes Minister* limbo we all went our separate ways, taking other jobs; but all of us, I think, were hoping to get notice that the series would be made. We got the green light in 1980.

When the time came for us to make more episodes we discovered that Stuart Allen had stepped aside and Sydney Lotterby was to be our new director. Sydney had directed a string of TV hits: *Some Mothers Do 'Ave 'Em*, *Porridge*, *The Liver Birds* and *Comedy Playhouse*.

For the pilot episode, 'Open Government', we had had a warm-up man – the actor, Felix Bowness – who told a lot of crude jokes. (Paul and Nigel were appalled when it was suggested that the comic got more laughs than we did.) After that we didn't have a warm-up man; instead we had a great floor manager called Brian Jones who simply welcomed the audience by explaining various technical bits and why they were there. He explained what would happen, what the different sets were and pointed to the overhead television monitors so they could follow the show on screen as well as watching it on the floor.

He introduced Paul, who liked chatting to the audience. Then Paul introduced Nigel (who didn't initially like chatting), then Nigel would introduce me.

Brian would then interrupt and explain that Derek was not allowed to talk. 'But if we have a tape break we may let him tell his one joke,' he went on. 'The thing about Derek's joke is that the only person who laughs at it is Derek. We may test you out.'

Sometimes, the tape did break so they said, 'Come on, Derek.'

I used to go out and tell this joke to the audience. It goes: 'A white horse went into a pub and said, "Could I have a glass of whisky?"

'The barman said, "Certainly. By the way, we have a whisky named after you."

'And the horse said, "What? Eric?"'

Nobody ever laughed except me.

*

And so began seven wonderful years, working with the brilliant Nigel and Paul. We never had a cross word. I don't think we ever had an argument.

I've read accounts of so-called rifts between Paul and Nigel on set, claiming they didn't get on. Rubbish! I was there. I worked with them for seven years. There were no arguments, no cross words, no envy, no jealousy. The chemistry between them just couldn't have happened had their mutual respect and admiration been anything other than genuine. They were professional, kind and considerate human beings as well as being talented actors.

We became close friends and socialised on and off the set. When we were doing other projects we always wanted to know how each other was doing. It was such a happy time.

We often visited each other. Jo and I used to go down to Hertfordshire and walk around the grounds of Nigel and his partner Trevor's house. They were very much the dogs and gumboots sort.

The bright idea of inviting employees of the Civil Service and other Whitehall people to make up most of the audience was so right. Secret cameras recorded the audience's response – unashamed hilarity.

With a glint in his eye Paul used to say to me, 'This is a master-class for you, isn't it?'

'What are you talking about?' I asked.

'You must know,' he said. 'Standing between me and Nigel every week – that must be a masterclass for you.'

There were many times Paul had a glint in his eye. In a gap in proceedings Paul asked me, 'Derek, where do you see yourself in football terms?'

'What do you mean?'

'What division do you think "Team Derek" is in?'

'I'm not sure. What do you think?

'Well, Nigel and I are about half way up Division One.'

'Really,' I said. 'Where do you think I am?'

'Probably at the top of Division Two, waiting for a promotion.'

I have no doubt that every fan of *Yes Minister* and *Yes, Prime Minister* will have their favourite storyline. I (as an insider) have my favourites. Some include my participation in a scene but others – mostly, but not always – embrace the extraordinary chemistry between Paul and Nigel.

Someone said that life is made up of moments and I think I have always agreed with that. You can read a book, see a film or play, listen to music and although you don't recollect the whole of the experience you do remember the special moments. The times you hear people say, 'Do you remember that bit when … ?' and 'What about, you know, when she did that?' … 'That moment when …?'

During my participation in *Yes Minister* and later *Yes, Prime Minister* there were so many moments of joy, hilarity, anxiety – the complete range of emotions. These were not confined to a few episodes, not even to the majority of episodes, but all of the episodes. So for every single moment I write about, there are dozens more I don't. The choosing of the moments is like trying to weigh one favourite song against another favourite song: an impossible and fruitless task.

The tense moments were always just before our break for supper that preceded the recording. Not much was eaten from that table. We knew that at 7:30 the audience of 250 would be in. During and after make-up the three of us hardly spoke and found dark corners to hide in.

I once saw Nigel swallowing a pill before we went on.

'What are you taking?' I asked.

'It's a beta blocker.'

'What's that?

'The nerves,' Nigel said. 'It helps settle the nerves. Try one.'

I did take it, and soon after I didn't know if it was Sunday night or Monday morning. Thank goodness I don't remember what episode it was for I really wouldn't want to see that one back. I don't think Nigel made a habit of taking one, but my first was my last.

Looking back there were episodes that had stronger, more sub-stantial storylines, while one or two now look dated. But there are a few that could have been written in recent times and reflect what goes on in today's corridors of power.

Of course, the first episode, the pilot, is prominent in my mind for many special moments; after all, these were the first special moments of the entire series. Character establishment was paramount along with the settings and the nature and spirit of the plot.

In 'Open Government', Jim Hacker wins his parliamentary seat, so contributing to the election victory of his party. He anxiously awaits a call from the Prime Minister hoping that a Cabinet post will be offered. On being appointed Minister of Administrative Affairs, his first decision is to have 'open and transparent government'. He immediately faces opposition: Sir Humphrey and the Civil Service.

By devious document placement Sir Humphrey invites his new Minister's wrath and reaction which, as it unfolds, antagonises

Hacker's boss, the Prime Minister. With Bernard's help Sir Humphrey saves the Minister's bacon.

As with every drama, comedic or tragic, the early dialogue is key to establishing character traits. By saying 'this' in a certain way rather than 'that' in a certain way you can, if the dialogue is concise and clever, receive a big clue to the character's personality and hints at what can be expected. Actors as well as the audience can take a giant leap forward in the plot if the dialogue is 'just right'. This is successfully illustrated by the first meeting of the Minister with Sir Humphrey:

Bernard (me): 'I believe you know each other.'

Sir Humphrey: 'Yes, we did cross swords when the Minister gave me a grilling over the estimates in the Public Accounts Committee.'

Minister: 'I wouldn't say that.'

Sir Humphrey: 'You came up with all of the questions I hoped nobody would ask.'

Minister: 'Well, opposition is about asking awkward questions.'

Sir Humphrey: 'And government is about not answering them.'

Minister: 'Well, you answered all mine anyway.'

Sir Humphrey: 'I'm glad you thought so, Minister.'

The relationship of the Minister and Sir Humphrey was fixed in that first encounter.

In this episode the first of Sir Humphrey's verbose speeches appeared. To a simple request from the Minister as to how many people worked in 'his' department Sir Humphrey replied: 'Well briefly, sir, I am the Permanent Under Secretary of State, known as the Permanent Secretary. Woolley here is your Principal Private Secretary; I too have a Principal Private Secretary and he is the Principal Private Secretary to the Permanent Secretary. Directly responsible to me are ten Deputy Secretaries, 87 Under Secretaries and 219 Assistant Secretaries. Directly responsible to the Principal Private Secretary are plain Private Secretaries, and the Prime Minister will be appointing two Parliamentary Under Secretaries and you will be appointing your own Parliamentary Private Secretary.'

The Minister asks, 'Do they all type?'

Sir Humphrey replied, 'None of us can type, Minister. Mrs MacKay types. She's the secretary.'

And the quote that unveiled my character's comic side:

Bernard: 'It used to be said there were two kinds of chairs to go with two kinds of Ministers: one sort that folds up instantly, and the other sort that goes round and round in circles.'

In a scene where political advisor Frank Weisel is discussing the new Cabinet appointments with Hacker and his wife, Annie, her cynical, sometimes mocking, view of her husband's 'business' was seen in three lines – eleven words:

Weisel: 'Did you know that Martin has got the Foreign Office? Jack has got Health, and Fred has got Energy.'

Annie: 'Has anyone got brains?'

Hacker: 'You mean Education?'

Annie: 'No, I know what I mean.'

Hacker: 'Well, what's left? I mean, what have I got?'

Annie: 'Rhythm?'

One episode that I enjoyed doing and even more enjoy recollecting was 'The Compassionate Society', in which Hacker finds out that there is a new hospital in London that is staffed with 500 administrators and staff, but has no doctors, nurses or patients. When the Minister shows his disbelief, suggesting that the hospital should shut down, Sir Humphrey argues: 'Why should we close a hospital because it has no patients? We don't disband the Army just because there isn't a war.'

Hacker tells him, 'The National Health Service, Humphrey, is an advanced case of galloping bureaucracy.'

Sir Humphrey replies, 'Ooooh, certainly not galloping. A gentle canter at the most.'

The hospital's chief administrator, Mrs Rogers, argues that the hospital is a superbly run organisation.

Rogers: 'Minister, it is one of the best run hospitals in the country. It is up for the Florence Nightingale Award.'

Hacker: 'And what, pray, is that?'

Rogers: 'It is won by the most hygienic hospital in the area.'

The Minister wants to sack half of the workforce and use the money to employ some doctors and nurses. When the union hears that 250 people will lose their jobs they threaten to strike. Eventually Hacker wins the bout by housing 1,000 Cuban refugees in the hospital building.

In 'Doing the Honours' the Minister, much to the horror of Sir Humphrey, suggests that honours will only be awarded to civil servants who have cut their budgets. Bribed by the possibility of receiving an Honorary Doctorate from an Oxford college, Hacker is seduced by Sir Humphrey's promise that expenditure cuts could be achieved providing the threat to awarding honours was withdrawn. The Minister accedes.

During this episode Hacker and Bernard travel to Oxford for a high table dinner at the college. As they drive Bernard explains to the Minister the honours available to senior civil servants.

Hacker: 'Well, what has Sir Arnold to fear, anyway? He's got all the honours he could want, surely?'

Bernard: 'Well, naturally he has his G.'

Hacker: 'G?'

Bernard: 'Yes; you get your G after your K.'

Hacker: 'You speak in riddles, Bernard.'

Bernard: 'Well, take the Foreign Office. First you get the CMG, then the KCMG, then the GCMG; the Commander of the Order of St Michael and St George, Knight Commander of St Michael and St George, Knight Grand Cross of St Michael and St George. Of course, in the Service, CMG stands for Call Me God, and KCMG for Kindly Call Me God.'

Hacker: 'What does GCMG stand for?'

Bernard: 'God Calls Me God.'

Qumran was a fictional Middle East sheikhdom that had made a deal with a UK company but received a bribe in doing so. In the episode 'The Moral Dimension' the Minister finds out about the skulduggery only after he arrives at a grand reception to finalise the contract. As the country is dry, liquor is to be made available on the sly in an adjacent communications room.

As Bernard, I had to keep visiting the room, where bottles of booze were laid out, and return to interrupt the Minister or Sir Humphrey (who was dressed up as a sheikh) telling them that an urgent message awaited them in communications. They would then pop out to top up their glass and return. Many messages came through that night with calls from a Mr Haig ('the one with the dimples'), a Mr Johnnie Walker ('from the Scotch Office – Scottish Office'), a Mr Smirnoff ('the Soviet Embassy is on the line'), and a call from the VAT man ('your 69 returns, Minister').

The Minister began to show that he had reached his limit on taking messages.

I think I'm heard laughing on the actual take for there are few actors who can do 'drunk' as good as Paul. From the first slur to the embarrassing stagger, Paul could play it wonderfully.

In the storyline Annie is given a valuable antique bowl by the Qumranis, but for her to be able to keep it Bernard arranges a valuation of less than £50. On their return home news gets out about the bowl, the press suggesting it must have been a bribe. The Minister announces that the bowl will be presented to his constituency's museum.

In 'The Bed of Nails' Jim Hacker is made Transport Supremo and soon has second thoughts. He tells Sir Humphrey and Bernard of his worries.

Hacker: 'Sir Mark thinks there might be votes in it, and I do not intend to look a gift horse in the mouth.'

Sir Humphrey: 'I put it to you, Minister, that you are looking a Trojan horse in the mouth.'

Hacker: 'You mean if we look closely at this gift horse, we'll find it's full of Trojans?'

I then come in with my pedantic corrections: 'Um, if you had looked the Trojan Horse in the mouth, Minister, you would have found Greeks inside. Well, the point is that it was the Greeks who gave the Trojan horse to the Trojans, so technically it wasn't a Trojan horse at all; it was a Greek horse. Hence the tag *"Timeo Danaos et dona ferentes,"* which, you will recall, is usually and somewhat inaccurately translated as "Beware of Greeks bearing gifts," or doubtless you would have recalled had you not attended the LSE.'

Hacker: 'Yes, well, I'm sure Greek tags are all very well in their way; but can we stick to the point?'

Bernard: 'Sorry, sorry: Greek tags?'

Hacker: '"Beware of Greeks bearing gifts." I suppose the EEC equivalent would be "Beware of Greeks bearing an olive oil surplus."'

Sir Humphrey: 'Excellent, Minister.'

Bernard: 'No, well, the point is, Minister, that just as the Trojan horse was in fact Greek, what you describe as a Greek tag is in fact Latin. It's obvious, really: the Greeks would never suggest bewaring of themselves, if one can use such a participle (bewaring that is). And it's clearly Latin, not because *timeo* ends in '-o', because the Greek first person also ends in '-o' – although actually there is a Greek word *timao*, meaning 'I honour'. But the '-os' ending is a nominative singular termination of a second declension in Greek, and an accusative plural in Latin, of course, though actually *Danaos* is not only the Greek for 'Greek'; it's also the Latin for 'Greek'. It's very interesting, really.'

I supposed the episode that bordered on farce was 'The Key' when the key to the door connecting the Cabinet Office to 10 Downing Street is taken away from Sir Humphrey. Jim Hacker does so in order to make a point, and Sir Humphrey doesn't like it. There were hilarious scenes of Sir Humphrey trying to find a way in, going around the front and through the back garden; and forever I will remember the moment when Nigel appears outside on the balcony, tapping on the window while we inside ignore him. Priceless humour. When he does get to Hacker he blurts: 'Prime Minister, I must protest in the strongest possible terms my profound opposition to the newly instituted practice which imposes severe and intolerable restrictions upon the ingress and egress of senior members of the hierarchy and will, in all probability, should the current deplorable innovation be perpetuated, precipitate a constriction of the channels of communication, and culminate in a condition of organisational atrophy and administrative paralysis, which will render effectively impossible the coherent and co-ordinated discharge of the function of government within Her Majesty's United Kingdom of Great Britain and Northern Ireland!'

Hacker: 'You mean you've lost your key?'

*

Yes Minister can be described as a slow burner. It was on BBC2 (first broadcast 25th February 1980) before it went to BBC1. But we heard that after only three or four episodes audience ratings had shot up. We also heard that the programme was genuinely popular with politicians of all persuasions and vast numbers of the Civil Service.

We were all sad when, at the end of the first series, Sydney Lotterby went on to do other things. Peter Whitmore who had produced, among others, *Terry and June* and *The Two Ronnies* was brought in. Although very good at his job, Peter didn't have that Sydney touch – whatever that is.

We did three series of *Yes Minister* and an hour-long special, 'Party Games', a brilliantly written episode in which we had to elevate Paul's character from Minister to Prime Minister and, in so doing, find skeletons in the cupboards of the other front runners, which we achieved. Jim Hacker duly became Prime Minister.

The storyline and writing in 'Party Games' surpassed anything that Jay and Lynn had done before. Sydney Lotterby returned to direct and stayed right through the *Yes, Prime Minister* series.

Sir Humphrey is told that he is to be Sir Arnold Robinson's successor as Cabinet Secretary. When he tells the Minister about his promotion, Hacker misunderstands, thinking that Humphrey is dying:

Sir Humphrey: 'Minister, I have some very grave news. The relationship which, I might tentatively venture to aver, has been not without some degree of reciprocal utility and perhaps even occasional gratification, is approaching a point of irreversible bifurcation and, to be brief, is in the propinquity of its ultimate regrettable termination.'

Hacker: '... I see.'

Sir Humphrey: 'I'm ... on my way out.'

Hacker: 'What?'

Sir Humphrey: 'There comes a time when one has to accept what fate has in store. When one passes on.'

Hacker: 'Passes on!'

Sir Humphrey: 'To pastures new, perhaps greener, and places oneself finally in the service of one who is greater than any of us.'

Hacker: 'Humphrey ... I'm so sorry.'

Sir Humphrey: 'Oh, thank you, Minister.'

Hacker: 'Does Lady Appleby know?'

Sir Humphrey: 'Well, she's suspected it for some time, apparently.'

Hacker: 'When did they tell you?'

Sir Humphrey: 'This afternoon.'

Hacker: 'How long did they give you?'

Sir Humphrey: 'Oh, just a few weeks ...'

Hacker: (getting upset) 'A few weeks!'

Sir Humphrey: 'Well, it'll give me enough time to sort everything out.'

Hacker: (filling up) 'Oh Humphrey, you're so terribly brave.'

Sir Humphrey: 'Well, one is a little anxious of course. One is always rather wary of the unknown, but I have faith somehow I'll muddle through.'

(Hacker starts crying.)

Sir Humphrey: 'Minister, what's the matter?'

Hacker: 'I'm sorry, Humphrey. Just, well, we've had our ups and downs, but ...'

Sir Humphrey: 'Oh Minister, don't take on so! We'll still be seeing one another regularly. Yes, once a week at least.'

Hacker: 'What?'

Sir Humphrey: 'I haven't told you where I'm going yet. I have been appointed Secretary to the Cabinet.'

Hacker: 'Secretary to the Cabinet?'

Sir Humphrey: 'What did you think I meant?'

Hacker: (pointing skyward) 'I thought, I … I …'

At Sir Humphrey's goodbye Christmas drinks party Hacker gets extremely drunk but manages to remind everyone of the Home Secretary's campaign, 'Don't drink and drive at Christmas'. The police stop Hacker on the way home but he gets away with it because of his silver badge. Annie Hacker drives home.

The Home Secretary is picked up for drunken driving after causing an accident with a lorry loaded with nuclear waste, forcing his resignation. Hacker asks Sir Humphrey what will happen to the former Home Secretary.

Sir Humphrey replies: 'Well, I gather he was as drunk as a lord. So, after a discreet interval, they'll probably make him one.'

Then suddenly the Prime Minister announces he is going to retire in the new year to give his successor a good run-up to the next election. The two front runners have dodgy 'baggage' so Hacker's name is put forward.

Over drinks Sir Humphrey broaches the subject: 'Bernard, what would you say to your present master as the next Prime Minister?'

Bernard: 'The Minister?'

Sir Humphrey: 'Yes.'

Bernard: 'Mr Hacker?'

Sir Humphrey: 'Yes.'

Bernard: 'As Prime Minister?'

Sir Humphrey: 'Yes.'

(Bernard looks at his watch.)

Sir Humphrey: 'Are you in a hurry?'

Bernard: 'No; I'm just checking to see it wasn't April the First.'

Jim Hacker seizes his opportunity when the EEC proposes to ban the British sausage, by renaming it the 'Emulsified High-Fat Offal

Tube'. In a televised broadcast Hacker refuses to accept the EEC regulation. He champions the British sausage which turns out to be a vote winner with his party.

At that point *Yes Minister* became *Yes, Prime Minister*.

One day Paul Eddington took me aside and said, 'Derek, this is our pension. They'll be showing this programme forever.'

'Is it that good?' I asked.

'Well,' said Paul thoughtfully, 'we are!'

The series featured a number of extraordinary and formidable actresses. Judy Parfitt played Betty Oldham in 'A Question of Loyalty' in 1981; Deborah Norton appeared in six episodes as Dorothy Wainwright, the PM's advisor, referred to by Sir Humphrey as 'that impossible woman' although when they met he would smile and address her as 'dear lady'; and Eleanor Bron, Brenda Blethyn and Gwen Taylor all had memorable parts.

All the regular cast and crew felt fortunate to have leading actors in guest roles. Frank Middlemass, whose stage career included Polonius in *Hamlet* for the Royal Shakespeare Company and the Fool in *King Lear* at the Old Vic, appeared in two episodes. I had worked with him in the play *Spitting Image** in 1968. Nigel Stock had taught me at RADA and it was quite astonishing to have him as a friend when he played Sir Mark Spencer in the episode 'A Question of Loyalty'. We had many enjoyable social gatherings that included his (then new) wife, actress Richenda Carey. Also featured were Edward Jewesbury and Robert Urquhart whom I had worked with in my first 'live' television drama in 1960, *The Assassins*.

The catchphrase of 'CJ', Leonard Rossiter's boss played by John Barron in *The Fall and Rise of Reginald Perrin*, was: 'I didn't get where I am today by ...' John played Sir Ian Whitworth, the DHSS Secretary in 'The Smoke Screen'.

John Fortune, fully recovered from his heart attack, played Major Saunders in 'The Whisky Priest'.

---

* See page 82

Among the many terrific guest artists who appeared over the years several well-known broadcasters played themselves, including Robert McKenzie, Ludovic Kennedy and Sue Lawley. Robert Dougall regularly played a newsreader, which was his own real-life profession.

In 1980/81 when Lord Tonypandy was the Speaker of the House of Commons, Paul, Nigel and I were invited a couple of times to sit in the gallery of the House to watch proceedings. We always had tea in Lord Tonypandy's quarters where he would relive his favourite moments from our programme, repeating some of the lines word for word. He was an unashamed fan. Another time, at dinner with other guests, Lord Tonypandy announced that over coffee we were all going to watch a taped episode of *Yes Minister*. Our faces must have dropped – we, the cast, were far from happy – but our misery didn't last long. The episode had barely started when a bell rang loudly and everyone except Paul, Nigel and myself shot to their feet and started rushing in all directions. It was pandemonium.

'It's a crisis,' said Lord Tonypandy as he hurried out leaving the three of us watching ourselves on the telly.

I can remember Paul saying that none of us was very good in this episode. A little later someone burst in to say the crisis was because an attempt had been made on President Reagan's life. We never knew, and never asked, why an attempted assassination on Ronald Reagan, over three and a half thousand miles away in Washington, DC should cause such an immediate and animated response in London with people running from one room to another. What were all these panicked politicians and civil servants supposed to do?

Paul, Nigel and I were invited to Number 10 on three occasions and on the third, when we met Margaret Thatcher and John Major, Jo came along.

*

Some years after *Yes, Prime Minister* had finished Paul Eddington and I found ourselves in Australia together. We were both on stage in two different productions. We used to meet up and often appear on local television. *Yes Minister* was very popular Down Under.

I always used to walk slightly behind Paul, he being the superior under all circumstances. I once asked a hotel manager if I could borrow a car as I was going to pick up Paul Eddington. 'We're going to do a TV interview,' I said.

'You can have the Rolls Royce,' he said.

'What?'

Minutes later the chauffeur of the hotel picked me up and I said, 'When I ring Paul's bell he will come down and I want you to say, good morning, Prime Minister. He won't budge. He'll just say, good morning and get into the back of the car. I bet you.'

And that's exactly what happened. Off we went to the interview.

On one occasion I was chatting to an Australian politician who told me he was a great fan of our programme.

'The difference,' he said, 'is that in the UK *Yes Minister* is viewed as a comedy show. In Australia we see it as a documentary.'

Overseas productions of *Yes Minister* and *Yes, Prime Minister* included the Dutch version in which Sir Humphrey is a woman and Bernard is Mohammed, a Moroccan. There was an Indian version produced in Delhi in collaboration with BBC Worldwide. It closely follows the original but adapts to Indian circumstances. The producer, Smeeta Chakrabarti, says: 'The things that the British serial looks at – why the system never changes and nothing ever happens – all that is the same here, in fact it's exaggerated.' Russia in the UK version was changed to Pakistan, football to cricket.

The series has been repeated everywhere: Scandinavia, the Czech Republic, (what was then) West Germany, Australia and most English-speaking countries. In the United States it was a success on Public Broadcast television. The *New York Times* deemed it to be 'the funniest, wittiest and truest piece of political satire to be published on either side of the Atlantic in the post-Evelyn Waugh era'.

The Complete Yes Minister BBC book was published in Chinese in 2012. Copies have been discovered in Beijing bookshops.

In 2006 the programme got a boost from British MPs voting *Yes Minister* the greatest political comedy of all time.

When Paul and Nigel both got the CBE I was phoned up by the *News of the World* saying they wanted my reaction to the news. 'What news?' I asked. They told me that my co-stars in *Yes Minister* had been awarded the CBE.

'What for? I asked.

A few days later a headline in the *News of the World* read: 'Bernard says what for?'

I really was thrilled for them both. Then they were honoured with Honorary Doctorates at Sheffield University.

'Sorry Derek,' they said, 'we've been offered Honorary Doctorates.'

'Brilliant,' I said. 'Have I got anything?'

'No, sorry.'

The programme was Margaret Thatcher's favourite. We always believed that she thought the characters in *Yes Minister* were her government. I think she went off the show when it became *Yes, Prime Minister*, with Jim Hacker taking her job.

In 1984 Paul and Nigel performed a sketch with Margaret Thatcher at an award ceremony for the writers of *Yes Minister*, in an event for Mary Whitehouse's National Viewers' and Listeners' Association. Paul and Nigel were far from happy, resenting Thatcher's attempt to 'make capital' from the programme's popularity, appealing to Jonathan Lynn to get them out of it. Jonathan couldn't help. Lynn called it a 'dreadful sketch'. Four people laid claim to writing it: Bernard Ingham, Margaret Thatcher, Michael Cockerell and Charles Powell. In his speech after the sketch was performed Jonathan thanked the Prime Minister 'for taking her rightful place in the field of situation comedy'. No one knew how Margaret Thatcher took that.

Paul and Nigel followed up *Yes Minister* by doing posh projects like *Uncle Vanya* for the National, *Who's Afraid of Virginia Woolf*, *The Magistrate* and, of course, *The Madness of George III*. Nigel was in the film version and was nominated for an Oscar that he should have won.

There were always thoughts about a follow-up series for *Minister*, taking Hacker into Europe – perhaps a film. But by this time Paul was most unwell and unable to take on new projects.

I remember the moment Paul told me of his illness. 'I've got this skin problem,' he said. 'I've seen a specialist. It's melanoma.'

Early on in my *Heartbeat* career, one Sunday evening, I got a phone call from Paul saying, 'I've just watched *Heartbeat*.'

'Are you slumming?' I asked.

'No,' said Paul. 'I enjoyed it. You were very good in it.'

'Paul, thank you so much. Coming from you that's very special.'

And after a pause he said, 'Don't stay too long.'

Alas, *Heartbeat* kept making me offers I couldn't refuse.

Towards the end of his life Paul gave a moving interview in the BBC *Face to Face* programme with Jeremy Isaacs. Typically, Paul made light of his illness. He was asked how he would like to be remembered. His reply brought tears to my eyes, and still does:

'He did very little harm.'

A week or so before Paul died I visited the hospital where he was being treated. Trish, his dear wife, welcomed me and said, 'We're trying to get him home.'

At Paul's bedside I waited for him to open his eyes.

'Hello,' he said.

'We're trying to get you home,' I said.

'I fucking hope so.'

They were the last words Paul said to me.

Paul's autobiography, *So Far, So Good*, came out a couple of weeks before he died.

*

In 1997 I was asked to audio record *How to Beat Sir Humphrey* written by Antony Jay. It was subtitled 'Every Citizen's Guide to

Fighting Officialdom'. It was rewarding but far from easy persuading my tongue to accurately provide insight into the workings of the official mind and the behaviour of bureaucracies.

In 2001 Nigel, who at the time was recovering from cancer, had a heart attack in his bath and died. It was a tremendous shock to all of us, just six years after losing Paul.

So we never did any more. However, in the published *Hacker Diaries*, Bernard Woolley finally reaches his destination and becomes Sir Bernard. 'Sir Bernard Woolley, Head of the Civil Service'. It would have been nice to play that.

We won, I think, four BAFTAs for Best Comedy Programme; and Nigel won four BAFTAs for Best Comedy Performance. I'm certain that Nigel was embarrassed that Paul never got an individual award.

Nigel got his knighthood and I'm sure Paul, had he lived, would have got one. Antony Jay was also knighted. I'm still awaiting my OBE. Still awaiting anything!

I think of the boys often and wish they were here, like so many of us. They both died too young. They were two wonderful people as well as being great actors. Rest in peace, boys.

In October 2014 Theresa May, the Home Secretary, was Kirsty Young's guest on *Desert Island Discs*. Along with music by Elgar and Abba she chose an excerpt from *Yes Minister* in which Hacker discovers the hospital empty of patients. As Bernard I tell the Minister that the press is unaware of the situation.

Hacker replies: 'Fortunately, Bernard, most of our journalists are so incompetent they'd have the gravest difficulty in finding out that today is Wednesday.'

Bernard: 'It's actually Thursday, Minister.'

For a while I felt comforted that the most powerful female politician in the country wanted to take me to a desert island!

Chapter 13

IN THE YEARS THAT SPANNED *Yes Minister* and *Yes, Prime Minister*
there were periods of weeks or months that I filled doing other jobs.

In 1982 I got a call from my agent to go to the BBC to meet the
director Gavin Millar. I was rather excited as the play, called
Intensive Care, was written by Alan Bennett. I had read Alan's books
and his plays and had always thought him a genius. The play was
somewhat autobiographical – one of the characters was Alan himself
and auditions were being held for someone to play Alan Bennett!

When I met Gavin he said, 'Alan has made a shortlist and you're
on it. But, as of this moment, Alan is on a train from Leeds; he is
coming down to audition to play himself!'

'Well,' I said, rather bemused. 'Alan is a great actor as well as
being a great writer. Still, it was nice to make the shortlist.'

Two days later I received a letter from Gavin saying that Alan
had got the part but they wanted to offer me the part of his cousin,
Hartley.

I grabbed it and we were in Leeds for a few weeks. I worked with
a wonderful cast: Alan of course, Julie Walters and Thora Hird. It
was a joy to do.

I did remind Alan that I was on the shortlist to play him.

'But I got the part,' he replied.

*

In 1983 I went down to the Thorndike Theatre in Leatherhead to do a play written by a friend of mine, Robin Hawdon, called *Birthday Suite*. It was there that I met the director Stephen Barry for the first time. Stephen and I became very close friends over the years. Sadly he was to die far too young in 1997.

When we were doing *Birthday Suite* he asked if I would join a small company of actors he was taking to Santa Fe in New Mexico. The actors would be performing two plays: *Betrayal* by Harold Pinter, and Willy Russell's *Educating Rita*. They were also going to teach at the University in Santa Fe, running a summer school for American students, and this was a huge attraction to me. The classes would encompass the whole curriculum of an English drama school, ranging from Shakespeare, modern drama and voice technique to singing and speech.

I was always attracted to working on auditions and working on speeches and monologues from different plays, so I decided to teach 'audition technique', which was a class I attended at RADA run by Denys Blakelock. (After all, I had won the Denys Blakelock Audition Technique Prize.)

The part I was going to play on the stage in the evenings was Frank in *Educating Rita*. I love that play and always wanted to play Frank; and I was blessed with my Rita, a very talented girl called Melanie Hill.

She and I worked so well together and she was brilliant as Rita. A real joy to work with.

We rehearsed and performed *Rita* for a month in Leatherhead, and then we flew off to New Mexico – first to Albuquerque and then to Santa Fe.

I remember the students gathering in front of us for the first time. We sat on the stage and told them about the plays we were doing.

A day or two later I gave a speech on the History of British Theatre. Anyone who knew me would have known that such a learned piece couldn't have been penned by me. A friend – actor and academic Ian Lindsay – kindly wrote it for me before I left England. As I read, my guilt grew; so, after enthusiastic applause at the end, I owned up but told the audience that I would pass on their acclamation to Ian on my return. For some reason this got me another round of applause.

We performed in the evenings – *Betrayal* one evening, *Educating Rita* the next – and during the day the students would come to different classes. It was a wonderful experience to sit there on my own, thinking, this is my class.

In my audition technique class I stressed the importance of what I called 'the three "d"s'.

'If you want to make it in theatre as an actor,' I used to say, 'the first "d" is desire. Like any job or profession you have to have that initial desire. You've got to want to do it, want to embrace it. If you desire it, you give it one hundred per cent. Then, the next big "d" is dedication. Body, soul and mind dedicated to your work.'

I gave the students the opportunity to guess the final 'd' but none did.

'Discipline!' I exclaimed. Sometimes a concept difficult to explain to young students but one made clear to us at drama school; you must never be late, you work on your lines until they're perfect, you study your character, you respect (and learn from) older actors.

Most younger actors have the desire and a bit of dedication but fall short on discipline. The great actors have all three 'd's.

I covered many aspects of performance, actively giving examples when I could: using space, getting in touch with themselves, building a monologue, duologues, and so on.

I so enjoyed being in New Mexico, especially in Santa Fe. The university was strikingly modern, beautifully designed with departments for most of the arts. We were all billeted out in various homes, the owners of which had decamped for the summer season.

In the evenings it was a treat to be appearing in that great play by Willy Russell, *Educating Rita*, with Melanie Hill who I felt was destined for really big things. Although it was thirty years ago I can see my Rita, Melanie, making her first appearance. She was quite brilliant. As you probably know, it's a two-handed play; and I would not have wanted to do it with anyone else. I still see Melanie in various dramas on the television and always look back at the friendship and comradeship that she and I had.

I really enjoyed teaching the American students. There was one girl in particular I kept noticing. She sat there, very quiet, not saying very much but totally absorbed. After a couple of weeks she came up to me and asked if I would work with her on a song. I said yes, and when I'm not playing in *Rita* in the evening, I'll stay behind. This remarkable young girl, Anna Gunn, sang 'Memory' from the show *Cats*. I thought she was so gifted – an extraordinary talent.

Anna and I became very close friends, and one day one of her fellow students came up to me and said, 'Derek, you know Anna is only 16?'

'What!' I shouted. 'She is so talented. So mature.'

Near the end of our stay the students and I put on *A Chorus Line*. It didn't have to be a musical but the class jumped at the chance. Although we had spent only a short time together the performance, culminating in the song 'One (Singular Sensation)', made the hairs on the back of my neck stand up. The reception that greeted the solo bows at the end, leading to a seemingly never-ending ensemble curtain call, completed a truly creative encounter for us all. A wonderful payoff for the work we had done together.

It was hard to say goodbye to all the students, and especially to Anna.

There was talk about returning to Santa Fe the next year to do another summer school. I was keen and so was Melanie. Back in England we were casually discussing what plays we might take back to New Mexico when I heard from the organisers, a Santa Fe University board, that I wouldn't be welcome. Anna Gunn's father, a member of the board, had decided I was *persona non grata*.

It may have been a father's wish to protect his daughter; but, apart from a (wine-induced) party kiss, nothing had happened between us. We were close, but that often occurs when working beside someone in drama when emotions can be exposed. It can 'feel' intimate without intimacy taking place.

Some time later Jo was innocently going through my desk to arrange a surprise birthday party for me and found all my letters from Anna. Anna had written to me as only a 16-year-old would. They were lovely letters and I kept them. Jo scrawled across them 'explain this'.

'Look, Jo,' I said. 'Nothing happened between Anna and me.'

I told Jo how talented she was and that we became good friends but I don't think Jo ever believed me.

In 2012 my son Jeremy gave me a box set of the American television drama series *Breaking Bad*. It stars Bryan Cranston as Walter White, a chemistry teacher who lives in Albuquerque with his wife, Skyler, and son, Walt Jr, who has cerebral palsy. Plots around terminal cancer, the illegal drug trade and the family's efforts to plan for the future are enhanced by wonderful scripts and outstanding performances. I was really stunned when watching it to see the actress playing Skyler, Walt's wife. It was that same girl who sat in my class in Santa Fe – Anna!

I just had to write to her, thirty years down the track, saying how thrilled I was to see her work. I reflected that, once upon a time, she sat in my class; and I wished her continuing success. I never got a reply. I didn't write the letter to get a reply; I wrote the letter to remind her that I knew she had a special talent when I first met her in 1984.

While I was in Santa Fe I got a phone call from Lionel Blair who asked me if I would do pantomime with him in Birmingham. He was directing and playing Buttons in *Cinderella* at the Alexandra Theatre, and wanted me to be one of the Ugly Sisters.

'Panto? Me?'

'Of course, you.'

We agreed to talk as soon as I returned to London.

*

When I followed up Lionel Blair's telephone call I had to point out that pantomime, to me, is a craft and a skill all of its own. 'I tried it once,' I told him, 'and I don't really enjoy the genre.'

'I promise I will teach you,' said Lionel.

'Will you have the time,' I asked, 'to teach me how to do drag as the Ugly Sister?'

'Of course.'

Eventually I said that I would do it providing he had time to coach me.

'Don't worry, Derek,' he said, 'I will.'

On the set of *Yes Minister*, I told Paul and Nigel that I was going to do pantomime.

They both said, 'Are you serious?'

I said, 'Yes. Lionel said he would teach me.'

'When do you start rehearsals?' they asked.

'The 10th of December.'

They both looked decidedly doubtful.

In early December I decided to pop in to a rehearsal for the pantomime dancers. To my shock, they were all there: the dancers, the whole cast, everyone.

Lionel was there, surprised to see me.

'Hello Derek,' he said. 'Come in, come in.'

He introduced me to everyone and asked if I wanted to have a rehearsal.

The other Ugly Sister, Fred Evans, knew exactly what he was going to do; I don't think he had a script.

'Lionel,' I said, 'I'm not supposed to start rehearsals until next Monday.'

'We haven't got time,' he said. 'We're rushed.'

I pressed him. 'You promised to coach me, to teach me how to do it.'

'Haven't got time,' he said. 'Haven't got time.'

'What do you want me to do?' I asked.

Fred and I were playing Alexis and Krystle from *Dynasty* – this was six days before I was due to start rehearsals. They played the music from *Dynasty* and Fred walked in and did the whole act.

I walked in with my pencil and my script asking, what do I do? There was a stony silence. I think they expected me to have an act. You walk down here, someone suggested, you do a twirl. So I wrote it down in my script. I thought, this is ridiculous.

The next morning I told Paul and Nigel what had happened and they both said, 'Get out while you can.'

I said, 'Oh no, I've got to work on this.'

So I went to the wardrobe at the BBC and got a blonde wig and high-heeled shoes, put them on and stood on the set of *Yes Minister*.

I said to Paul and Nigel that I should've played Bernard in drag. The boys looked at me and said, 'Derek, *get out.*'

Lionel phoned me and asked if I could go in.

I reminded him that I was to start on the Monday.

'You've broken the ice,' said Lionel, 'now come in.'

I went in and he told me they were going to do a run-through on that Saturday afternoon.

'Lionel,' I said. 'I don't know the script.'

'Well,' he said, 'we're going to run through the first act. Can you learn it?'

'Can I take you back,' I said, 'to the conversation that you and I had when you promised to teach me?'

'Derek,' he said, 'I haven't got time and I have to say I'm slightly worried about you. Can you really see yourself doing this?'

I said, 'I don't know what to say. Because I wouldn't have done it had you not promised.'

He admitted it required special skills and promised to show me. So we had another rehearsal. I looked at my script, saw some moves I had to do and where we did the song. Not much else.

I knew Lionel was a bit pissed off with me because he knew it should be wonderfully funny, and I had no idea what to do with it.

So I went back and put the blonde wig on. I learned the lines and suddenly I felt I knew how to do it. I thought, I'm going to play a beautiful Ugly Sister who is kicked around the stage by the ugly one.

I knew that Ronnie Corbett had played a nice Ugly, a sort of dumb blonde.

On the Monday morning, on a run-through of the first act, I knew my lines; so when it came to our entrance, the music started and Fred played the typical Ugly Sister and I played it fey.

Dame Anna Neagle, who was the Fairy Godmother, wet her breeches saying, 'Derek, it's so funny.' Veteran film actor Anthony Steel, who was playing Baron Hardup, agreed.

While everyone was saying that's wonderful, Lionel was looking daggers. He took me into the kitchen after the run-through.

'Lionel,' I said, 'before you say anything this should have been my first day of rehearsal. I was due to rehearse on this day. You were going to coach me. I've just done a run-through of the first act.'

He said, 'But you can't play it like that.'

'What do you mean?'

'You're a nasty, horrible, Ugly Sister.'

'You don't have to be nasty. He can kick me around. Ronnie Corbett did a wonderful Ugly Sister.'

He said, 'But you can't do that in this production.'

'I'm sorry, Lionel. That's the way I want to play it.'

'You can't. I can't sack you but I'm asking you to resign.'

I really couldn't believe it. I said, 'Why don't you and I swap parts? You play me and I'll play Buttons.'

I don't think that went down very well.

So in the end I said that I would go.

I left, on the day that would have been my first day of rehearsal, realising it wasn't for me. I tried my best and I certainly made Anna Neagle and Anthony Steel laugh. But it wasn't right for Lionel.

What was sad was that in Birmingham, where I had already been billed on the posters for the show, there was some publicity saying that I'd given up because I didn't like being hated by the children. It was total rubbish. I just wanted to play it a different way. I left because Lionel asked me to. Artistic differences!

So I went back to Jo and told her I wasn't doing it and she said, 'Thank God for that.'

When I told Nigel and Paul what had happened they were thrilled.

'We told you,' they said. 'You should never have got involved.'

*

At that time Jo and I were very happy in our house in Strathearn Road, Wimbledon; or so I thought. I began to feel that she was unsettled. Out of the blue she said that she would really like to move.

I was stunned. 'Where to?' I asked.

'I'd like to move to Bath.'

'Why Bath?'

I cannot recall her reply, but we agreed to visit Bath and have a look around and have tea with our friends, Sheila and Robin Hawdon.

Funnily enough, while we were with them they asked if we were thinking of moving.

'I don't think we can,' I said.

'Oh, yes, we can,' said Jo. 'We'll put our house on the market and move down here.'

I said that we didn't know anybody down there apart from Sheila and Robin. Then Robin told us of a house in the middle of Bath owned by two friends of theirs who were going around the world for a year and wanted someone to rent it.

'Let's go and see it now,' Jo suggested.

So we went. It was an idyllic, wonderful cottage in Widcombe, close to the middle of Bath. It had flowers around the door and an inglenook fireplace, open-plan ground floor and a beautiful sunken garden. We just flipped. Jo said that she didn't want to see anything else, that she wanted to move in straight away.

We successfully negotiated with the owners, Crispin and Denise Raymond.

On the way back to Wimbledon Jo said that Bath was where she belonged.

'I feel I want to move away from London and live in that cottage for a year.'

So that's what we did. By the time we found a buyer for the house in Wimbledon, Jo had already moved to Bath. I joined her as soon as I could.

Yew Tree Cottage, Widcombe. Another change. Certainly a change in both our lives.

I think Jo was much happier with the move to Bath than I was. Little did I know that I would grow to know and love the city, and many years later still choose to live there.

After we moved to Bath, the longest period of me being out of work began. I became very frustrated. I remember Jo and me going to parties in Bath when Sheila and Robin were trying to introduce us to more people. We didn't know anybody in the city, and at one party somebody came up to me and said, 'What are you doing here? You know what they call this place?'

I said, 'I don't, but it's a very beautiful city.'

'They call it ambition's graveyard,' he said.

'Why?' I asked.

'This is a place where you don't want to do anything else – you don't want to move, you want to stay here and enjoy it.'

*

In a period of inertia I got a call from my friend, Derek Nimmo. Would I tour with the play *There Goes the Bride* by Ray Cooney and John Chapman? I was sent the script, which I liked; we were going to Dubai, Abu Dhabi, Bangkok and other venues.

In the play the main character invents a beautiful young lover for himself just as he is about to marry off his only daughter. Many implications arise from this. There was no way of knowing how a clever British sex farce would go down in these exotic locations.

I said to Jo, 'I'm off on this long tour; I'm very sorry but I've got to earn some money.'

'That's okay,' she said, 'don't worry.'

Derek Nimmo had assembled a wonderful cast of superb actors: the great Michael Denison and Dulcie Gray, lovely Jennie Linden, Jennifer Lonsdale, Tony Anholt, Ewen Solon, and a young girl called Christina Barryk. Jan Butlin directed the play with Derek Nimmo overseeing the whole operation.

Before we left Derek arranged, without consultation, a public performance. The cast weren't happy, for none of us felt well rehearsed. It went ahead, we got a few laughs, then we waited for our departure date.

We had the most wonderful tour of the Middle and Far East. After a great Christmas together with my mum and Jo's mum, Babs and the kids, I flew off to our first stop, Dubai, where we were put up in a luxury hotel with all expenses paid. The play took place in the ballroom of the hotel after guests had eaten in the restaurant. At five minutes to nine in the evening we were called from our rooms and assembled in the kitchen to be led 'backstage'.

After the first night Derek came up to me saying, you could be a lot funnier.

I said to Derek, my comedy is not like your comedy. I like to play for the truth. I don't like to do funny walks and funny voices in order to make people laugh.

I spoke to Michael and Dulcie about it and they both said, 'Oh, darling. Don't change a thing.' They were very supportive.

I did say to Derek (I love Derek and had known him for a long time), if you want me to be funnier you do it and I'll go home. In the end he did come around to me and said that it was getting funnier.

I always had the support of the cast. They were lovely friends.

We went to Abu Dhabi, Bangkok, Bahrain, Singapore, Kuala Lumpur, Jakarta and Muscat, one of my favourite venues. We even got to Papua New Guinea – the National Theatre of Papua New Guinea in Port Moresby.

It was in Port Moresby that I got chatting to an Australian pilot who delivered the mail to distant outposts.

Without any twisting of arms the pilot agreed to take Jennifer Lonsdale and myself on his next flight. We landed on a pebble landing strip in between rough mountains and endless jungle. The first thing I saw was a mass of people emerging from nowhere. As they got closer I could see that all were smiling with mouths of bright red. I asked what the red was.

'Betel nut,' said the pilot. 'It's an areca nut wrapped in betel leaf with lime. It's a stimulant, but it rots your throat.'

When we were in Bangkok we went to Patpong Street, the red-light area. Jennie Linden, Tony Anholt and I took Dulcie and Michael along. Following Tony's lead we found ourselves in a nightclub witnessing a sex show. We got drinks and sat near the stage area where fully naked women were shooting ping-pong balls at each other from parts of their bodies that were never designed for that task.

At one point a ball went astray and flew past Dulcie. Such was the alarm on her face that Jennie, Tony and I went to comfort her. We were stopped by Michael (forever the English gentleman in manner and voice) who leaned over to his wife and, with perfect timing and tone, asked: 'Dulcie, darling, would you like another gin and tonic?'

For some reason the three of us found this hysterical.

As we left I asked Dulcie if she enjoyed the show.

'Not really,' she replied, 'but it was interesting. It was very, very interesting.'

I suspect that today such a tour couldn't take place; political and religious obstacles, even wars, standing firmly in the way. Sad.

We ended up in Singapore.

In the same year – 1985 – my sister, my darling Babs, was getting married and I had to give her away.

I was worried because the wedding was arranged for 5th May. Babs knew I was away on tour and was worried that I would not make it back. I was worried too.

When we were about to leave Singapore, there was a strike at the airport and we had to depart in pairs – we could not go back together. Most went before me but I did get home in time.

*

My sister's wedding: what a day. Off we all went to our old Congregational Church in Berkhamsted.

Jo and I were there, and the boys, Jeremy and Jamie, were ushers.

Dear Babs married Alfred Young. Babs had nursed Alfred's wife while she was ill with cancer. They kept in touch, got close and later fell in love.

'Forever Young,' I said, 'keep her forever Young.'

Babs looked absolutely fantastic: she was so beautiful in her wedding dress. It was a proud moment for me to walk her down the aisle at our old church. My friend David Kernan sang at the service.

We had a reception afterwards at the old scout hut opposite the Congregational Church. It was a beautiful day shared with our family and friends.

At the beginning of 1986 Jo got a job teaching. She was an inspiring teacher. Her first job was at a place called Twerton. I remember the name 'Twerton' as one which you can use to wrap your tongue around to get a Somerset accent. I used to love that.

Jo wasn't truly happy in that first job, and soon after she got another one in Corsham. She really settled there in a position she enjoyed.

It was then I was offered the chance to take over the lead in Ray Cooney's play *Run for Your Wife*. It was a well-written play. Ray Cooney was a brilliant farceur and had written many successful plays.

Ray was directing and tried to impose a great deal of business on me which I found pretty uncomfortable. I had to find my own way into the play which turned out to be a very difficult process. Most of the cast had done it before: they were already up to performance level. My request for three weeks' rehearsal was turned down – we had two weeks to get it right. At that point I was beginning to panic. I needed time and space, I had to get 'closer' to the part. I think I asked for a complete change of cast so that we were all beginners. Ray would have none of this.

When I arrived for the first morning's rehearsal we had a read-through until Ray offered a lunch break. As we gathered together for the afternoon, to my astonishment Ray announced that we would now be 'blocking' (the precise movement and staging of actors).

I thought that we might have sat around and talked about the play: how we were going to approach the play, what the situations were, form some character relationships. Not 'blocking', not yet, not yet for me.

'You're outside,' Ray said to me. 'We want to hear you come in so you do a sort of, oooh, oooh.'

'Why?' I asked.

'You've had an accident and been in hospital overnight. You'll have a bandage around your head.'

As Ray gave his directives I found myself asking, 'Why?' many times.

Ray's answer was always the same: 'It'll get a laugh.'

I did find a way of playing the character but for me it was often fraught, particularly when Ray insisted on telling me how my part should be played and about the success of others who had performed my role. We did fall out over a few things and I recall telling him he was directing the play as 'music hall' rather than 'farce'.

There was a moment (nothing to do with Ray's directing) when a cast member accidentally spilled tea over a member of the audience. He handed over a handkerchief, watched as the liquid was cleaned up, then carried on as if nothing had happened. The audience loved it – laughter, screams of delight, and applause. I was appalled. Farce, for me, had to be played in the 'real', it has to be true.

I got used to being appalled as, throughout the run, acting or performing 'over the top' became a regular occurrence.

I didn't really enjoy it. There were some lovely people in the cast but I was quite grateful when it came to an end. It was a long six months. I think I tried to get out of it after three months but Paul Elliot, our lovely producer, said, 'No, no, Derek. Please stay.'

Years later when Ray was making a film version I did a cameo and thoroughly enjoyed it.

*

Our landlords, the Raymonds, were coming back to take over their house at the end of the year. We knew that we would have to move, and soon.

Doing the play in London enabled me to get money together to put a deposit on a flat in Prince of Wales Drive, Battersea. It cost me £64,000. I laid out ten grand and took out a mortgage.

Jo said, 'What am I going to do?'

We found a cottage in Pera Place in Bath that Jo liked so I said, with my flat in London and you in Bath, we'll have two homes. We can commute from London to Bath.

Jo thought that was a good idea and so, with her money from the sale of the Wimbledon house, Jo bought Pera Place.

So, another change in our lives – our commuter period. Up and down from London to Bath. I enjoyed the travel, but Jo didn't enjoy coming to London. I appreciated that and the way she felt. I loved her dearly. It was a great love match between Jo and me. She was my best friend as well as my soulmate. We laughed every day, tackled things head on and made decisions together; and she was a joy to be with – a total joy.

I was offered a part in the tour of *Compo Plays Cupid*, the stage version of the long-running BBC sitcom *Last of the Summer Wine*. Peter Sallis, who played Cleggy on TV, didn't want to do the play. Bill Owen, who I'd met before and always admired, rang me up. He asked if I would come into the play and do the tour playing Peter Sallis' role and I said I would.

I was a great fan of the television series and knew most of the characters in it. We had a wonderful time. It wasn't the greatest play in the world, but they were a lovely company and we did have enormous fun doing it. Bill Owen was a bundle of energy; he was in his late seventies, yet when he came on the stage he bounced around like a 20-year-old. He was so dapper off the set, immaculately dressed; very left-wing, very Labour. He loved the working-men's clubs.

I laughed a lot in that production. We didn't get big audiences, though. I remember one matinee in Sheffield, Bill was looking through the curtain.

'Anybody there?' I asked.

He said, 'Two nuns and a monkey.'

So, from then on, every matinee I've done I've called it 'the two nuns and a monkey show'.

I was reminded of Oscar Wilde's quote when we had bad reviews but enjoyed doing the play. 'The play was a great success,' said Oscar, 'but the audience were a disaster.'

I used to go around with Bill a lot and share digs, and got to know him very well. Between us we could recall some of the best quotes that came out of our profession.

One was from dear Katherine Hepburn who was reported to have said, 'Acting is the most minor of gifts and not a very high-class way to earn a living. After all, Shirley Temple could do it at the age of four.'

I enjoyed Bill's company and his energy on stage. It was a treat to act with him. A great guy, Bill. Rest in peace. God bless you.

Robert Fyfe was also in the cast; I'm still in touch with Robert. Also, the wonderful Jean Fergusson and Lizzie Elvin. It was a lovely tour.

After I went back to Bath I was out of work for a few months. Jo and I were happy. It was that Christmas that Jo decided she would never go back to London.

So there we were. We had two homes – two small homes. My flat in Prince of Wales Drive had only one bedroom, but it was very cosy and in a lovely position near Chelsea Bridge, just opposite Battersea

Park. Being a Chelsea football supporter I used to walk across to Stamford Bridge to watch Chelsea play.

Jo was very happy, but after a while we were beginning to think that having two properties that were too small to entertain the whole family was not ideal. So at some point we were going to have to think about getting a bigger place. And we didn't know which property to sell.

It didn't come to that. At the end of 1986 a job came up, beginning early in '87. They wanted me to go to Australia in the play *Rattle of a Simple Man*. It was a two-hander. I was to play Percy, a 39-year-old virgin who has come up to see his football team play in the Cup. His mate sets him up with a lady of the night. She takes him back to her apartment and that's when the play begins.

The girl I did the play with was called Abigail: just one word – Abigail. She had done quite a few television shows in Australia; they sent me over a tape of some of her work and I thought she was terrific.

It was a really good play. I so enjoyed being in it, and I loved being in Australia for the first time. It was a country I came to love deeply: the climate, the light, the space and the friendliness of the people.

It was 'dinner theatre' which means the audience would come into the hotel, sit down and have a three-course dinner and at 9:30 the curtain would go up and we did the play. We also stayed in the hotel where we were working.

I had a wonderful time. It really was a journey of discovery for both Abigail and me. She hadn't acted much on the stage and we just bonded through the ups and downs of rehearsing. However, she did have a very strange husband and I was slightly suspicious of him – although her own behaviour could be odd at times too. I often wondered whether she was on anything, whether she was taking any stimulants. I know that she loved her white wine. I loved her enthusiasm, her energy and her sense of fun. I did find her very attractive and thought she was happily married.

*

In 1987 we did the last series of *Yes, Prime Minister*. It was a time when we all got together to say goodbye: Paul, Nigel, Diana and Syd and all the boys. It was at once very happy and very sad. I knew dear Paul wasn't at all well. He was so brave and I think he was relieved that the series was coming to an end. But nevertheless, I look back on those seven years with great joy and great love.

I received a call from Australia saying that they wanted me to return to tour the play, *Rattle of a Simple Man*. I was excited about going back to Australia and doing the play again, but having been away a lot I was missing Jo. I wanted to spend more time at home.

Jo was very happy living in Bath and teaching at the St Joseph's Primary School. She agreed that I should go back to Australia.

For some time I had been thinking about changing agents. I'd been with my present agent, Barry Burnett, for ten years. I had a chat with him and suggested that maybe it was time for a new voice. He was very understanding, saying that I could think about it and let him know.

I talked briefly with another agent, Caroline Dawson, and went to see Nigel Hawthorne's agent, Ken McReddie. I knew Ken because he used to be the junior in the office of my first agent, Al Parker. It was so good meeting Ken again and he was very interested in taking me on.

*

In Sydney, there was Abigail, Kerry Jewell our producer, Edgar Metcalf the director, and a great stage crew. We rehearsed and then toured all the way up from Woolongong, Wagga Wagga, Canberra, Newcastle, to the Gold Coast of Brisbane, then to glorious Surfers Paradise.

While we were in Canberra I got an invitation to address the National Press Club lunch party. My producer told me it was a very prestigious organisation.

'What shall I address them on?' I asked. 'I don't do speeches.'

'Say whatever you like. They just want an appearance.'

I told the organisers that I would prefer not to address the club, but they persisted, calling me daily with new angles.

Eventually, after telling me that Paul Eddington had appeared the previous year, they offered a question-and-answer session, and I said I would do it.

I had the foresight to wear a jacket and tie, for it was a formal gathering of a hundred and fifty or more. After food, sitting at the top table, I grew increasingly nervous.

A spokesman got up from his seat and said, 'Ladies and gentlemen: we're very privileged today to have, as our guest speaker, the Prime Minister of the United Kingdom's Principal Private Secretary, Mr Bernard Woolley.' And he sat down. There was some applause; then – silence!

I knew that the *Yes Minister* and *Yes, Prime Minister* series had topped Australian ratings, so for a moment I wondered how many in the banqueting hall knew that I was merely the actor who played the part of Bernard Woolley.

Somehow I got started. I said, 'I've never done this before, never given an after-lunch or after-dinner speech, however good the lunch or dinner was, because generally, actors are terrible at it. Mainly because very few members of an audience know who we are. This gentleman on my left introduced me as Bernard Woolley. I'm not Bernard. I'm an actor, Derek Fowlds, who played Bernard and I'm in Australia doing a play at the Hyatt Regency Hotel and I would like to know how many people here have been to see it.'

Nobody responded.

'That's terrible,' I said. 'We've got four more performances so as soon as you leave here make a booking.'

I rambled on until I could ramble no more.

The nature of the questions that followed revealed that the audience had been less attentive than I hoped.

'How would you handle Prime Minister Bob Hawkes' government?'

Although I had met Bob Hawke a year earlier in the company of Paul and Nigel and found him a delightful man I was cautious with my reply. 'Very carefully,' I said.

'Would you accept sponsorship from a tobacco company?'

It was a loaded question, for I knew that Paul was part of an anti-smoking group and would have spoken about it. Nevertheless, I said what I thought.

'If it's a question of keeping a theatre open I would accept sponsorship from anybody.'

I must confess I have little recollection of all the things I said during what seemed an endless hour.

As I left two ladies came up to me and said, 'Mr Fowlds, we gotta tell you, you're a bloody lot funnier than Paul Eddington.'

I told Paul this story but he just stared in complete disbelief.

I think at that time Abigail was having marriage problems and I detected that she was not as happy in 1988 as she had been the year before. I liked her company and I enjoyed working with her. She became a very close friend.

One evening in Sydney, Danny La Rue was in the audience and later sent me some flowers suggesting that we must perform on stage together.

I remember a very funny moment from the tour, when we were performing in Brisbane at the Key Theatre. On this day Abigail told me she couldn't speak. She said, 'I can't go on stage tonight.'

I think it was in the afternoon, when it was too late to cancel the performance, and we didn't quite know what to do.

I said, 'I'll go to the theatre, bring the curtain up and I'll talk to the audience. We'll have to give them their money back, or suggest that they could come later in the week when Abigail is better. We'll give them that choice.'

There were about sixty or seventy people in the audience and they must have been very surprised when the curtain went up to reveal me sat on the bed, saying, 'Hello, and good evening.'

It wasn't *Rattle of a Simple Man.*

I talked to them for about half an hour, mentioning Abi – that she wasn't well and we were going to offer them their money back, or hopefully they could come another day. I talked to them about *Yes Minister* and *Yes, Prime Minister*, about Paul and Nigel and other shows that I had done.

They asked questions, were very interested and it was a jolly time with just me sitting on a bed. I think most of them came back and saw the play. Abi was on the next evening and there for the rest of the week.

One day Abi and I went to a clairvoyant. It was extraordinary because, before I left to come to Australia, I was in the process of changing my agent but I had told no one of my thoughts.

The clairvoyant knew nothing about me yet; she talked about my mother and she asked me what I did for a living.

'I'm an actor.'

'Would I know anything that you've been in?'

'*Yes Minister.*'

'Of course, of course,' she said. Then, 'Your mother has been very ill.'

'Yes,' I said, 'and I worry about coming away and leaving her.'

'Don't worry, she is not going to go yet. She doesn't want to go yet. You can relax and be sure she's okay.'

We talked a little, then she continued: 'You've just told me you are an actor and are thinking of changing your agent. Have you decided who your new agent will be? Ah, I see. It is a woman.'

'No, it's a man.'

'Don't go to him. There is a woman who wants to look after you. Go to her.'

I told Abi that I had had an extraordinary experience with this clairvoyant; apparently, so had she.

At the end of the play my character, Percy, has to kiss Cyrenne, Abigail's character. On tour I had only kissed her gently on the lips but on the last performance I thought, well, this is the end, so I turned to Abigail and I just kissed her with my tongue right down her throat. And it went on for a long time and we both knew that it was the last time we would ever do this play together.

When the curtain came down she looked at me and said, 'What took you so long?'

Dear Abi. It was wonderful to be in her company and I wish her well.

On my return to London I had to ring up Ken McReddie.

I said, 'I've got to be honest with you, Ken. I've got a tale to tell but you won't believe it.'

He laughed when I told him I had seen a clairvoyant and I had to go to a woman agent.

He was very generous. 'Derek, don't you worry,' he said. 'I am here, whenever.'

I had been dreading the conversation, but Ken made it easy.

I phoned Caroline and asked if she was sure she wanted to take me on.

'Of course, Derek,' she said.

It was wonderful to join that agency. I'm still with them twenty-five years on. Sadly Caroline passed away a few years back; she is really missed by all of us. The agency still has her name: Caroline Dawson Associates.

Chapter 14

Back to Oz – Filming with Olympia Dukakis

IN 1990 I APPEARED IN *DIE KINDER,* a mini-series aired on the BBC and on PBS in the USA, written by Paula Milne and directed by Rob Walker. Miranda Richardson played a character whose children were kidnapped by her German ex-husband. She hires Lomax (Frederic Forrest, an American actor) to help her find them. I played Crombie, a detective.

Frederic had worked with Jack Nicholson and Al Pacino and had been nominated for awards by the Academy and others for his roles in *Apocalypse Now* and *The Rose.*

I had a scene with him in an auditorium in which he had to appear out of breath as my character interviewed him.

Rob, the director, had warned me: 'When I say action, Derek, be careful, watch what Freddie does.'

We rehearsed the scene and Rob told us we would shoot the take.

'You gonna go for a take?' said Freddie. 'Give me a minute.'

Suddenly Freddie took off, running at some speed around the auditorium until he was breathing heavily. Arriving at my side he shouted, 'Turn over, I'm ready.'

I had great difficulty hiding my amusement.

It reminded me of the celebrated story that Dustin Hoffman's character in the film *Marathon Man* had to appear tired, as if he hadn't slept for days. Dustin, a method actor, stayed up for three nights so as to look realistic. When he told Laurence Olivier what he had done and why, Olivier paused for a moment, then said, 'Try acting, dear boy. It's much easier.'

After *Die Kinder* there was a period without work until the beginning of 1991. I got a call inviting me to go back to Australia to make a film with the wonderful American actress Olympia Dukakis. I suppose they asked me because of the success of *Yes Minister* and *Yes, Prime Minister*. When I was offered it I initially thought that they wanted Nigel or Paul. No, they wanted Bernard. Which, of course, was me.

This was a pretty exciting job for me. For a while I thought it would be my opportunity of breaking back into films as it was years since I had done any. In my dreams, Hollywood was calling.

Olympia had starred in the film *Moonstruck* with Cher and Nicolas Cage, a great success in 1987. Cher won an Oscar for Best Actress in a Leading Role and Olympia, Best Actress in a Supporting Role. It also won the award for best screenplay. So Olympia was hot property. I was simultaneously excited, flattered and nervous about the prospect of working closely with her – and, according to the script I had read, working very, very, very closely with her.

The film was called *Over the Hill* although, as filming got under way, I was told someone had suggested a new title, *Round the Bend*. I was far from certain that the producers knew of the British connotation of the phrase. It had been based on a book, *Alone in the Australian Outback*, by Gladys Taylor.

Part of my excitement was that my travel arrangements were all 'first class' – the flights, the limousines, the hotels; and, so, so, wonderful, they would pay for Jo to come out and join me. Both of us couldn't wait.

Timing and circumstances meant that I would have to fly out ahead of Jo. She hated flying and she had to summon up a lot of courage to travel alone. I was by then filming in Alice Springs, and friends of mine met Jo in Sydney after her twenty-four-hour flight, showed her around and then put her on a plane to Alice Springs. I remember being there at the airport and watching her come off the plane. She was shaking. I think she was shaking when she boarded the plane. She never got used to flying. It was so lovely to see her and have her with me in Australia. She met all the cast and stayed with me throughout the shoot.

My first shock after my arrival was to learn that the director, George Miller, and the writer, Robert Caswell, had decided that I must have hair extensions. I was to play an English retired dentist who wanted to 'loop the loop', driving around Australia in an RV just for the hell of it. A sort of 'walkabout' but in a camper van.

I must confess that after hours and hours of attractive girls fixing hair extensions to my head I began to like it. Jo didn't, and made her view clear, but she had to help me every night spreading the hair out over the pillow and tying it up into a bun. Every time she did this she muttered, 'What a terrible sight.'

The extensions had to stay in until filming had finished.

The big joy for me was meeting and working with Olympia. Not only was she a great actress, she was also a great person. We had many chats and walks along the beach, talking about this and that and life's disasters and triumphs. Olympia's cousin was Michael Dukakis, the 65th and 67th Governor of Massachusetts; in 1988, he was the Democratic nominee for President. He lost to the Republican candidate, the then Vice President, George H. W. Bush.

It was wonderful to be out in Australia, a truly fabulous country. We started off in Sydney, went to the Red Centre, then on to Melbourne and then to Alice Springs. The crew were a wonderful group of people. Bill Kerr played Maurice in the film. We talked about his time in *Variety Bandbox* and *Hancock's Half Hour* on British radio. In Alice Springs we met his very young wife and baby. I think Bill was nearly 70 at the time.

A highlight for me was that I met and got to chat to the Aboriginal actors taking part in the film. We didn't talk much but I've always found it rewarding to share even the smallest thing with people from a vastly different cultural background to mine.

In the film Olympia's character, Alma, upset at not being able to see her estranged daughter on her birthday, decides to take a supercharged motorcar on a voyage of self-discovery. Along the way, she meets con-men, crooks and a pony-tailed ex-dentist in a camper van, little knowing that through this short adventure and even shorter romance she would find the courage to return and set family matters right.

I think my part was seen by the writer as a 'white knight' in Alma's plight.

In one scene Olympia and I had a love encounter in the sea. It called for me to lift her up and carry her into the bowels of a shipwreck. She complained of pain around her ribcage shortly after filming. What nobody knew was that somehow, during the carry, I had broken one of her ribs. This was diagnosed a long time afterwards.

After viewing the rushes the director decided there was an acute lack of kissing between Olympia and me, so he demanded some close-ups.

In make-up, before the take, the girls were teasing me about kissing Olympia. 'How you gonna do it, Derek?'

My reply was intended to be a bit of fun. I said, 'What do you think I should do with my tongue? Should I keep it to myself?'

'Derek,' one girl said, 'do you want a demonstration?'

I thanked her for her kind offer but I declined it.

A little later Olympia went into make-up and was immediately told what I had said about my tongue. She didn't tell me then that she knew, but during our clinches I got a very clear message of how far I could go but no more.

The crew built a revolving rostrum on which Olympia and I knelt facing each other, pretending we were waist deep in the sea.

As the rostrum was slowly turned toward the hovering camera the director shouted, 'The first kiss is gentle, the second passionate and the third – well – just go for it big time.'

When we had a couple of days free of filming, the company paid for Jo and me to visit Ayers Rock (now known by its Aboriginal name of Uluru). It's a huge sandstone rock formation in the southern part of Australia's Northern Territory.

It really was so extraordinary for both of us. After checking into our hotel we hired a car and drove out to watch the sun set over this magnificent and impressive landmark. It certainly is an icon of Australia. We returned very early the next morning so we could catch the sunrise. It was breathtaking. Rising red for 2,800 feet to the blue, blue of the sky, it is easy to understand why Uluru is listed as a UNESCO World Heritage Site.

Although others did, we were never tempted to climb. People were beginning to be aware that the rock is venerated by the Anangu, the Aboriginal people of the area. The area around the rock has a plethora of springs, caves and paintings.

One day I took Olympia to visit the clairvoyant I had met three years before who remembered me and was thrilled to meet Olympia. I told her that my mum was still with me and that I had taken her advice and joined Caroline Dawson as my new agent.

She told Olympia that our film would not have great success but it would be a very enjoyable experience. She was right.

She also told me I would be offered a part in a uniform and boots, a sort of 'Hitler' character. She got that right, too; I realised that when I took the part of Sergeant Oscar Blaketon in *Heartbeat*.

I received a note from Olympia soon after we parted. It read: 'Whatever happens to the film it can never take away the joy and the wonderful experience of working with you.'

It was a strange film really, *Over the Hill*. After its premiere in Australia (I think it grossed no more than $90,000 at the box office) it went straight to video.

Some years later Jo and I were in New York and went to see Olympia's husband, Louis Zorich, in a musical, *She Loves Me*, on Broadway. We saw Louis backstage but Olympia was away filming.

I still cherish the time Olympia and I had together and I still hear from her every Christmas.

Chapter 15

Heartbeat

I WAS HAVING DINNER AT CAROLINE DAWSON's house one evening in 1991 and among the guests was the casting director Malcolm Drury. We were all having fun gossiping and talking, then suddenly Malcolm looked at me and said, 'I've got an idea that may include you but I'm not going to tell you anything about it.'

'You can't say things like that,' I said.

'No,' he replied. 'It's just come to mind. Leave it with me.'

As we went on chatting I couldn't get Malcolm's words out of my head. We had a lovely evening and said goodbye to each other.

The next day Caroline said, 'There's a script coming your way. It's Malcolm's idea. I've read it. It's a six-part series set in Yorkshire, being shot in Leeds and Whitby, and a little village nearby. At the moment it's called *Aidensfield*. The title may change but it's six episodes, about six months' work. I'm sending it over.'

I got the script and read it. The only London character in the storyline was someone called Nick Rowan, a young and very new copper, who was moving up to Yorkshire. I thought, I'm far too old to play this part. I phoned Caroline and said, 'Look, there's only one Londoner in this and he's 28.'

'Don't be ridiculous,' she said. 'They want you to play the Sergeant, Oscar Blaketon.'

'But he's from Yorkshire,' I protested.

'Last time I looked,' she said, 'you're a bloody actor.'

I had played North Country characters on the stage but never on the telly and there were many good Yorkshire actors. Why me?

'Why not go down to meet them at Yorkshire Television if you're worried?' said Caroline.

So I did. I met Malcolm, Keith Richardson the executive producer, and Stuart Doughty, who was the producer on the first series.

I told them of my concern.

'Listen Derek,' they said, 'take the weekend and think about it and call us on Monday morning. The part is yours if you want it.'

That Saturday evening I was fated to go to a show given by my friend Philip Stone and in the audience was the director, Jimmy Ormerod, who, funnily enough, was going to direct the first two episodes of this new series in Yorkshire.

He asked me if I was going to sign up.

'I'm not sure I can pull it off,' I said.

Jimmy, being a blunt Yorkshireman, said, 'For goodness' sake. It's only six episodes. Just cut your hair short, grease it back and shout.'

I thought, I know, I'll base the character on my drill sergeant when I did my National Service. He was a bastard when we did square-bashing at West Kirby. His name was Corporal Maund. He took great joy out of belittling all of us. I thought, right, that's how I'm going to play Oscar Blaketon.

One of my oldest friends, Bill (William) Simons, was cast as PC Alf Ventress. I first met Bill in the early 1980s when he was starring in a TV programme called *Cribb*, a drama series about police work mostly based in Victorian London, with Alan Dobie as Detective Sergeant Cribb, a member of Scotland Yard's newly formed CID unit. Bill played Constable Thackeray. I played a voyeuristic hat-maker called Albert Moscrop (falling in love with Fenella Fielding) in 'Mad Hatter's Holiday', an episode that takes Cribb and Thackeray to Brighton to experience the sea air and solve a gruesome murder.

I spent ten days with Bill in Brighton and we promised to get in touch again as soon as we could. We had mutual friends in Fulham: Belita and Jimmy, who ran a garden centre.*

---

* See page 100

Over the years our friendship grew and after I'd accepted the part of Oscar Blaketon I had a phone call from Bill telling me he had been offered a part in a Yorkshire-based television series, *Aidensfield*, and had heard that I had been offered one too. He was far from sure as to what to do.

I told him that I had accepted. 'Come on, Bill,' I said. 'Do it. It's only six episodes, only six months.'

He signed up for the role and it wasn't long before I found myself travelling up to Leeds to meet Bill and the rest of the cast including Nick Berry, who played the young PC Nick Rowan, and the other copper in our 'station', the lovely Mark Jordan as PC Phil Bellamy.

Bill bought a cottage not far from the village of Goathland where the outside scenes of the series were filmed and I enjoyed many days and evenings in the company of Bill and his wife, Janie. My Jo used to travel up to Leeds and the four of us would get together. Jo and Janie got on so well that they joked about leaving Bill and me as they had saved enough 'going away money'. At least, we thought they were joking!

When Janie passed away in 2002 it was tragic for Bill and devastating for us all. There was the most moving ceremony for Janie in St Mary's Church, Goathland.

Bill carried on in the programme, as I did, and by the time of the last ever episode we were the only characters to have stayed the eighteen-year run.

Several years after Janie's death, Bill remarried; he and his second wife Jackie both love travelling, and now spend most of their time in France.

The call on the telephone saying, 'Hello, Derek – it's Bill,' is a simple greeting but one I will always cherish.

I first saw Peter Benson playing Dauphin in Shaw's *Saint Joan*, with Gabrielle Lloyd as St Joan. I had also seen him in the BBC Television Shakespeare series, including *Henry VI* and *Richard III*. So it was a delightful surprise to meet him on the set of the Aidensfield Arms pub during early filming.

It took me some time to latch on to Peter's sense of humour. Most actors moan 24/7 but Peter's moaning, delivered in a low, slow, doom-filled voice, is really unique in the acting profession, perhaps in the human race. He never fails to make me laugh over seemingly the most innocuous matters. Dawn, in the make-up room, typically began with Peter complaining about something that had happened in the short time since he awoke. Or it could be about something that was going to happen, or might happen. Any complaint, however, would always end with laughs – sometimes eye-watering laughs.

My visits to London will always include meeting up with Peter, having lunch and going to matinees and shows if we can.

He truly is a great character in life and on the screen.

*

We began work on the first series on 18th November 1991, the day after Bill Simons' birthday. We had a read-through and rehearsed for the first week, which was unheard of but we didn't really know what we were doing.

We kicked off and started filming. I remember after the second episode we were crawling through the undergrowth playing coppers at two o'clock in the morning when Nick Berry turned to me and said, 'What do you think, Del? Do you think this will run?'

'Not a chance,' I said. 'It's a pile of poo. So, let's enjoy it while we can.'

I loved playing Oscar and I loved working with the boys. It proved to be a great team, Blaketon, Rowan, Ventress and Bellamy. As the weeks, months and years went by the camaraderie between us 'coppers' just grew and grew.

One day early on a chap walked up to me and said, 'Hello, I'm the props man. My name is Dougie Vince.'

'Dougie Vince,' I said, 'I know you.'

'No,' he said, 'you know my dad. He was your stage manager in 1979 when you did *No Sex Please, We're British* in the West End.'

'Of course, Dougie Vince! How is he?'

Sadly, Dougie Vince senior had passed away; but I got to know his son very well, along with Arthur Lake, another props man. Arthur was to become one of my closest friends.

When Keith Richardson, our producer, changed the name of the series from *Aidensfield* to *Heartbeat*, a recording of the Buddy Holly song 'Heartbeat' sung by Nick Berry was played over the opening titles.

It was extraordinary. The programme just took off and before we finished the first six episodes we were asked to do another six, and then another twelve and then fifteen; it just went from strength to strength. They were very special, the first six years.

The first series (which was a little more risqué) went out on a Friday night, but once the programme shifted to what became its regular Sunday evening slot we got almost eleven million viewers and it soon became one of the most popular drama series on television. I shudder with the thought that I almost talked myself out of nearly eighteen years' work.

During the filming of *Heartbeat* we did the interiors at the studio in Leeds for the first week and then we used to travel up to Goathland where we stayed at the Mallyan Spout Hotel and various bed-and-breakfast digs. We all looked forward going to Goathland every other week. Nick and I called it 'Brigadoon' – it just came out of the mist every ten days.

When we were filming outside the 'garage' or the 'Aidensfield Arms' we always got a big crowd watching. They were all jolly and obviously great fans of the show. Arthur Lake, our property master, would get all the crowd going by telling them it was someone's birthday. Sometimes we had five or six hundred people singing 'Happy Birthday' to whoever Arthur randomly chose.

One afternoon when we were filming outside the garage Arthur pointed out a woman in the crowd waving to us.

'Derek, Derek,' she shouted, pointing at a woman next to her in a wheelchair. 'This is my mother.'

I went over to say hello.

'She's been in love with you for years,' said the daughter.

'I'm so pleased to meet you,' I said.

'Oh,' said the mother, 'I do love you.'

'You've made my day,' I said.

She had a bright face. We chatted and talked about why she was in a wheelchair.

'How old are you?' I asked.

'I'm 91,' she said.

'91!' I exclaimed. 'You look amazing.'

'Thank you very much.'

Without thinking I said, 'Are you sexually active?'

The moment I said it I knew I shouldn't have, but her face lit up. 'Now *you've* made *my* day,' she said.

But a number of the crew heard all this, so from then on whenever I walked into the make-up wagon all the girls would shout, 'Are you sexually active?'

My reply was usually, 'Not today, I'm not.'

The books by Peter Walker that *Heartbeat* was based on were about a country copper: *Constable on the Hill*, *Constable on the Land* or *Constable* here, there and everywhere. The producers of *Heartbeat* changed the original idea to bring in a conflict (you can't have good drama without conflict). At the beginning the conflict was between North and South: the London copper joining the police force of a sleepy town in North Yorkshire with a curmudgeonly, old-fashioned, 1960s sergeant. There was also the conflict created by the modern medical doctor Kate Rowan (Niamh Cusack) joining a long-established practice run by Dr Ferrenby (played by Frank Middlemass).

Over the first few years any 'guest' appearance was subordinate to the plots headed by the regular characters. So the leading actors had storylines built around them, which allowed each of us the chance to get under our character's skin and develop the part. Initially, the relationship between the doctor and the copper (Niamh and Nick) was paramount, and we policemen and the rest of the cast responded to the central story.

In series two the beautiful Tricia Penrose joined us as the pub landlord's niece, Gina. Trish was only 21, full of fun, a constant joy to work and socialise with. She is a naturally gifted girl, a wonderful mimic with a phenomenal singing voice. In fact, I always thought that singing was (perhaps should have been) her career, rather than acting. I can remember her amazing rendition of the song 'Shout' in one episode. The whole cast and crew were spellbound as she belted the song out. Often, if Trish and I were in make-up together, we would rehearse the song 'You Don't Bring Me Flowers' which would, if we were ever asked, be our triumphant duet. We never, ever, got it right so the duet never happened.

Years later, in 2001, Trish, David Lonsdale and myself did a play at the Edinburgh Festival.

When, after three years, Niamh decided to leave it was quite a blow; but she had a wonderful episode where, after giving birth to a daughter, Katie, she contracted leukaemia. She played that magnificently and it gave all the regular characters something to play to. Nick was superb in those episodes.

A teacher came into Nick's life which created a different kind of drama, with the changing education of that period.

So it was still character driven with the regulars vitally important.

*

At the beginning I stayed at Oulton Hall Hotel just outside of Leeds; then I rented a cottage that Jo hated. Some years later (after much toing and froing) Jo did stay in the flat I bought in Whitehall Waterfront in Leeds. She loved that flat.

After six years Nick came up to me and told me he was leaving. At that time I was thinking of leaving too. I'd done six years and I thought, it's time for me to move on, to do other things. Nick suggested we leave together.

The producers had other ideas, however. They took me out to lunch and asked me to stay, telling me they had plans such as retiring me from the police and putting me in the post office. (Eventually, I was to buy the pub, but that came later.)

I was aged 60 at the time and, after considering my options, decided that I should stay with it for the financial security.

Meanwhile Nick's character left the series, taking his second wife Jo and daughter Katie with him to start a new life in Canada.

Nick's part was taken by Jason Durr. Jason was great. He had his own ideas about how to play the copper which made the character completely different from Nick; and of course he didn't have a partner in the series so he was open for all sorts of ladies coming into his life.

Slowly the conflict between 'North' and 'South' disappeared. So the cultural differences, so ably exploited in the early series, played no part in the storylines.

One of the stalwarts of the series was Bill Maynard who created the wonderful character, local villain Claude Jeremiah Greengrass.

I had met Bill years previously when I was doing *Basil Brush* and he was doing all sorts of other things. I knew that Greengrass and Blaketon would have continuing conflicts. Blaketon would always want to 'nab' him, lock him up and throw away the key. Feedback suggested that the viewing audience loved the relationship between them.

The movement of my character from the police station to the post office didn't quite come off. It lacked bite. At that time I don't think the writers knew what to do with Oscar. So I 'bought the pub' where some of the conflicts with Greengrass continued.

After a series of small strokes Bill Maynard left the programme. With Bill gone, something else went out of the show; it was never really the same again. Geoffrey Hughes (as Vernon Scripps) came after Bill, and Gwen Taylor (as Peggy Armstrong) took over from Geoffrey.

*

In 2003 Bill Simons said that he had to go to an award ceremony in Blackpool and that he had to fill a table of ten. He wanted me to join him.

'Why are you going?' I asked.

'I've been nominated for an award. What's more, I've been told I've won.'

'What for?'

'The best actor in a series.'

'What series?'

'*Heartbeat.*'

'What about me?' I asked. 'Wasn't I nominated?'

'No, you weren't. Our producer is coming and some of the cast and crew.'

I agreed to be part of the ten.

I found out that the Michael Elliott Trust Awards ceremony helps fund a charity providing sanctuary for neglected donkeys and a safe place where children with special needs can adopt a donkey. Sponsors included June Brown MBE, Dame Judi Dench, Martin Shaw, Jenny Seagrove and Hayley Mills.

The hotel food and wine at the pre-ceremony dinner were first class and, as one or two of us were recognised, the free bottles kept coming. Bill accepted his award and others followed. As the ceremony was drawing to a close the MC announced that we had arrived at the special moment of the evening when the two Lifetime Achievement awards would be presented. 'Who's got them?' we all asked.

Within seconds and to tremendous applause, the female winner was revealed to be Barbara Windsor.

Barbara said a few words, thanked people then walked off leaving the MC to announce the male winner. 'This actor,' said the MC, 'trained at the Royal Academy; his first West End play was *The Miracle Worker.*'

I think I said aloud, 'I was in that!'

Bill started laughing – everyone started laughing. The penny dropped that I had been set up as the MC went through my entire career. My 'friends' cheered and chortled; I, meanwhile, was having an 'out of body' experience.

I did manage to say something like 'You knew all the time!' to Bill, but I suspect I put in a few colourful words as well.

Somehow I made my way up to the rostrum, received my award and said how honoured and surprised I was. I also explained that I hadn't prepared a speech so didn't really know what to say.

From the audience came a loud shout, 'What about "boom, boom"?'

'Okay,' I said. 'Who can remember Basil Brush?'

There was uproar, a clamour of protest. I'm not sure how but we all started singing the Basil Brush song: 'Basil de Farmer, the knight in shining armour …'

On the way home I reflected on receiving a 'lifetime achievement' award, thinking, 'Is this it?'

In 2004 the *Yorkshire Life* magazine held their annual food and wine awards. The Pub Landlord of the Year went to Oscar Blaketon of the Aidensfield Arms. I was presented with a certificate signed by the publishers, the regional director and the wine editor. I think it might have been pushing plausibility a shade too far to have had it signed by a food critic!

*

During my time with the series there were three young actors that stood out for me. It's so difficult to know exactly why one actor stands out and another doesn't. You have so little time with them on set and it's often no more than a few lines between you, but stand out they do. They stood out when I worked with them and they now stand out in any company.

After appearing as a lovestruck schoolboy in the 'Wall of Silence' episode in 1993 John Simm went on to play Sam Tyler in *Life on*

Mars and the Master in *Doctor Who*, among many other roles. He has starred in *Cracker*, *The Lakes*, *Sex Traffic*, *State of Play*, *Crime and Punishment* and *The Village*. He has been nominated twice for the BAFTA Award for Best Actor and is a Laurence Olivier Award nominee.

And what can you say about Daniel Craig? He got a chilly reception in the episode 'A Chilly Reception' when he played thwarted lover Peter Begg, whose granny was found dead by his old flame, Susan, who was about to be married to someone else. Angry at this, Begg breaks into Susan's home and steals her wedding presents. Begg must have got away with it for Daniel, among many other things, went on to play a secret agent called James. Even in those early days there was a 'still' quality in Daniel's work and, coupled with a granite face that was designed to fill a screen, it was inevitable that success awaited him.

I'm certain that no one could have predicted that the actor who played both Toby Fisher in the episode 'No Hard Feelings' and Lord Ashfordly's nephew Charles in 'The Good Doctor' would be, in a decade or so, the best known and loved 'Sherlock' on television. Benedict Cumberbatch is a very talented actor and the son of the beautiful actress, Wanda Ventham. Wanda and I had parts in the 1962 film, *We Joined The Navy*.

I only had one scene with Benedict but I was more than impressed with the confidence he had. Before he left the set I wished him well with his career. After his impressive portrayal of Alan Turing (the gay mathematician who broke the Enigma Code used by the Germans in the Second World War) in the film *The Imitation Game*, I think I got my wish.

As time went on the drama just wasn't there between the established characters and there appeared to be no plans for development. The emphasis of the show had completely switched to guest actors. Plots were written for the 'guests'. Over the years, a number of well-known guest stars have made one-off appearances in *Heartbeat*, either in cameo roles or more substantial single-episode parts. These include Richard Todd, the legendary actor and Second World War hero. (On 6th June 1944, Captain Todd participated in the British Airborne Operation Tonga during the D-Day landings. He was among the first British officers to land in Normandy as part of Operation Overlord.)

I remembered clearly going to the cinema to see *The Hasty Heart* with Richard starring alongside Patricia Neal and Ronald Reagan. There was *The Dam Busters* in 1955 with Michael Redgrave and Robert Shaw; *The Story of Robin Hood and His Merrie Men* in 1952. At that time Richard was a huge box office star.

We were all star-struck when Richard walked on to the set of 'Seeds of Destruction' playing Major Harold Beecham. I regret that my only scene with him was in the Aidensfield Arms with me behind the bar. We didn't know then but this was to be Richard's last appearance on screen. He died in December 2009.

Back in the 1960s, George Baker (subsequently of *Wexford* fame) had offered me a part in a production for a theatre company he was running. I recall I was unable to do it, but we had an opportunity to catch up and talk about the 'old days' when he played Maurice Dodson in the episode 'Vendetta'. His character was an old flame of Peggy Armstrong who turned up after twenty years, causing more than one heart to flutter.

George reminded me he was in *The Dam Busters* with Richard Todd.

I know that, as a good-looking young actor, he was raved about. Some called him 'the new Cary Grant'. I believe Ian Fleming wanted him to be the first James Bond but George couldn't commit. When he died in 2011 an obituary reminded me of a grand recollection of his: that, for six weeks in 1954, he had a brief fling with Brigitte Bardot. 'Imagine that,' said George. 'Brigitte Bardot, the world's number one sex bomb, in a clinch with me, George Baker, jobbing actor! I was completely dazzled.'

Another George, George Cole, played an old crook Albert Hallows – aka 'The Professor' or 'Prof' – who had escaped from prison and returned to Aidensfield to settle a score with the police in the episode 'England Expects'.

In the 1970s, after seeing one of his plays, I'd written a fan letter to George. I had admired his work ever since the black-and-white film *Cottage to Let*, a wartime spy movie starring Leslie Banks, Alastair Sim, John Mills and George, playing cocky teenager Ronald.

In real life George had been adopted, and after appearing with Alastair was taken in by the Sim family along with his adoptive mother. There are so many films on George's CV, with a huge variety of parts, from Flash Harry in the St Trinian's films to Arthur Daley in Thames Television's *Minder*. One of Britain's best loved character actors, he passed away in August 2015, aged 90, after a career spanning more than 60 years.

I'd had a cameo part in *Minder* back in 1982. It was quite wonderful working with George and my old friend Dennis Waterman. The only bit I remember about the story was that Terry (Dennis) had to collect a coffin from the airport and store it at Arthur's lock-up. 'Nuff said!

When Leslie Phillips joined us I reminded him that I nearly played his son in a play. Leslie's voice could only have been Leslie's. 'Did you really, darling?' he said.

'You didn't want me,' I complained.

'Oh, darling, darling! What a mistake!'

(I did get to work with Leslie again in Central Television's *Chancer*.)

Some of our guest actors were better known for their singing careers. In 'Harmony' Lulu played singing star Deborah Vine, the cousin of Sergeant Merton; and there was David Essex who played the tinker, Johnny Lee, in 'The Traveller'.

The real delight for me when welcoming 'guest' stars was when they were old chums.

Clive Mantle played famous cricketer Vinny Sanders in the episode 'A Gentleman's Sport'. His car breaks down in the village so he must stay at the Aidensfield Arms while the car is fixed. My character, Oscar Blaketon, is beside himself with joy and organises a match between The Aidensfield Arms and another pub, with Sanders playing for the 'home' side (Oscar's pub).

There was one outside shot with Clive and me in the distance supposedly discussing the upcoming match. In fact, we were catching up. 'How's Jo?' Clive asked.

'Good,' I replied. 'How's Zoe?'

From way away we heard someone shout, 'Action!'

'What was that?' I said.

Clive smiled. 'We are to walk toward the camera over there and start acting.'

For some reason we found it tough to switch the conversation from private to professional. It took us a good fifty yards to get it right.

Sylvia Syms! What a lady! What an actress! It was years – decades – since we filmed *East of Sudan*.

As Peggy Tatton in 'Where There's a Will' Sylvia resorts to drastic measures to stay on the family farm. Fortunately for me the shooting schedule allowed Sylvia and me plenty of opportunities to sit in the pub to endlessly reminisce, catching up with so many things in our lives. There was non-stop giggling.

It was always difficult for me to avoid giggles. Some were stifled and it showed. Some could be entirely suppressed (after a few takes). But others went beyond control. I only had to look at Michael Cochrane for the first cracks to surface. In fact, the very thought of Michael starts me laughing.

In the first of his appearances in *Heartbeat* I was then still the police sergeant and Michael played a man, Derek Lightfoot, whose wife Jean is 'stalked' by a woman claiming to be Derek's old sweetheart.

In one very sombre scene (I think I had been inspecting a body) Michael walked in, looked at me and I started laughing.

I apologised and tried again. Same result. The director, Tim Dowd, was normally a very patient man but not that day, not after so many failed takes. In the end he announced that filming was now halted and that Michael and I had to leave the studio and return the next morning fully composed.

We did do the scene – just.

When Michael returned for another episode he requested that he and I should be kept apart. The director wholeheartedly agreed to his request.

When I got notice that Judy Parfitt would soon arrive on set it filled me with joy and dread until I saw I was not to be in that particular episode. In fact I was away during the shoot. Judy (belying her role as Sister Monica Joan in *Call the Midwife*) is one of the world's worst gigglers. It was fortunate that we didn't have to repeat a former scene together when a large obstacle was put between us.*

When I got back to work a note awaited me. It said, 'Darling, what a pot of cream you've fallen into. Love Judy.'

Harry Towb appeared as Hugo Cummins in the episode 'Mastermind'. Dear Harry, husband of Diana Hoddinott, was a remarkable character actor of Irish and Russian-Jewish descent who grew up in Belfast. Over the years he was attached to the National Theatre, the Abbey and Gate Theatres in Dublin, and the Royal Shakespeare Company. His face and his talent graced many television dramas: *Eastenders*, *The Bill*, *Casualty* and that wonderful mini-series *The Camomile Lawn*.

Three cricketing heroes of mine made appearances: Ray Illingworth, Brian Close and the great umpire, Dickie Bird. As it was near my birthday, Ray and Brian signed a cricket bat for me. I still have it in pride of place.

We also had Freddie of Freddie and the Dreamers, Twiggy, Charlotte Church, Philip Glenister, Celia Imrie and many others.

In 1993 Dora Bryan appeared, and the following year Thora Hird. I'd never worked with Dora, but I went way back with Thora to the Alan Bennett play, *Intensive Care*. Some time later the BBC

---

* See page 89

were interviewing people for a showbiz programme and after Thora had done her slot she asked who was coming in next.

'Derek Fowlds.'

'I'll wait,' said Thora. And she did, for almost an hour, just to say a brief hello.

Another of the guest stars in *Heartbeat* was Gary Barlow. He played Micky Shannon in the episode 'The Son-In-Law', which we all referred to as 'the Barry Garlow story'. Micky is travelling around the country collecting old folk tunes. He also has seeds for thousands of rare orchids and wants Greengrass to grow them for him!

Gary was terrific company, mucking in with the crew and always laughing along with us.

When in Goathland we used to gather at the Mallyan Spout Hotel to party and sing a few songs. 'Nessun Dorma' was a favourite, as were 'When You Walk Through a Storm', 'I Believe', 'Danny Boy', and my song, 'Sweet Caroline.' We had been singing through empty bottles for years, but when Gary agreed to play and sing with us, microphones and recording machines suddenly appeared. I said, I've been singing in this bar for eighteen years and now Gary Barlow arrives we get sound!

I can proudly announce, I'm delighted to say, that Gary Barlow and I have made music together.

When I was at RADA there was a very influential teacher called Peter Barkworth. He joined us for a guest part in the second series. To my great honour I had a scene with him.

I started off with: 'Mr Barkworth …'

'Derek,' he said. 'For goodness' sake.'

We had long chats, and during one I asked how long he thought I should stay in *Heartbeat*.

He replied, 'As long as you want to.'

I didn't know, and neither did Peter, that I would stay another sixteen years.

We were good friends and always got in touch over Christmas. Sadly, he is no longer with us.

Two years before the series ended we lost our associate producer, Pat Brown. She was, in essence, *Heartbeat*. She loved her crew, loved her cast and loved the show. She was sorely missed when she got ill and passed away. We were all there to bid her farewell. In Goathland, there is a tree where we always go to say hello to Pat. Thanks for the memories.

In 1995 *Heartbeat* won the Television and Radio Industries Club award for ITV Programme of the Year, and again in 1998. Also in '98, we were nominated for a National Television Award (for Jason Durr as Most Popular Newcomer). In 1999 the series was named as the Best Performing Peak-time Drama.

In 2007 we were still popular in Norway where viewers voted us the Best European Drama.

Over the years there were actors who didn't take to the series. One of them said that *Heartbeat* was low-brow fare, a 'soap' which looked as though it had been filmed in a fog. The *Daily Mail* journalist Lynda Lee-Potter responded with a glowing review of the show, saying that *Heartbeat* had gripping scripts and was superbly well-acted by Nick and Niamh; she went on to say that 'the programme also has the glorious character actor, Derek Fowlds as a filthy-tempered sergeant'. In a later article she wrote for the newspaper she asked why Derek Fowlds didn't have his own series.

Lynda and I kept in touch. A lovely lady who is also sadly missed. A brilliant journalist who earned the success she received.

Heartbeat would be still running today if it wasn't for the powers that be at Independent Television, who felt they needed to save money and decided to bring down four programmes: *The Bill*, *The Royal*, *Wire in the Blood* and *Heartbeat*. The last programme was in 2009.

For me, as an actor, *Heartbeat* never really finished. In the final scene Oscar was in hospital, his life in danger. Even to this day people come up to me to ask if Oscar died.

I have to say I have no idea.

Chapter 16

'I want to see you on the front cover of the *Radio Times*' –
This is Your Life

DECADES AGO I RECALL MY MOTHER SAYING, 'There are three things I would like to see happen to you.'

'What are they?' I asked.

'I would really like to see your name in lights.'

She did, many times; at least, if they were not exactly 'lights', they were giant billboards. She was thrilled. The first was in 1961, *The Miracle Worker* at Wyndham's Theatre. Notices were outside the Royal Court and that was followed by another dozen staged in the West End. Mother saw them all.

'Now, I want to see you on the front cover of the *Radio Times*.'

And she did. In January 1986, to mark the launch of *Yes, Prime Minister*, I was photographed with Paul and Nigel outside number 10 Downing Street.

It wasn't the gated and guarded street it is now, and we were able to pull up in a car outside number 10 where a photographer was waiting for us. We posed and smiled for the camera and then sped off to have lunch.

'One more to go,' Mum said.

'What's that, Mum?'

'I want to be alive when they do you on *This is Your Life*.'

I said, 'I'm sorry, Mum, I don't think that will ever happen.'

In 1992, while filming *Heartbeat* in Goathland, we were rehearsing a new scene. My lines, although not lengthy, had required a lot of practice on my part. But no one else, it seemed, had learned *their* lines properly. Niamh Cusack had to walk into the bar and twice fluffed her lines.

For a moment or two I wondered if the whole cast and crew had been on a boozy bender the night before and not invited me. People were shuffling and mumbling and appeared to be in a hurry to get away. They certainly were not concentrating.

'I think we should try again tomorrow,' I said.

'No,' I was told. 'One more try.'

I said one of my lines which should have been the cue for Niamh Cusack to come in but she didn't. Deciding that the director was about to shout 'cut' and start again, I turned around to see Michael Aspel walk in.

I immediately looked at Bill Maynard, convinced it would be for him.

'No,' said Bill. 'It's not me.'

Michael, microphone in hand, walked up to me. 'Derek Fowlds,' he said, followed by the immortal words, 'This is Your Life.'

I was so stunned. I couldn't believe it.

I knew Michael as a neighbour when my boys were very young and played with his twins. The boys tried to out-brag each other:

'My dad's on *Crackerjack*!'

'My dad's on *Basil Brush*!'

After the shock of seeing Michael on set I was taken to the Leeds studio by car. I wasn't allowed to see anybody before we began the show; they were all backstage. They had come from all over the place to be there. Family – my mum and sister Babs, her husband Alfred and a few cousins. My friends and colleagues. My old English teacher, Enid Watling, was there, as was my dear Jo.

Jennie Linden, Benjamin Whitrow and Derek Nimmo came on.

Although the half-hour programme could hardly cover all events and all the important people in my life, there were many who they had tracked down. My old flight sergeant from Malta came with his wife, and I know they tried to get Byck from America. But Byck's state of health and his need for constant care ruled him out.

Paul Eddington, now very ill, came on at the end of the show. We chatted and joked as we had always done. I even got to tell my 'White Horse' whisky joke.

It was informal, funny and most of all, for me, very moving.

We all stayed in the Queen's Hotel in Leeds. It was a bizarre but wonderful evening with so many people I hadn't seen for a long time.

I went to Mum at the end and said, 'Well, Mum. That's the third wish you had for me.'

'Yes,' she said, 'I can go now.'

I just laughed and told her she wasn't going to go yet. She waited another year.

On 15th December 1993 my dear mum died. A huge wrench and one I know I'll never get over.

Chapter 17

Wonderful years in Colerne – A broken heart

IN 1991, AFTER FILMING OVER THE HILL in Australia and before I accepted the part of Oscar Blaketon in *Heartbeat*, Jo and I came back to Bath and thought about looking for a bigger house. I had this thought that the fees from six episodes of *Heartbeat* would give us the deposit for the new property.

We thought it wise to keep my flat in London, so we decided we would sell Pera Place.

One evening Jo said she had found this house in a village called Colerne.

'Where's Colerne?' I asked.

'It's a few miles out of Bath. Come and see it.'

So we went to see this property which turned out to be a bungalow.

I hate the term 'bungalow'. People retire in bungalows.

I told Jo I didn't like it.

She said, 'Let's go around the back and look at the view.'

The view, I had to admit, was sensational; but there was something about it I thought wasn't for me.

Jo was really keen on it.

I said 'no' but Jo suggested we had another look.

As we went through all the rooms I kept thinking about what we could do with it. The asking price was £159,000 and I told Jo that it was far too expensive.

She said, 'I really love it. I think we can do things to it.'

'I'll make an offer,' I said.

'What will you offer?' asked Jo.

'£140,000.'

'That's ridiculous. That's almost £20,000 less.'

'Let's just try it.'

Of course they turned my offer down.

Okay, I thought, that's fate.

Jo was disappointed, suggesting I should have offered more.

'We'll keep looking,' I said. 'We'll find the house.'

'That was the house,' said Jo.

About a month later they came back to us and asked if we would offer £145,000. Jo was so excited, so I agreed. We got it. Number 11 Eastrip Lane in the lovely village of Colerne. When we bought it, it was called Martindale. We changed it to Jodderek – Jo and Derek: Jodderek House, affectionately known as Jodders. We always called it Jodders.

We bought it September/October 1991.

I started *Heartbeat* in the November and we moved in on Valentine's Day. We decided to paint the whole house white, the idea being that white would give us a blank canvas onto which we could contemplate how to decorate.

Later, when I heard I was getting another series, I asked Jo what we should do next on our new home. Lots, she decided. Eventually she called it the house that *Heartbeat* built. We lived there very happily for eleven years, and each series we would add something else: a large conservatory, then a studio and a new garage. We went up into the roof so Jodders did become a house. The whole of the top floor became our master bedroom, with a balcony and a bathroom en suite.

The garden dropped sharply from the house, wonderful for sledging in the snow but quite difficult to negotiate on ageing legs. We had it landscaped into a series of terraces, with a vegetable patch and a small goldfish pond. It really was a lovely house, one that saw happy times and many parties with friends.

One new friend came into our lives when I got a job on television. I met Clive Mantle in 1994, shortly after I had started

Heartbeat, when I was offered a guest role in the *Casualty* series in which Clive played Dr Mike Barratt, one of the regulars. I played Mr Croft in the episode 'Value for Money'. I seem to remember I was beaten up in a car park, but I don't recall if Dr Mike Barratt treated me.

I had previously seen Clive as Little John in TV's *Robin of Sherwood* with Michael Praed and Jason Connery. I also remember him as a Frankenstein monster in a TV advert for electricity shares. So I did know of him when we first met, in the canteen on the top floor of the BBC's rehearsal studio in Acton. It was a very tall building, used for years by actors and known as 'the Acton Hilton'.

I saw Clive come in. He stopped, looked straight over to me, and immediately changed from walking pace into a trot. Quite a sight, Clive, even at medium speed. You don't often have to face a very tall and well built man charging at you.

Screeching to a halt inches from me, he bowed to the point of kneeling, saying, 'Mr Derek!'

'And you are Clive,' I said.

'Mr Derek, my hero. I was always a fan of yours. I grew up with Basil Brush and Mr Derek. It's such a pleasure to meet, as you and I have things in common.'

'Really?' I asked. 'What are they?'

'I know you're a Chelsea supporter. I am too. And I play golf.'

'So do I.'

'And,' he said in triumph, 'we're neighbours. You live in Colerne, and two miles across the valley is Box, where I live.'

After I finished work on the episode, Clive and I promised to keep in touch; and we did, playing golf whenever schedules allowed. And we socialised as a foursome: Clive and his wife Zoe, and me with Jo. As time went on Zoe and Jo became very close.

I was invited to attend Clive's *This is Your Life*.

As we worked away a lot, golf became a very rare occurrence for us; and, as we both gave up our season tickets, visits to Stamford Bridge to watch Chelsea play stopped completely.

Although Clive has moved away from Box we still see each other on birthdays and other special occasions.

A top man, Clive, and a close friend.

*

Jo was a great hostess, very popular with new and old friends. She had a special knack of pushing complete strangers into one room and making them bond like long-lost friends. She loved organising parties and dinner parties as much as she loved going to them.

Somehow, I never knew how, Jo would serve up delicious plates of food despite her limited culinary skills. The big surprise always came when pudding was served. During the main course I would ask Jo what was following, and she would reply that she hadn't yet decided.

The first big party we had was in November 1994, the night of the maiden National Lottery draw. We had just discovered an open fireplace in the living room, previously hidden by a gas fire and boarding. Paper, kindling and logs were stacked ready. Our guests arrived with a bottle of wine in one hand and their lottery ticket in the other, and we gathered in front of the fireplace as Jo set light. We all cheered, toasted our new discovery and watched as the flames leapt upward. Unfortunately, the smoke had other ideas. Instead of rising up the chimney it began wafting into the room. Within minutes we could hardly see one another. With laughter and much coughing, we all beat a hasty retreat and adjourned to the kitchen. If anyone won a million that night they never told me.

Jo's ability for fun parties knew no limits. She arranged a 'French' party, a 'Spanish' party and a 'Chinese' party. Guests had to 'dress' for the evening: black berets, red neckerchiefs and bands of onions for the 'French' men and tight blue-and-white striped tops and short black skirts for the women; sombreros and castanets for the 'Spanish'; and for the 'Chinese', Suzie Wong frocks, Japanese kimonos and one chap in a Chairman Mao suit.

To add to the spirit of the occasion Jo insisted that, for the first hour, English could not be spoken; we were all required to converse in the theme's native tongue. There was a little French, rather less Spanish, and round-mouthed oriental mutterings that had no relation to Mandarin or Cantonese, but there were plenty of hilarious attempts at sign language.

One gloriously sunny day in August 1996 we held a lunchtime party to celebrate our 20th 'getting together' anniversary. Everyone that we wanted to come and who could come was there. Family members arrived, mine and Jo's. Clive Francis, an old actor mate, his wife Natalie, Benjamin Whitrow, Clive and Zoe and Roger Hammond mingled with tens of old and new friends. We hired musicians, people got up and said a few words and Jo, Zoe and Clive sang a song they had written. I cannot remember all the lines; just the first two which went: 'Many years have gone by, since you first caught my eye/You are handsome and lovely and mine.'

Two regulars to our parties were close friends of Jo: Nerys Hughes and Pattie Brake. Nerys brought along her husband, Patrick, and Pattie brought her husband, Michael.

We also got into a marvellous habit of inviting actor friends who were performing in Bath to come for a 'luvvies lunch'. Nigel Hawthorne came with the cast of *The Madness of George III*, Richenda Carey and Harold Innocent. Joanna McCallum joined us, and one day Paul Eddington, his wife Trish and Richard Briers. Although Paul was unwell and the play, *Home* by David Storey, was to be Paul's last stage appearance, the joy and laughter around that lunch table that day was one of the highlights of my life.

Family visitors grew in numbers the more we extended the house.

One of Jo's many talents was her skill at drawing and painting. Her cartoons were brilliant, topical and invariably whimsical and funny. She would capture a seemingly innocuous moment and reveal its heart and soul.

She did, however, on occasion get carried away with her paintbrush. I returned one Saturday from filming in Leeds to be met outside the house by Jo who announced, 'I've done something. I hope you'll like it. It's a surprise.'

There was a long corridor running down the centre of the house connecting the kitchen and the living room with other rooms to the left and the right.

Jo opened the door to a corridor that I didn't recognise. Instead of framed theatre posters and family photos, there was a floor-to-ceiling-and-back-to-floor mural of the four seasons. It was a shock but it was resplendently done, in colours and shades I didn't know existed. I always went along with Jo's creative side so I said I loved it. I didn't: not here, not in a narrow corridor, not in the spine of the house.

A year or so after we moved in, Jo's mum and my mum came to stay for a few days. One afternoon Jo took them both for a trip into Bath. It was a gentle, sunny day, one of those when you count your blessings, and I settled down in a deckchair to read.

On their return, when the two oldies had gone indoors for a rest, Jo dragged a seat next to me and announced that she had called into the Registry Office.

'What for?' I asked.

'For us to get married while our mums are still alive. We can do it next week.'

My reaction was not what Jo had expected. 'I can't do that!' I blurted out. 'It's too soon. I can't go through with it.'

At the time I really couldn't see the point of getting married, no matter how much Jo wanted to. Jo was very upset and no words of mine could sensibly explain my feelings to her. I've never had the words that could explain my feelings, even to me. Jo knew I loved her deeply but at that moment it wasn't enough. It took weeks for the hurt to subside and for us to begin carrying on as before. But carry on we did.

*

Slowly, but surely, Jo and I got more involved with the village and its activities, especially Jo, who taught at the nearby school. I fitted in when I could: weekends mostly, as my working week was up north.

One year I was honoured to be asked to present the prizes at the village fair, and while I was there a bearded man came up to me. I noticed that he was carrying a professional video camera. He said hello and asked if I would say a few words to camera about the village as he was filming a documentary about its day-to-day life.

I said a few things: how I liked the village, the pub, the church and the friendly atmosphere. He thanked me and went on his way.

A few months later he called me. He was Stewart Mackay, a wildlife cameraman with his own film company. He had a proposal that he wanted to pitch to television.

'Six thirty-minute episodes,' he said. 'It's a format that you're not used to and may be out of your comfort zone.'

I was all ears.

Stewart's idea was for me to travel the West Country, get behind the obvious and find out how things work and meet the people who still carry out traditional handicrafts. His suggestion that we approach it from a position of general ignorance of country matters was not far short of the truth. I was to ask the questions that naive 'townies' would ask.

It was presented to HTV West in 2001, and in 2002 we got the green light. We began shooting in May, starting in the Cotswolds and working south over the weeks, ending up in Cornwall. Called *Fowlds in the Landscape*, the series covered people and wildlife – snakes, butterflies, fossils. We touched on ancient farming techniques, dry stone walling, hurdle making; and, on a river, otters, crayfish, trout, fly fishing. Mud fishermen, beachcombers and falconers made an appearance.

The last scene of the series was with me on the 'battlements' of the open-air Minack Theatre. It's a theatre cut into rock, and over the years I visited many times as part of the audience. Once, in the company of Jo and my sister, I took my mum to a performance that she obviously couldn't focus on as, covered in blankets, she fell asleep after ten minutes.

As the light faded, the cameras slowed and I recited the Prospero speech from *The Tempest*.

I grew very fond of Stewart during the filming, and his crew were a joy to work with: Robin Smith, Laura and Julian.

We did achieve over two million viewers; but in those days HTV, like much of the ITV network, was in a state of flux and decided that the series would not carry on. A great shame for us as, a decade or so later, there are many similar programmes being shown with well-known people as hosts: Stephen Fry, Griff Rhys Jones, Adrian Edmondson. Walking around the country talking and looking at rural life has become a second career for many personalities. I think our series might have been the start of televising such a successful format.

However, Stewart and I did get to work together again two years later by filming a short drama called *Pigeon Post*.

*

Fowlds in the Landscape was filmed while I was on leave from *Heartbeat*. The journey from Wiltshire to Yorkshire had become second nature to me, but the parting from Jo was always very hard. We pressed on doing the same sort of things until 2003.

Something really very odd happened in that year, something that I regret to this day.

I'd been endlessly commuting, and tried to persuade Jo to join me in Leeds. She didn't want to come up. She used to say, 'What do I want to go up there for? There's nothing there.'

'Well, I am,' I said.

'I can see you when you come home.'

She really loved her home, but we were beginning to grow apart because I was spending so much time away. It was often impossible to get home every weekend. I did it as much as I could.

In January that year Jo gave me an ultimatum.

She said, 'I think we should get married.'

I said, 'Please don't go there.'

Jo pressed. 'We've been together twenty-seven years now and I really think it's time we got married. If you don't then I'm going to leave.'

I said, 'You can't leave.'

'I'm going to be 60 soon,' she said, 'and if you don't marry me I'm going.'

'I'm sorry,' I said. 'I really am sorry. I can't do it, Jo.'

I didn't think that she would really leave, but when I came back from Leeds she told me that she had been looking at properties. I said I didn't believe her and joked about it, but pretty soon I realised she was serious.

I didn't know what to do; I didn't know how to handle it and hoped that it would turn out all right.

Jo had her 60th birthday. She saw a number of properties – some with Laurence, her son – and came back to tell me what she had found; hoping, I think, I would change my mind, while I continued to hope she would change *her* mind. I still couldn't believe we were going to break up after all this time. It didn't make any sense, for we both still loved each other. It was just the most awful time.

One weekend she said to me, 'I've found a property and I want half the value of our house to pay for it.'

'You're serious,' I said. 'You're making a huge mistake, Jo.'

'I want security and you're not giving me any.'

It wasn't entirely true, for we had everything written down and if anything happened to me, Jo would have inherited almost everything.

'I want a house of my own,' she said. 'I want to leave something to my kids.'

I said, 'I still can't believe you're doing this, Jo.'

She said, 'Well, it's your fault.'

I didn't really understand that, as we were so happy and all the legalities had been drawn up so that Jo wouldn't have lost out if anything happened to me.

As all this was going on I was negotiating to buy a flat in Leeds. It was planned that the show, with me in it, would go on for years, so buying rather than renting seemed the best option for me.

Reluctantly I went to my accountant and arranged for Jo to have half the value of our house in Colerne that she was entitled to. I gave her the £250,000 in October and she planned her departure.

She said, 'When I leave I don't want you to be around.'

I agreed, saying that I would stay in Leeds until she had moved out.

When Jo left me I was totally shattered. I missed her so much but I knew I couldn't call her.

Zoe, Clive's wife, phoned me and said that I could go back into the house.

'Thanks, Zoe.'

She said, 'I'm sorry to have to tell you this, Derek, but your house is very empty.'

So I went back home to Colerne. The house was almost totally empty. Jo had taken so much and I just sat there not believing it had happened. The house was so bare it echoed.

Luckily, my older son, Jamie, and his girlfriend were living on a boat nearby and they came over and cleaned every room thoroughly which was a great help to me.

I knew I had my flat in London, and another in Leeds; but this was the house, the home that Jo and I shared for so many years.

I had a choice. I could take out a bigger mortgage and refurbish it completely, or I could sell it. I talked to friends who reminded me that I loved the house and its position.

I pointed out that that was when I shared it with Jo.

Well, make it yours, they suggested. Just make it yours.

Then I talked to my dear friends Eileen and Michael Sellers, who recommended an interior designer called Jennie Reeve who lived nearby. We met up and discussed the house, and I asked if she would undertake the refurbishing. It was going to cost quite a lot and I took out a big mortgage – I was then earning good money.

We discussed colours and fabrics, the look and the style. That was all. I left the project to Jennie. She would start on 5th January 2004. I told her that I would leave a couple of days before and that I would live in Leeds and London until she told me that it was all complete and I could return to a new home.

Christmas was awful without Jo. I went to stay with my sister Babs and her husband, Alfred, and we went out to a nice restaurant, just the three of us. It was a sad occasion for us all as Jo and Babs were very close, like sisters. Babs couldn't believe this had happened. Neither could I, but there was something deep in me that I can't explain that stopped me from marrying again. But, looking back, it is one of the biggest regrets of my life.

After Christmas I planned to come back to the house and do something different for New Year. I didn't want to spend New Year's Eve at home without Jo, so I booked into Cedar Falls – a health farm near Taunton – just to get away, be on my own and have some treatments. To my astonishment, who should turn up at the health farm on New Year's Eve but Eileen and Michael who couldn't bear the thought of me being alone.

It was a bizarre evening and I met some extraordinary people, but I was so grateful to the two of them for being there with me. They've been wonderful friends. At quarter to twelve I said that I couldn't wish people a Happy New Year and would have to go to bed. They understood and off to bed I went. It was New Year's Eve, 2003.

Chapter 18

Women in my life

I'VE ALWAYS BEEN HAPPY IN THE COMPANY OF WOMEN, I've always adored women and have often thought they should run the country. I much prefer the company of women to that of a whole crowd of men – although I did enjoy the days going to watch Chelsea football with my great friends Basil, Harvey, Danny and, in the early days, my five-year-old son, Jeremy. I enjoyed that, but I was never a pub man; I took delight in vodka and good wine, I never got into beer.

When I was growing up I was surrounded by women. I was given so much love by them.

My father died when I was five. In the opening chapter of this book I explained how, in my mother's absence, my gran became my 'mother' figure during my formative years. My mother was out most days being our breadwinner and so became my 'father'. There were the many cousins and maiden aunts who used to come to tea on Thursdays. They all adored me when I was young and I loved their company.

My love for women never ceased throughout my life. They say that when you are surrounded by women there is a chance that you may turn out gay or even a sex addict. I don't think I'm either, but I know that in the past I leant more to one than the other.

I can recall all my girlfriends going right back to my very earliest schooldays. Way back in primary school there was Margaret, Valerie and Olive and, in secondary school, Cynthia, Sybil and Ruth. When I left school at 15 there was my wonderful dance partner, Vivien King. She was five years older than me and I thought her the most amazing woman I had ever met. When I was 17 she provided my first sexual experience.

Vivien and I belonged to the Crown School of Ballroom Dancing in Berkhamsted. Harry Gibson, a chum from work, also belonged along with his girlfriend Janet.

I passed my Silver Medal exam with Vivien as my partner.

In the summer of 1955 the head of the dancing school, Albert Rudge, advised us that we were all going to Butlin's Holiday Camp as entrants to the All England Dancing Championship.

A coach was provided to take us all off to Filey in North Yorkshire. Harry and I climbed aboard to be greeted by Vivien and Janet.

Our participation in the competition didn't last beyond the first round, so the four of us had plenty of time swimming, riding horses and enjoying ourselves.

We were in separate chalets, Harry and I in one and Vivien and Janet in the one next door.

One night, after dark, Harry and I could hear giggling that got closer and closer to our chalet. Suddenly the door opened and I heard a whispered voice say, 'Shush!'

'Who's that?' I asked.

'Don't,' came the whisper, 'don't say a word!'

I felt the bedclothes rise from me and a completely naked Vivien slip in.

A second or two of panic overcame me but it was quickly quelled by Vivien taking my hand and (excuse my poetic account) I was able to touch and explore paradise.

Vivien had a boyfriend in the army so I knew that a long-term relationship wasn't possible, but when I was called up to do my National Service she wrote to me, wishing me 'good luck' for my two years away. I never saw or heard from her again.

When the RAF posted me to Malta I met a Maltese WAF called Maria. On our first date in Valetta she turned up with her mother, grandfather and brother and they walked a short distance behind.

They never let her out of their sight. We did manage to sneak away on occasions.

Then I went to drama school. There was a Patti, Susan, Suzanne and Susie (Susie one, two and three); then there was Erica.

In my first film *We Joined the Navy* there was Joan O'Brien;* and shortly after that I met my first wife, Wendy. Although Wendy and I lasted eight years it was like two opposites meeting. Shortly after that Jo made a short appearance in my life. She was married at the time to Ian Lindsay.

Then I met Lesley, my second wife. This lasted a little over a year.

During the *Heartbeat* years I did form very close friendships with some beautiful women. There was Julie and Caroline, Janet, Sally and Helen (who owned a beautiful rocking horse). But what stopped me from taking these relationships further was my love for Jo.

*

So, it was no surprise to me or anyone who knew me that, being alone that New Year after Jo had left, I felt somewhat desperate and – after Eileen and Michael had departed from the health farm – terribly isolated.

The next evening, my friend Zoe Tolfree phoned me. She was on a night out with girlfriends; I could hear them all screeching in the background. Karen, whom I had met socially with her husband, was in the car and came on the phone to talk to me.

She said, 'I'm so sorry about you and Jo. I can't believe it.'

'That's life,' I said. 'I don't know why it's happened. It's knocked me for six. But I've got the show, thank goodness, and I'm refurbishing the house.'

And then I said something quite facetious: 'I think you and I should have an affair.'

She laughed a lot. I said goodbye and wished them a nice evening.

---

* See Chapter 4

The next morning I rose to find I had a text message from Karen saying she'd never been to the health farm before, she was in the area and could she pop in and meet me for lunch?

'Of course you can,' I wrote.

Karen arrived: gorgeous, all 4 feet 11 inches of high maintenance, really. It was fun. We had a lovely lunch and talked about everything. She told me she wasn't happy in her marriage. She had been with her husband since she was 16 – a lifetime.

'I'm sure it will work out,' I said.

As we said goodbye I told her that I was going back to work on 4th January and I wouldn't be coming back to Colerne until the house was ready, meaning it could be three months before I returned.

She said, 'That's fine, good luck,' and left.

The next day I left the health farm and went home to Colerne with one more night to spend there before going up to Leeds. This was 3rd January. It was seven o'clock in the evening when the doorbell rang and I opened the door to Karen carrying a half bottle of champagne and a daffodil. I must have told her that my favourite flower was a daffodil.

It was lovely.

I said I could show her the house as it was now, before refurbishment, and when I came back in three months she could see it finished.

I gave her a tour of the house, we drank champagne and chatted. She was thinking about changing her job (she was in animal health, though I never understood what that was) and going back into the hotel business which was what she had been doing before.

I wished her well, and she wished me well and hoped that everything worked out for us both. I said goodbye, thanked her for coming round and said I would see her in three months.

So I left the next day and drove up to Leeds and started work. I was renting a cottage which wasn't very far from the studios.

I had been back a week or so when Karen phoned to say she would be in Leeds. I told her to come over and see me at the cottage, which she did. She was a delight, great company, good fun, and I felt she enjoyed being with me.

Although Karen was lovely company I couldn't get Jo out of my head or my heart and thought about her every day, wondering how she was getting on, if she was missing me, how she was coping; but I kept telling myself that I had to move on because that was Jo's choice. She was happy, had her own house and was doing her own thing.

Karen said that she would be up again in two weeks, so I suggested she stayed with me next time. She made a list of food items for me to buy, saying she'd never seen such an empty fridge.

Anyway, she came back and this time she stayed. I put her into the spare bedroom but she came through to mine and I kissed her.

I suppose I was desperately lonely after Jo left and Karen was like a breath of fresh air. She was funny, generous, giving, kind, and she helped me enormously. She and I began an affair, which seemed crazy and quite surreal given the fact that Jo and I had separated only six months before, but I was so grateful and I enjoyed Karen's company enormously. In 2004 we had some happy times; she used to come up at weekends to Leeds and she began to meet members of the cast.

One of my great mates in *Heartbeat* was Arthur Lake, who was the prop master extraordinary. Arthur did me the honour of asking me to be his best man; he was going to marry the lovely Jen in Scotland and I asked Karen if she would come with me. She did, and that was a very happy time.

It was my dear Babs' 70th birthday in May that year and Karen came too. She adored Babs, and they took to her very quickly and felt that she was very good for me at that time. She met my boys. So, it was good.

I was now back in my refurbished home. I must say Jennie had done the most fabulous job – it really was wonderful. It cost a fortune but I was very happy with it. I was so pleased I had kept it.

In the summer Eileen and Michael asked if we would go to Spain with them on holiday. Karen was still living at home with her husband which seemed odd to me.

A couple of days before we left for Spain, I was sitting on the balcony enjoying the morning sunshine when Karen came up with the post, including a letter from Jo.

'What does she want?' asked Karen.

'I don't know. I'll open it.'

It was a lovely letter. Jo was saying she knew I had moved on, so had she, but we had shared so many years together she thought it would be silly for the two of us not to be friends.

I understood the letter, but Karen got very upset.

'She wants you back,' she said.

'No.'

During the holiday in Spain she remained concerned, continually asking Eileen and Michael if they thought I or Jo wanted to get back together. It became very childish. Eileen and Michael were not inclined to indulge her and I didn't know how to handle it.

We kept going, Karen and me; but from then on unpleasant things began to happen. Whether it was jealousy I'm not sure, but she began to behave strangely. She would do weird things like tear up photographs and push them through letter boxes, or put ham in my toilet bag; and she used to send really horrible texts to me. The next day she would be sweetness and light, kind and full of apologies.

I told her that if she was going to separate from her husband she should do something about it. 'Go to a solicitor,' I said, 'to prove to me you really intend to divorce.'

She told me she had meetings but nothing happened.

By now Jo and I had begun to rebuild our relationship and we had met up a number of times. It was 2007, shortly before my 70th birthday. I was still seeing Karen and also seeing Jo. I found myself in love with two women and didn't know how to handle it; but I knew that Karen would never leave her husband, and there was a huge twenty-seven-year age gap. I knew it was going to end.

One day I met Karen over a drink; she was on her way to do some business somewhere with her new job.

I said, 'I'm going to have an operation on my hip.'

'Don't worry,' she said, 'I'll be there. I'll be there for you.'

'No need,' I said. 'The crew will be great. They'll look after me.'

She gave me a short embrace and drove away. I think it was a few hours later I got a text from her saying, 'Derek. I'm sorry, this is the end. I cannot be there for you. It's time for your family. I wish you well and good luck with the operation. I'm erasing your contacts from my phone. Goodbye.'

By then Jo and I had hugged each other.

Chapter 19

My 70th birthday party – A priceless gift from Jo – Illness strikes

IN THE YEAR LEADING UP TO MY 70TH BIRTHDAY I was getting an incredible pain in my left hip. Only a lot of painkillers helped. I decided after the birthday I would seek advice.

Jo had been writing to me and in 2006 we met in her son's house, just two and a half years since we parted. It was really extraordinary.

I asked her how she was.

'I'm working,' she said. 'I've got two jobs; I can't afford not to work. I don't teach any more.'

'Tell me what you're doing?'

'Well, I work in a gym, as a receptionist and I clean the toilets.'

I said, 'Jo, you can't do this.'

'I have no alternative.'

'I'm very sorry,' I said.

'But, how are you?'

'The show's going very well, we're getting millions of viewers; and I've bought a flat in Leeds, on the Waterfront.'

'Are you still seeing Karen?'

'Yes, but not as regularly.'

'What does that mean?'

'We've had our problems. She's having problems.'

Anyway, I got up and asked if there was anything I could do to help.

'No, you carry on,' Jo said. And I gave her a hug and I left.

About four hours later Jo called, asking if we could meet again. 'I just really would like to see you again.'

'I'm not sure that's a good idea, Jo,' I said.

'Just once more,' she said. 'There are things I must say to you.'

So the next day we met again.

She said that she was sorry she hadn't behaved very well, and added, 'When you hugged me I just remembered all the happy times we had spent together. And I'm so sorry.'

'So am I,' I said. 'I just wish things could have worked out differently.'

And I left.

Before Christmas I decided to take the boys, Jeremy and Jamie, on holiday. We went to Mauritius and I asked Jo. By then we were talking to each other regularly, and I was helping her out in various ways.

So the four of us went to Mauritius. We had two wonderful weeks, a lot of fun. Jamie kept talking about India at every mealtime. He and Jo bonded and were having script ideas while Jeremy and I used to go off and play golf every afternoon. It was a wonderful hotel; there was much swimming in the sea. It was a gorgeous time for all of us.

On my 70th birthday I decided to have two parties. I had a wonderful gathering in the Queen's Hotel in Leeds with the whole of the *Heartbeat* crew, about sixty of us, all dressed up to the nines – dinner jackets for the men and evening gowns for the girls. I loved every one of them; it was fabulous, a night to remember.

There were speeches, and they did a wonderful video of the song 'My Way' with all of them taking a line. I've still got it – it makes me laugh a lot and, sometimes, brings a tear to my eye.

Then I had another party in London at the Pink Flamingo in Dean Street for all my London friends. It was organised by my friend in Leeds, Shanti Bhatia. She did most of the work.

It was a beautiful sunny day. We took over the whole restaurant and, for a while, spilled out onto the pavement.

Jeremy came, but not Jamie: he was in India. He was a cameraman and had done a small film in the UK with an Indian producer. The producer asked him to go to India to work, so he did.

Many of my friends came to my party, friendships that dated back decades. Syd Lotterby from *Yes Minister* was there, as were John Nettleton and Diana Hoddinott. From *Heartbeat*, there was lovely Trish Penrose with her husband, Mark; and Mark Jordon with his brilliant actress wife, Siobhan Finneran. Clive Francis came, as did my cousins, Beryl and Geoffrey, and my old friends Ann and Basil.

From Leeds came Harry, Jerry, Ian and Del. And, of course, my best pal, Arthur Lake with his wife, Jen.

My friend Ken Parry was also present, and Penni Harvey-Piper with husband, Derek.

My dear friend Clive Mantle and his wife Zoe were there. I know that Clive made an inspiring and humorous speech but I can't remember it. After his research I think Clive knew more about me than I did. I do remember it going down very well.

My friends Eileen and Michael came. Without Michael I wouldn't be doing this book. I know that. He and Eileen have been among my closest friends.

I remember two things stand out from that day in London.

One was when my son Jeremy's girlfriend, Cecily, knelt at my feet and said, 'Can I have your permission to marry your son?'

'Please,' I said. 'He's 39. Please take him.'

They later produced a wonderful son, Marlon: my grandson, who I am very proud of.

The other outstanding memory of that day is the sheer joy of having Jo by my side. A birthday gift like no other.

It was the first time we had been together at a party since we broke up. I think on that day we both realised we should never have parted and would always be together. Jo gave me a huge hug and wished me happy birthday. It was magic to hold her.

Perhaps my next party will be my 80th. Golly, that's not far off. Time flies by so vividly you can almost see it go.

I've still got Clive Mantle's speech somewhere; maybe I'll bring it out again.

After my parties I was still getting great pain in my left side. I knew I had to do something about it. I went to see a doctor in Leeds who referred me to a specialist, and he arranged an X-ray.

'Your hip is shot to pieces,' they said. 'You need a new hip.'

Blow me, I thought. I don't want to take six weeks off work. I talked to my producers who insisted I had it done and said they would write me out of two episodes. So, that's what they did.

About that time I went with Jo to see a plastic surgeon in Bath, hoping to arrange a simple nip and tuck on what our family traditionally called 'Fowlds' Jowls'.

'It's not as straightforward as that,' said the surgeon. 'I do not recommend it, as it will probably alter your appearance significantly. And,' he added, 'I do not want to be responsible for changing the face of a national icon.'

I dined out on that for a long time.

*

By this time my sister, Babs, had suffered a series of strokes and Alfred, her husband who was 90, couldn't look after her, so we decided to place her into a lovely home in Pinner. It was 14th May, her birthday. After settling them both I went back to Leeds.

Jo heard about my operation and called me.

'I'm having it done on the 28th,' I said.

'Who's going to look after you?' Jo asked.

'They're giving me two episodes out,' I said. 'I'm fine.'

'I'm coming up,' she said. 'I'll stay and look after you.'

'You don't have to do that.'

'No, I want to.' And she did. She used to leave Bath on a Friday at 5am and a few hours later was cooking my breakfast in Leeds. She helped me walk. I had to go to physio. Every weekend she was there, and we used to enjoy those weekends.

We both realised we loved each other, always had and always will.

When I went back to work after six weeks the crew were great. They used to lift me from set to set because I couldn't walk too far. There was such a wonderful feeling in that show that never changed.

Jo still came up and we had some wonderful times in Leeds. I asked her why she hadn't come up before, and she said she didn't like where I was living. We made up for it.

At this time we began hearing that things were changing, that *Heartbeat* was threatened. It was touch and go whether it would be recommissioned in 2008; we did manage to get another year out of it, but in 2009 we were told that this would be the last series.

We couldn't believe it. The management came up, we had meetings. They said, it's so expensive, we haven't got the money, we have to cut back by axing four or five shows. Unfortunately, *Heartbeat* was one of them. 'How can you do this,' we asked, 'when we're getting seven million viewers?'

All they said was that they didn't have the money to make any more programmes.

And that was it.

I came back to see Jo. She had this lovely cottage in Bradford on Avon that she'd bought with her share of the money from our old house in Colerne. She had her new home set up very well.

I told her that *Heartbeat* was coming to an end in May.

And that's when she told me that she had been diagnosed with myeloma.

'What is myeloma?' I asked.

'It's blood cells, a cancer of the bone marrow. I think I've got to go through chemo and stem cell transplants.'

'I'm so sorry, Jo.'

'They tell me it's a treatable cancer.'

So we were in high hopes.

I said, 'Look. I'm not going to work after *Heartbeat* ends in May. I'm coming to live here with you and we are going to get through this. That's what I want to do. You looked after me and now it's my turn.'

And that's what happened.

Ending *Heartbeat* was traumatic for all of us. It was very sad. It was so tough saying goodbye to everyone who had been part of my life for eighteen years.

Isn't it funny when you say goodbye to someone and you don't see them again? You've been emotionally involved with them, you've loved them; you've gone through births, marriages and deaths; you just say goodbye and they go out of your life.

While Jo was ill I didn't want to take on more work; I just wanted to be with her. We got closer and closer to each other. We spent so many hours driving back and forth to the hospital in Bath where Jo was treated. Jo never, ever complained. My car could probably have found its own way to the hospital, such were our many visits. Jo was very strong. She put up with so much.

I sold my flat in Leeds and stayed with Jo.

And so began the two years of ups and downs of Jo's treatments.

When Jo lost her hair I bought her a wig which I thought was terrific. She had such a noble head – she looked amazing. She rarely used scarves but didn't use the wig very much either. I had my head shaved too (though I didn't have much to begin with). We were a couple of baldies together.

We were with each other 24/7. We seemed to spend our lives going to movies, going to the hospital and seeing the children: Jo's granddaughter Alice and my grandson, Marlon.

There were times when she did rally, when she almost felt well.

At a high point we went to Cape Town to stay with Jo's friend Patti Brake and her husband, Michael.

Jo had met Patricia Brake, the actress, and her close friend Nerys Hughes back in 1961 when they were playing fairies in *A Midsummer Night's Dream* with the Royal Shakespeare Company in Stratford. Jo's husband Ian Lindsay was an actor with the company and Patti and Nerys adored Jo with her two children, Amanda and Gemma, then both babies. I think Nerys is godmother to one of them. Patti married a lovely man called Michael Kennedy who was a dour Scot.

I'd never really met Michael until he called Jo to tell her he was suffering from the same cancer as she was. They bonded instantly. Patti was thrilled as he and Jo used to talk non-stop on how they were coping with their illness, and one day in 2010 Michael said to Jo that she needed a real break. They had a lovely house in Cape Town and asked us to visit for two weeks, sit in the sun, see Cape Town and spend time with them.

We had a wonderful ten days. And Jo was really well, she had rallied. The thing about her cancer was that it was treatable, and never for a minute did I think we would lose her; and I'm sure Patti felt the same way about Michael.

We joined our friends for lunch, drinking and eating far too much. We visited wineries for tasting, and Jo and I went to Robben Island and up Table Mountain. Jo hated heights and clung to the pole of the cable car. But she was thrilled to be up there.

We also managed to go that year to France and stay with my old friend, Donald Douglas. We had always kept in touch. He now lived in France with his partner, Emma. We had a wonderful week with them. We met up with Bill Simons and his delightful wife Jackie, who also had a home in France. Amanda Rice, whom I had worked with in the 1960s, was also there with her husband, as was Robin Ellis. Donald and Emma were terrific hosts; we sat on their balcony and played silly games.

I knew that, every now and again, Jo was suffering badly. She got recurring pneumonia which was very difficult, and she had to keep going into hospital to deal with infections; and for eleven months she had shingles which was terrible. But although she was suffering, she always laughed, never moaned. We laughed every day. She made me laugh every day I was with her.

Chapter 20

Sister Babs

I OFTEN THINK ABOUT THE IMPORTANCE of people in my life, both family and friends of all ages and backgrounds. They have always been there for me in life's ups and downs. Whenever they come to mind there is always my sister, Babs, my longest-serving friend. How lucky I was to have Babs as my sister.

The whole family called her Babs, but her real name was Ann: Ann Elizabeth Mary. Elizabeth was after my father's mum, and Mary after my mother's mum. I've never called her Ann in my life, nor did my children or immediate family. When Ann was mentioned I used to ask who that was.

She and I were as close as you can be as brother and sister. She was the kindest, gentlest, warmest, loyalest person you could ever wish to meet. I often used to say that if there were angels on this earth Babs was certainly one of them. Apparently she pushed me off the kitchen table when I was two and broke my arm. I don't remember that, of course. I think it might have been the only confrontation we ever had. I can't remember having a cross word with Babs or a fight or an argument. She was three years older than me, and my hero in many ways.

All her life she wanted to be a nurse. But when she left school at 15 Mum, being alone and not at all well off, told her that she must learn a skill and start earning some money. So Babs went into a solicitor's office and became a shorthand typist and started to earn money. But after a year Mum gave in and told her she must do what she really wanted to do, and so Babs went to West Herts Hospital in Hemel Hempstead to begin her training.

I think it was about this time that I introduced Babs to a friend of mine. I had started work at a printing company and I introduced her to John from the art department. She fell madly in love with John, and I think he with her, and they got engaged. Then John got a job in London and started to commute; Babs was very busy training, and he broke off the engagement. He met someone else and I think he now lives in Australia with six children. Good luck to him.

Babs was very hurt and channelled all her energy and skills into her life as a nurse. She went from probationer to staff nurse and decided she wanted to become a midwife, so she moved to Pinner in Middlesex and concentrated on midwifery.

She was a midwife for over thirty years and delivered thousands of babies, among them my firstborn, Jamie. A day we shall never forget, Babs and I and Wendy. I was the assistant midwife.

After thirty years of midwifery, Babs decided to go 'on the District' and so became the District Nurse. She was greatly loved wherever she went. She'd had a few boyfriends: I can remember a Lyndon and a couple of Charlies.

While she was on the District she nursed a Mrs Young in Pinner and got to know the husband, Alfred. Babs was present when Mrs Young died and helped Alfred through it. Later Alfred proceeded to chase her, turning up on corners unexpectedly. We called him the stalker. Although she liked him, Babs wasn't too keen at first. In the end he was persistent and courted her pretty well. They fell in love and were married.

Although Babs was 50 years old she said she was going to do it as if she was 21. I was honoured when I gave her away in our old congregational church which became the United Reformed Church. Babs wore white, my sons were the ushers and it was a wonderful day. Mum was there and my dear Jo.

They had twenty-five years together. Babs was very happy. She raised so much money for charity – the Save the Children Fund – every year. She organised vegetable and plant stalls and raised money wherever she could.

She was the actress in the family, performing in amateur productions of *Yeomen of the Guard* and *HMS Pinafore*. She joined a concert party and did her monologues. We will never forget her *pièce de résistance*, 'Nobody Loves a Fairy When She's Forty', for which Babs used to get dressed up with a wand and a tutu. She was a very special person, a very special sister.

In 2007 she had to go in to have a hip replacement as it was giving her a lot of pain. The replacement was really successful and she was so thrilled, but she needed her other one done. She was told she had to wait for at least three or four months.

Shortly after her second operation she was hit with a series of strokes. We did wonder if there was a problem with oxygen to the brain, if something had gone wrong during that second op. We had no proof. It was a horrible time for Babs. She didn't deserve that at all. Neither she nor Alfred could cope.

We found her a nursing home and after a while she seemed content. Alfred used to go every day. As he weakened he couldn't cope, and eventually he went into the same home. I used to go and visit them. They always sat together holding hands.

It was awful that in the space of a few short years they had lost their lovely home and were both in care.

In 2010 Alfred was not well, got a chest infection and just died. By this time Babs had a tumour on her tongue and had to have it cut away which was so hard for her.

Babs never complained about anything: the strokes that she suffered, going into a home, losing Alfred. She just was the most wonderful human being. She kept asking where Alfred was after he passed away, but the strokes had taken their toll. Her health and quality of life were diminishing each time I went to see her. It was painful and upsetting, and she used to talk out of the corner of her mouth because of her tongue. And then she got a secondary tumour in her neck. She had to be operated on again, and that was the beginning of the end. She slowly became weaker and didn't want to eat. It was very hard for her to communicate.

I had recently had a botched knee operation and was unable to walk for weeks; and Arthur Lake, my friend from *Heartbeat*, came down from Leeds to look after me. He took over from my great friend, Kate.

Katy Manning. The great Katy Manning, my friend for over forty years. She's a brilliant actress, one of the original *Doctor Who* girls (Jo Grant), and she's been a wonderful friend to me. I always look forward to seeing her and I love her talent and her energy. Her whole attitude to life is something special.

I said to Arthur one day that I needed to see Babs, so he got me in the car and off we went to see her. We drove to the care home in Harrow and there was Babs in bed. She remembered Arthur.

The film *My Fair Lady* was on the telly and we started to sing, 'I Could Have Danced All Night'.

It was one of the shows that Babs had performed in her younger days, and she started to hum the tune. She opened her eyes and looked at me. Arthur said it was a very special moment. I kissed her goodbye and told her I would see her soon and to take care and that I loved her.

Arthur drove me back home and I knew, deep down, that I had seen Babs for the last time.

I got the call on the Sunday after our visit, telling me that our dear Babs had passed away. As Arthur said, it was as if she had been waiting for me to say goodbye. What a lady, what a woman, what a sister. We loved each other all our lives. Warmth, love and affection. Babs was my hero. God bless her.

Chapter 21

My darling Jo

WHEN I WAS LOOKING FOR A HOUSE TO BUY in 2010 Jo came with me to view quite a few, some of them very strange. In the one house I particularly liked, Jo looked out of the window across the valley. 'There's Colerne church,' she exclaimed. 'I'm not sure but I think I can spot our old house in Eastrip Lane. I'm sure it's Jodders.'

Jo thought that was an omen so I bought the house, 'King's Court', which, in the years that followed, has been a haven for me. It's very peaceful.

I knew that the house would need a great deal of work. I would need to change every room. The kitchen was at the back with no view. I wanted it in the front so I could see across the valley. The garden was like a jungle and needed redesigning with a patio and pathways.

'It needs a mountain of work,' I said.

'It'll be worth it,' Jo replied.

In the June of that year the builders started with my designer, Jennie Reeve, overseeing. Jennie had helped me with the properties in Colerne and London. She knew what colours I liked and what fabrics and I could say to her, this is what I like and this is what I would like to happen, and leave it to her.

I lived with Jo after *Heartbeat* had finished until my house was ready. I visited a couple of times – it was like a building site. I was so depressed. I told Jo I wasn't going to go again.

After five months Jennie told me it was finished. I was thrilled. I moved in in October 2010.

At the time Jo was still unwell, still living in her cottage, but my hope was that she would eventually move and live with me again. I knew in my heart that I would persuade her one day to move in to the new house but she was quite reluctant, although she was at my house more than her own. She still loved her independence, did Jo.

Her hospital visits became more frequent and in February she got shingles, which never left her. The shingles were very painful. She would often say that she couldn't bear it. They kept saying it would go, and then she got pneumonia just before Christmas. She was very weak. She moved into my house so that I could be hands-on with her. Sometimes she couldn't climb the stairs so slept downstairs. I still never thought that I would lose her.

When she next saw her consultant she was told the myeloma had come back and that her proteins were up and that she would have to start chemotherapy again.

Jo said, 'Oh please. I don't want to go through that again.'

She was told she had to.

I told her that we would face it together. She had to go through this. But they couldn't start the therapy until they had cleared the infection, the shingles and the pneumonia. Her system was very low.

We have had so many wonderful family Christmases. Without that three-year gap we would have had thirty-three Christmases together. This time we were going to the local hostelry with the whole family and we were all there: Jo's family, my family.

On Boxing Day everyone was at my house having a meal in the evening, playing silly games. Jo said that she wasn't feeling well so she went up to bed. The next day I called the doctor suggesting that Jo should be in hospital. An ambulance came and took her in; the consultant saw her, saying that she needed to stay in hospital while they treated the infection.

Jo's birthday was 23rd February (the same day as my mother, which always pissed Jo off although she adored my mother) and over the years I always tried to organise a birthday surprise for her – a show in London, a party with old friends, or a trip somewhere.

This year I had booked our favourite hotel in Cornwall, the Mullion Cove, which we'd been to many times before. I had to tell Jo when she was in hospital that the surprise this year was the hotel.

'I love it,' she said, 'but I can't, I'm not strong enough.'

I postponed the hotel trip and a few days later Jo came out of hospital. She wasn't well after her birthday and quite weak. I told her that this was crazy and took her back to hospital on the Wednesday after her birthday.

I'd just bought my new car and Jo hadn't seen it. When she looked at the colour (it's bronze) she said, 'It looks like shit!'

'You can't say that about my new car.'

When we got to the hospital we parked and Jo was violently sick.

'You can't be sick in my new car,' I said.

'Fuck the car. Go and get me some wet wipes.'

I found a wheelchair for her and we went into the waiting room. I went in with her to see her consultant, who insisted Jo be readmitted to hospital straight away so that they could treat the infection.

Jo had had shingles for almost a year, she kept getting pneumonia and the myeloma still had to be tackled. And even then it didn't occur to me that her condition could be terminal. It just didn't.

On the Thursday morning I went back with extra clothes, hairbrushes and various other things. I was due to play golf the next day with Peter Tory, Wendy's brother, a tremendous friend who had come back into my life. It was a real bonus for all of us to have Pete around. I asked Jo if I might slip away for a few hours.

Jo said, 'Of course, go and play golf with Pete.'

So Friday morning I went to Bowood, my golf club. Pete pulled in to the car park as I was putting my clubs on the buggy.

Just then my phone rang. It was Laurence, Jo's son, saying that I must get to the hospital straight away.

'What's up? What's going on?'

'Look,' he said. 'I can't talk. Just get down to the hospital.'

I said to Pete, 'Sorry mate. I've got to go.'

Pete took my clubs and said he would call later.

Laurence was at the hospital waiting for me. Later the reality hit me that, although Jo and I had been together for thirty-six years, we never married, so Laurence was her next of kin and he was the person the hospital authorities had to talk to.

He told me that they were transferring Jo into a side ward. I went in and Jo was sitting on the bed saying that she didn't know what was going on.

I said, 'Jo, it's the infection. They can't treat you until the infection is gone.'

Laurence took me to one side and said, 'They've told me she's got seventy-two hours to live.'

I was shattered but we had to keep up a pretence.

I didn't leave the hospital over the hours and days that followed. All her close friends came in: Eileen and Michael, Yvonne and Rog, Debbie, Joy and Henk. And, of course, her family. Her brothers, Mike, Paul and Julian were there as was Amanda, Jo's daughter.

We just stayed. We sat with her the rest of Friday until Sunday. She was breathing, asleep. She wasn't in any pain because of the morphine. In the end it was just Laurence, Amanda, Paul, Mike, Jeremy (my son) and me. They all left me alone with Jo late on Sunday night and I held her hand and said, 'I love you very much.'

She died early on Monday morning, 5th March 2012.

Chapter 22

An Act without script or rehearsal

THE DAYS AFTER JO PASSED AWAY I didn't know where I was or what I was doing. I remember endless calls from friends offering help, hoping to give comfort. They were all so understanding. Jeremy stayed with me. He provided much-needed strength.

Jo's funeral was really hard. I felt I had to speak. My knee was still troubling me so the boys, Fletcher and Jeremy, helped me up to the rostrum. The church was packed with mourners. I told them that Jo had been my soulmate, my best friend, the love of my life. I had asked Jeremy to take over if I couldn't manage the speech without breaking down. But I did, just.

My emotional state was not being helped by the pain from a near useless knee. Eventually I went into hospital to have an arthroscopy. It had been a bit of a gamble as I was on warfarin for a blood condition, but such was the pain I was more than willing to take a calculated risk. My cartilage was cleaned out and all seemed okay, but three days later I was in the worst pain ever and I went into hospital for a whole week. They had to swab out the cartilage.

I could hardly walk for three months. I was on a Zimmer frame, then crutches, then walking sticks. I found it hard and, with this coming right after Jo had passed away, I felt it was just one thing after another.

My friend Katy Manning came to look after me. Although she had been in Australia over the past eighteen years I've always felt Katy has been there for me. We met in 1972 when she was playing the part of Jo Grant, *Doctor Who*'s sidekick. We were both in Macready's, the actors' club, and got chatting. We became the best of friends; and years later, along with Derek Nimmo, I became godfather to her twins. She cooked and cleaned for three days and then Arthur Lake came down from Leeds.

A very strange thing happened. Wendy, my first wife, the mother of my children, came from Ireland where she had been living for twelve years. Every now and again she had to make trips to Bermuda to take over from her brother Mike, caring for their mother.

Wendy wanted to live in England, to spend time with her brother, Peter, and to be near our son and grandson, which meant she would be living rather close to me.

In 2007, when I left the house in Colerne, I ended up renting a cottage in Euridge which was lovely. When I moved into my present house Jeremy took over the cottage; and when he and Cecily, his wife, bought a house in Coleford, Wendy took over the cottage.

Wendy hadn't attended Jo's or Babs' funeral although she knew them very well. She felt she had been out of our lives for such a long time it was best if she stayed away. But it was nice to have her back in the area.

Nobody could have foreseen another twist in this awful journey of the last four years. I didn't. Peter and I had played a round of golf one morning and were having a drink when he said, 'I've got this condition. I can't swallow. I can drink, but I'm having difficulty swallowing. I'm going to see a specialist.'

News came through that Peter had cancer of the oesophagus and had to start chemotherapy treatment.

Wendy was so close to Peter. She was in bits. We visited him in hospital in Cheltenham every week.

Alas, he went downhill quickly and passed away in October.

So in the year 2012 I lost Jo, Babs and Peter. Wendy's father, my ex father-in-law, also died that year. It really was the most awful time.

But one nice thing was that, after all the years being apart, Wendy and I were forming a friendship. She and I had history. We could talk about families and try to ease the pain we both felt.

The extraordinary thing about meeting up again with Wendy was rediscovering how much we still had in common. There was the family, of course, but we both could easily admit that our marriage was not all bad. There were exciting and joyful times that were lodged firmly in our memory banks. We have sons in common, grandchildren in common, history in common and, alas, tragedy in common. I came to enjoy and value her company.

Jo always loved Christmas. A week before, we used to decorate the tree with lights and get absolutely hammered on whisky macs. On Christmas mornings we had breakfast in bed. Just two things on the menu: champagne and orange juice, luxuriously downed as we opened our stockings. Every year, for many years, we went to mass on Christmas Eve. A very special time, and Jo loved it; but since her death I couldn't face it. It's always difficult to partake in celebrations without Jo by my side. Even on the most joyous occasions – and there are few – there is always a moment to reflect on Jo's absence.

That Christmas didn't happen. I didn't send cards; I just wanted to go and see my eldest boy, Jamie.

Jamie had been in India for six years. He went as a cameraman in 2006. At the time I told him to use his contacts and try it for six months, see how he got on. He's done some wonderful work and has a great CV in feature films and commercials. And that's where his life has been, in India.

I asked Jeremy if he would come with me. Of course, he had to ask Cecily, his wife. She agreed to let him go.

So we flew to Goa, staying in a lovely hotel on the coast.

The first morning there was a knock on my door, and there stood Jamie, six foot four, thin as a rake.

'Hello, Daddy,' he said. 'What kept you? It's been six years.'

We had a lovely two weeks. By nine o'clock in the evening I was in bed while the boys bonded. They went to where Jamie was staying, a great beach where all these extraordinary people gathered smoking, drinking and enjoying themselves. It was great to see my sons together for the first time in six years.

For Christmas 2013 we went to a cottage in the Yorkshire Dales. When I say 'we' I mean Wendy, Jeremy, his wife Cecily and her parents, and my grandson Marlon. Liz Dawson was there too along with her sister Briony, her partner and their baby. Wendy's son Fletcher came; and number one grandson, Jacob, a successful wine merchant, arrived armed with a car boot full of fine wine.

On Christmas Eve, Fletcher got a telephone call and disappeared, saying he was going down to the local pub. After half an hour and (I suspect) two or three drinks Fletcher returned with my son Jamie in tow. He had flown from India for the occasion.

*

From the age of 12 I've always been a football fan. At that age, in the company of my cousin, I used to watch Chelsea play. Though still a 'Chelsea boy', I now watch them on television rather than live. Jeremy, my son, and Marlon, my grandson, are also fans. My eldest son, Jamie, never liked football.

In 2011 I got a call from Dave Gane, the commercial director of Chippenham Town Football Club, asking me if I would give an after-dinner speech.

I told him that I rarely did that sort of thing and if I did I didn't like it.

He explained that the annual dinner was one of the few ways in which the club were able to raise money to help meet essential costs and asked me to consider it. I declined, but he kept coming back.

'We'll pick you up and take you home,' he said. 'You'll have dinner with us and you'll receive a fee.'

I was persuaded, but I laid down one condition: 'Your team will have to wear blue strip for me. I'm a Chelsea man and won't support a team that doesn't play in blue.'

'It's funny you should say that,' he said. 'Chippenham Town FC are called the Bluebirds. We do play in blue. It'll be home from home for you.'

Any resistance on my part disappeared and in February I went to the venue, a restaurant called Revolutions. It was packed.

The people were so friendly, very hospitable. I felt so welcome.

We had a lovely meal, and afterwards I gave my speech. Not sure what I went on about but I remember it got a few laughs.

Afterwards they kindly invited me to the next home match.

Three weeks later I saw Chippenham FC play, but only after the 'committee' had wined and dined me and invited me to join them in the directors' section of the stand. I found myself thoroughly enjoying the event, and meeting the people again was very rewarding.

It really is grass-roots football, and the atmosphere is as good as it gets with three to four hundred people cheering their team on.

Whenever I can, I go and see them play. I find myself looking forward to my day out at Hardenhuish Park – although, as I write, I have to confess that since I started supporting the team, results have suffered, causing a rapid decline in the league table from 7th in my first year, down to 11th in my second, then down to 16th, then 18th. Before I began attending matches they were regularly 2nd or 4th. After a 9-0 drubbing by Stourbridge in 2013 the manager, Steve Winter, was sacked.

Mark Collier is now in charge and there are signs of improvement – the dizzy heights of 14th have been reached. 'Up you blues!'

*

As I moved into 2013 I thought, I haven't really worked for three years. I didn't want to work when I was caring for Jo, but I love my profession and love acting; now, no one was offering me work. I'd been out of the loop for so long. I think I said to my agent once, if you were casting me in *Upstairs, Downstairs* would you put me upstairs or downstairs? (They had no idea.) I suppose I could do both really.

At the start of the year I decided that I would do some work and told my agents that if something good came up I would like to be considered. I did a short interview on the Jo Brand show and, in April, I was offered a part in *Casualty*, which I took. I felt I could do something with it; it wasn't a big part but at least it would get me back on telly.

Some years ago Jo and Jeremy wrote a script. I can hear them now, laughing and giggling. They were talking about ghosts and graves and rabbits and a mother coming out of a car on a Zimmer frame. I thought, what is this all about?

The working title was *The Grave*. I read it; a lot of work was needed, but it was a nice story, a good idea. After three drafts it got better.

When the new script was finished I took it to Stewart Mackay who I had previously collaborated with on *Fowlds in the Landscape* and other projects. He thought it was a good story but wanted to think about it. He got another writer on board and the two of them got the story into a shooting script. We decided to go for it.

Arthur Lake, from Leeds, agreed to be prop master for the film; Diana Hoddinott and Peter Benson agreed to join the cast. Jeremy would play the lead and I would play a ghost.

In June 2013 we got a crew together and shot the film, which was now called *Kindred Spirits*. It was a great week. Peter and Arthur stayed with me in my house. We were up at 6:30 each morning, and shot 48 minutes in seven days. We cut, did titles, chose the music. We designed a DVD cover.

The film premiered the following year. We hired a suite in Bailbrook House near Bath and invitations were sent out for the evening of 28th September 2014. Over eighty people came.

It's happened for all of us, but it is in loving memory of Jo and my sister, Babs. Dedication too went to the wonderful actor Harry Towb who was married to Diana. People we loved and we lost. This film is for them.

Having been an actor for over half a century it's difficult, if not impossible, to kick the habit. I would love to feel that buzz again, to have an interesting and demanding role to play.

I see the success of most of my contemporaries: Jacobi, McKellen, Hurt, Courtenay, Gambon, Broadbent; actors I have known and admired all my career. At times I do wonder if I've been out of the loop too long, but a career is a marathon, not a sprint. At 77 years there is a certain amount of slowing up, but not yet giving up.

There was an occasion when I was reminded of the importance of 'having your face out there'. On 12th February 2014 the Prince of Wales, as Patron of the Actors' Benevolent Fund, and the Duchess of Cornwall gave an evening reception at Clarence House. Penelope Keith, President of the Fund, introduced us all; and what struck me most was just how vital the Fund is and how much people are benefiting from their work.

The Prince of Wales walked up to me (we had met before) and said, 'Are you still working?'

I think I replied, 'When I'm asked.'

As the Prince moved on a whisper came from behind, 'He thought you were dead, Mr Derek.'

At the end of 2014 I heard the sad news that the actor and writer Jeremy Lloyd had passed away. He and I spent an incredible ten weeks together in 1962 making the film *We Joined the Navy*. We were two of the three young lads training to be naval officers, the other being Dinsdale Landen. One of my abiding memories of Jeremy was his wonderful comment after my then girlfriend, the actress Joan O'Brien, left me to star in a film with Elvis Presley.

'You can always say,' said Jeremy, 'that she dumped you for Elvis.'

*

Jamie, my son, now makes trips from India to England. I've no idea how long each visit will be. As a film cameraman he must go where the work is. I haven't seen all his films but I've read glowing accounts of his many and varied skills in an industry that demands perfection.

Number two son, Jeremy, is a very talented actor who now seems to have the best of two worlds. He has a job which allows him time to follow his beloved acting. He has done some extraordinary work. He performs with leading amateur companies. Sometimes we work through his parts together. That is always a pleasure; to watch him create a new character – it reminds me so much of me. In the summer of 2014 he played Macbeth in a local production. I reminded him how, aged six, he used to sit in the stalls at the Young Vic and watch me rehearse the role.

He told me that he remembered the time clearly, but on this occasion it was his turn.

After *Macbeth* he went on a short tour of Emily Brontë's *Wuthering Heights* where he and an actress played all six parts. I know that to be an amazing feat.

Jeremy has been a rock for me. I don't think I would be here if it wasn't for him.

And there are my inherited boys. Wendy's son by her second marriage, dear Fletcher, who lost his dad when he was four – it was a joy for me to take him on. And Jo's son, Laurence. I took him on when he was nine and he is now in his late 40s. Losing his mum was really tough for Laurence and I'm very proud of him. He's been a great support to me. Very successful in his job, and he has the most beautiful daughter, Alice, Jo's granddaughter, who is the spitting image of Jo. Alice will break so many hearts.

My grandchildren: Jacob (great that he's come back into my life after so many years living with his mother in Norwich). He's now in his mid-20s. He looks like Jamie and has all the charm in the world.

Marlon, Jeremy's son. I saw him born and I watch him grow. Very strong and single-minded even at six. He's fearless. Lovely smile, very naughty. And there's Jo's grandchildren who I watched grow up: Jack, Tom, George. Great kids.

I wish all of them – sons, grandchildren, my family, my extended family – every happiness. I thank you all. I love you so much. I'm blessed to have you all in my life.

To my kids and grandkids, I hope you have the freedom of choice to do what you want to do, be who you want to be, go where you want to go; and remember the words of Shakespeare: 'We are such stuff as dreams are made on, and our little life is rounded with a sleep.'

That terrible year when I lost Jo and Babs I found a poem:

'Those special memories of you
Will always bring a smile
If only I could have you back
For just a little while
And we could sit and talk again
Just like we used to do
You always meant so much to me
And always will do too
The fact that you're no longer here
Will always cause me pain
But you're forever in my heart
Until we meet again.'

I just love that so I kept it.

*

So, as I contemplate the New Year of 2015, who knows where my career will take me. Is it fate? Or as my dear mother would say, 'just one of those things'?

The wonderful thing about being an actor is that you never know what's around the corner. It was always so. A call, a text, an email, a letter. A simple message that could change your life once more. Always remembering that the journey is more enticing than arriving.

Excuse me, I have to go. The telephone is ringing. I may be up for a part worth playing.